200

Other books by W. W. TIMMS, M.A.

A First Spanish Book
A Second Spanish Book
with MANUEL PULGAR
A Simpler Spanish Course

Advanced Spanish Course

W. W. TIMMS, M.A.
and
M. PULGAR

LONGMAN

LONGMAN GROUP LIMITED
Longman House
Burnt Mill, Harlow, Essex CM20 2JE, England
and Associated Companies throughout the World

© *Longman Group Ltd 1971*

First published 1971
Seventh impression 1983

ISBN 0 582 36480 9

*Printed in Singapore by
Huntsmen Offset Printing Pte Ltd.*

Contents

SECTION TWO

Passages for Translation from English into Spanish

SECTION THREE

Essays

SECTION FOUR

Exercises and Tests on Grammar

SECTION FIVE

Grammar

Acknowledgements

We are grateful to the following for permission to reproduce copyright material:
Aguilar, S.A. de Ediciones for extracts from *Tres Poetas Junto Al Mar* by Noel Clarasó; author for an extract from *Semblanzas* by Antonio Armendáriz; Jonathan Cape Limited for an extract from *Brazilian Adventure* by Peter Fleming; author for extracts from *El Molino de Viento* by Camilo José Cela; Chatto and Windus Limited and The Viking Press, Inc for extracts from *The Unicorn* by Iris Murdoch, Copyright © 1963 by Iris Murdoch; La Codorniz for extracts from *Dios le Ampare Imbécil* by Álvaro de Laiglesia; Collins Publishers and author's agent for extracts from *The Towers of Trebizond* by Rose Macaulay; Compañía Editora Espasa-Calpe Argentina S.A. for an extract from 'Una Novena en la Sierra' by Martín Gil from *Colección Austral No. 447;* The Cresset Press for extracts from *Mediterráneo* by Chapman Mortimer; authors for extract from *Historia de una Finca* by José and Jesús de las Cuevas; Ediciones Destino S.L. for extracts from *Historias de la Artámila* by Ana María Matute, *El Curso* by Juan Antonio Payno, *El Jarama* by Rafael Sánchez Ferlosio and *La Zancada* by Vicente Soto; Editorial Gredos, S.A. for an extract from *Mis Páginas Preferidas* by Juan Antonio de Zunzunegui; Editorial Joaquín Mortiz, S.A. for an extract from *Las Tierras Flacas* by Agustín Yáñez; Faber and Faber Limited and Harcourt, Brace and World, Inc for extracts from *Cortés and Montezuma* by Maurice Collis; author for extracts from *Lola, Espejo Oscuro* by Darío Fernández-Flórez; Fondo de Cultura Económica for extracts from *El Llano en Llamas* by Juan Rulfo and *La Región Más Transparente* by Carlos Fuentes; William Heinemann Limited for extracts from *The Spanish Pimpernel* by C. E. Lucas Phillips; author and author's agent for extracts from *So Well Remembered* by James Hilton; Hodder and Stoughton Limited for an extract from *Señor Saint* by Leslie Charteris; Horacio Sáenz Guerrero for extracts from an article by Sebastián Juan Arbo from *La Vanguardia* 21 October 1966, extracts from an article by Alberto Vázquez-Figueroa from *La*

Vanguardia, 21 October 1966; Hutchinson Publishing Group Limited for extracts from *The Spanish Dancer* by Sylvia Sark; Instituto del Libro for extracts from *La Situación* by Lisandro Otero; Little, Brown and Company and Paul R. Reynolds Inc for extracts from *Captain from Castille* by Samuel Shellabarger, Copyright 1944, 1945 by Samuel Shellabarger; London Express News and Feature Services for an extract from an article from *Evening Standard*, 19 May 1966; author's agent for an extract from *Fabled Shore* by Rose Macaulay; Macmillan and Company Limited for extracts from *The Golden Century of Spain* by R. Trevor Davies; Macmillan and Company Limited, Charles Scribner's Sons and author's agent for extracts from *The Masters* by C. P. Snow; The Literary Executor of W. Somerset Maugham, William Heinemann Limited and Doubleday and Company Inc for extracts from 'The Point of Honour' and 'The Mother' from *Collected Short Stories* by W. Somerset Maugham; John Murray for extracts from *Spanish Main* by P. C. Wren; John Murray and author's agent for extracts from *Don Gypsy* by Walter Starkie; The Literary Executor of Sir Harold Nicolson for an extract from *Miriam Codd* by Harold Nicolson; author's agent for an extract from *The Fell of Dark* by James Norman; author's agent for extracts from *Mary Lavelle* and *That Lady* by Kate O'Brien; Organización Editorial Novaro, S.A. for extracts from *El Indio* by Gregorio López y Fuentes, copyright 1960, 1967 by Gregorio López y Fuentes; author's agent for extracts from *Portugal and Madeira* by Sacheverell Sitwell; Taurus Ediciones, S.A. for an extract from *Una Exhibición Peligrosa* by Carlos Edmundo de Ory; author's agent for extracts from *Don Roberto* by A. F. Tschiffely; author's agent and Michael Joseph Limited for extracts from *The Midwich Cuckoos* by John Wyndham.

We have been unable to trace the copyright holders of the following, and would appreciate any information that would enable us to do so: *Ushanan-Jampi* by Enrique López Albújar; *Calixto Garmendia* by Ciro Algería; *Tigre Juan* by Ramón Perez de Ayala; *Otoño* by Fernando Benítez; *Funes, el Memorioso* by Jorge Luis Borges; *El estilete de Oro* by Francisco de Cossío; *Ha Entrado un Ladrón* by Wenceslao Fernández Flórez; *El Hombre Nuevo* by Ricardo León; *El Llamo Blanco* by Fernando Díez de Medina; *Diálogos con mi Enfermera* by Santiago Lorén; *El Delincuente* by Manual Rojas; *Bolívar and the Independence of Spanish America* by J. B. Trend and *Sangre en el Umbral* by Hugo Wast.

Introduction

This Advanced Level book is offered to students as a logical development of *A Simpler Spanish Course for First Examinations*.

Although it is traditional in form, providing translation and essay practice for those preparing for the present 'A' Level examinations, we hope that it will offer a challenge to all students at an advanced level who are faced with translation from or into the mother-tongue, a test, which, in fact, not many universities are ready to forgo in their final examinations.

The scheme of work recommended is briefly to go slowly, gradually and conscientiously from 'O' Level work up to 'A' Level. It is obviously a mistake to throw ex-'O' Level candidates into the deep waters of 'A' Level without teaching them to swim fluently at 'O' Level. So the passages for translation from and into Spanish have been roughly graded from the early stages, where ample notes are given to help the student not only to do the translations but also to find his way about the book, onwards to the later stages where very few, if any, notes are provided and more difficult passages are encountered.

The choice and presentation of grammar turned out to be our most exhausting and exacting task – it was evident there was no room for a complete grammar in this book when such excellent works by Harmer & Norton (*A Manual of Modern Spanish*) and Ramsden (*An Essential Course in Modern Spanish*) are already in wide circulation. We thought that a more practical approach, although limited in its survey, would be useful and acceptable. Therefore, the ex-'O' Level candidate will find here information and exercises which will help him in his study of the more difficult and complicated realms of the Spanish language such as prepositions, government of verbs, *ser* and *estar*, *para* and *por*, the order of words and, of course, the subjunctive mood. Lists of idioms, irregular verbs, etc. could not be excluded and will be found at the end of the book.

The essay section provides groups of titles suitable for all candidates, graded from narrative to philosophical subjects. During the first year after 'O' Level it is advisable to concentrate on straightforward narrative subjects so that fluency and ease of writing can be obtained before tackling more difficult and mature topics. It is hoped that the special hints on writing essays as well as translations will be welcomed especially by those students who may be working alone.

We wish to express our deep gratitude to all who have aided us in the production of this book, especially to Mrs Gerda Pulgar, Mrs Evelyn Timms and Mrs Shirley Watt who have spent long and arduous hours typing and organizing the manuscript during its preparation.

W.W.T.

M.P.

Passages for Translation from Spanish into English

These prose passages, taken from mainly modern Spanish and Latin American authors, provide not only practice in the examination technique of translation but also a store of knowledge for the student of the Spanish language. Here will be found examples of Spanish usage, vocabulary and idiom and much can be learnt if the passages are studied closely and if conscientious use is made of the footnotes which call attention to these examples and to background information about Spain and Latin America.

In translating, a good rule is to keep as near to the Spanish version as is consistent with normal English; a paraphrase is not necessarily a translation.

Here are hints for tackling 'unprepared' translation:

1. Read through the passage at least twice.
2. Concentrate on the difficult phrases and see if by intelligent guessing or perhaps grammatical analysis (finding the subject, verb, object, etc.) some reasonable meaning can be found which fits in with the context.
3. Translate the whole passage mentally, thinking of a good English version and, if it is dialogue, how you would say that particular phrase or sentence yourself in English.
4. Write out your final translation, neatly and legibly, leaving gaps for words and phrases you have failed to decipher. Perhaps you will be able to fill these in at the last minute as you read through your script before handing it in.

1 The golden tree (a)

Quizá lo que más se envidiaba de Ivo era la posesión de la codiciada llave de la torrecita.[1] Ésta era, en efecto, una pequeña torre situada[2] en un ángulo de la escuela, en cuyo interior se guardaban los libros de lectura[3]. Allí entraba Ivo[4] a[5] buscarlos, y allí volvía a dejarlos, al terminar la clase[6]. La[7] señorita Leocadia se lo encomendó a él, nadie[8] sabía en realidad por qué[9].

Ivo estaba[10] muy orgulloso de esta distinción, y por[11] nada del mundo la hubiera[12] cedido. Un día, Mateo Heredia, el más aplicado y estudioso de[13] la escuela, pidió encargarse de[14] la tarea – a todos nos fascinaba[15] el misterioso interior de la torrecita, donde no entramos nunca[8] –, y la señorita Leocadia pareció[16] acceder. Pero Ivo se levantó y, acercándose[17] a[5] la maestra, empezó a[5] hablarle en su voz baja, bizqueando los[18] ojos y moviendo mucho las manos, como tenía por costumbre[19]. La maestra dudó[20] un poco, y al fin dijo:

– Quede[21] todo como estaba. Que siga[21] encargándose Ivo de la torrecita.

ANA MARÍA MATUTE Historias de la Artámila

[1] diminutive of *torre*, *23*. [2] *situada*, used here to introduce a prepositional phrase. [3] *lectura*, *25*, *12*. [4] position of *Ivo* in the sentence, *12*. [5] why *a*? *9(a)*. [6] *al* + infinitive and subject, *11(a)v*. [7] *la*, *2(d)*. [8] negatives, *16*. [9] *por qué*, *26*. [10] *estar*, *19*. [11] *por*, *10*. [12] *hubiera*, used for *habría*. [13] *de* for 'in' after a superlative, *9(c)*. [14] 'asked to be responsible for'. [15] note use of active voice, *11*, *12*. [16] *pareció*, *11(b)* and *(c)*. [17] *gerundio*, *14*. [18] *los ojos*, *2(c)*. [19] 'as was his habit'. [20] *dudar*, *25*. [21] imperatives, *17*, *18(a)*.

2 The golden tree (b)

A la salida de la escuela le pregunté[1]:
– ¿Qué le has dicho a la maestra?
Ivo me miró de través[2] y vi relampaguear[3] sus ojos azules.
– Le hablé del árbol de oro.
Sentí una gran[4] curiosidad.
– ¿Qué árbol?
Hacía frío y el camino estaba[5] húmedo, con grandes charcos que brillaban al sol[6] pálido de la tarde. Ivo empezó a chapotear en ellos, sonriendo con misterio[7].
– Si no se lo cuentas a nadie[8] . . .

– Te lo juro[9] que a nadie[8] se lo diré.

Entonces Ivo me explicó:

– Veo un árbol de oro. Un árbol completamente de oro: ramas, tronco, hojas . . . ¿sabes? Las hojas no se caen nunca[8]. En verano, en invierno, siempre. Resplandece mucho; tanto, que tengo que cerrar los ojos[10] para que no me duelan[11].

– ¡Qué embustero eres! – dije, aunque con algo de zozobra. Ivo me miró con desprecio[7].

– No te lo creas[12] – contestó –. Me es completamente igual que te lo creas[13] o no . . . ¡Nadie entrará nunca[8] en la torrecita, y a nadie dejaré ver[14] mi árbol de oro! ¡Es mío[15]! La[16] señorita Leocadia lo sabe y no se atreve[17] a darle la llave a Mateo Heredia, ni a nadie . . . ¡Mientras yo viva[18], nadie podrá entrar allí y ver mi árbol!

ANA MARÍA MATUTE Historias de la Artámila

Investigate the examples of negatives, pronouns and subjunctives in the passage.

[1] ask, *21*. [2] *mirar de través*, *24*. [3] why infinitive? *11(a)*iii. [4] *gran*, *3*. [5] *estar*, *19*. [6] *al sol*, *9(a)*. [7] *con misterio*, *9(b)*. [8] negatives, *16*. [9] *lo*, *5* [10] *los ojos*, *2(c)*. [11] why subjunctive? *18(f)*. [12] imperatives, *17*. [13] why subjunctive? *18(i)*. [14] why infinitive? *18(b)*. [15] no article, *2(a)*. [16] *la*, *1(h)*. [17] *atreverse*, *11(b)*. [18] why subjunctive? *18(e)*.

3 The golden tree (c)

Ocurrió entonces algo que secretamente yo deseaba; me avergonzaba sentirlo[1], pero así era: Ivo enfermó, y la señorita Leocadia encargó a otro la llave de la torrecita. Primeramente, la disfrutó[2] Mateo Heredia[3]. Yo espié su regreso, el primer día[4], y le dije:

– ¿Has visto un árbol de oro?

– ¿Qué andas graznando? – me contestó de malos modos, porque no era[5] simpático, y menos conmigo.[6] Quise dárselo[7] a entender, pero no me hizo caso[8]. Unos días después me dijo:

– Si me das algo a cambio, te dejo un ratito[9] la llave y vas durante el recreo. Nadie te verá . . .

Vacié mi hucha y, por fin, conseguí[10] la codiciada llave. Mis manos temblaban[11] de emoción cuando entré en[12] el cuartito de la torre. Allí estaba[13] el cajón. Lo aparté y vi brillar[14] la rendija en la oscuridad. Me agaché y miré.

Cuando la luz dejó de cegarme, mi[15] ojo derecho sólo descubrió una cosa: la seca tierra de la llanura alargándose hacia el cielo. Nada más[16]. Lo mismo que[17] se veía desde las ventanas altas. La tierra desnuda y yerma, y nada más que la tierra. Tuve una gran decepción[18] y la seguridad de que me habían estafado. No sabía cómo[19] ni de qué[19] manera, pero me habían estafado.

ANA MARÍA MATUTE Historias de la Artámila

[1] infinitive, *11(a)*. [2] *disfrutar, 11(b)*. [3] position, *12(b)*. [4] adjectives, *3*. [5] *ser, 19*. [6] *conmigo, 4*. [7] *dar, 20(b)*. [8] *hacer, 20(j)*. [9] *ratito, 23*. [10] *conseguir, 11(b)*. [11] spelling, *26*. [12] *entrar en, 11(b)*. [13] *estar, 19*. [14] why infinitive? *11(a)*. [15] *mi ojo, 2(c)*. [16] negatives, *16*. [17] *lo mismo que, 24*. [18] *decepción, 25*. [19] why accent? *26(c)*.

4 The golden tree (d)

Olvidé la llave y el árbol de oro. Antes de que llegaran[1] las nieves[2] regresé a la ciudad.

Dos veranos más tarde volví a las montañas. Un día, pasando por el cementerio – era[3] ya tarde y se anunciaba la noche en el cielo: el sol, como una bola roja, caía a lo lejos[4], hacia la carrera terrible y sosegada de la llanura –, vi algo extraño. De la tierra grasienta y pedregosa, entre las cruces caídas, nacía un árbol grande y hermoso, con las hojas anchas de oro: encendido y brillante todo él, cegador. Algo me vino a la memoria[5], como un sueño, y pensé: "Es un árbol de oro." Busqué al pie[6] del árbol y no tardé[7] en dar con[8] una crucecilla[9] de hierro negro, mohosa por[10] la lluvia. Mientras la enderezaba, leí: Ivo Márquez, de diez años de edad.

Y no daba tristeza alguna, sino[11], tal vez, una extraña y muy grande alegría.

ANA MARÍA MATUTE Historias de la Artámila

Study the use of tenses in the passage.

[1] why subjunctive? *18(e)*. [2] position, *12*. [3] *ser, 19*. [4] *lo, 5(g)*. [5] *la memoria, 2(c)*. [6] *al pie de, 9(a)*. [7] *tardar en, 11(b)*. [8] *dar con, 20(b)*. [9] diminutives, *23*. [10] *por, 10*. [11] *sino, 8(b)*.

5 The Spanish football team in training

La selección nacional de fútbol se ha entrenado[1] con intensidad esta mañana en el campo de la Ciudad Lineal, bajo[2] la lluvia, con barro y ante[3] bastante público. El equipo *sparring* ha sido[1] el Plus Ultra, que jugó sin tregua un partido[4] de hora y media ante la siguiente[5] formación del equipo nacional:

Iríbar, Sanchís, Santamaría, Reija, Glaría, Violeta, Vavá, Luis, Ansola, Marcial y José María.

Dirigió el juego el seleccionador nacional, Balmanya, con "mono" azul y la cabeza protegida por un gorrito[6] de[7] lana multicolor. El Plus Ultra vistió de rojo[8] y azul y la selección, azulada por entero.

El entrenamiento se caracterizó por el juego efectuado por la selección, que no fue efectivo en forma de[9] goles, quizá porque los jugadores no tuvieran[10] órdenes de profundizar, sino[11] de mover la pelota con la máxima velocidad. Balmanya dedicó especial atención a Violeta, sometiéndole a un trabajo exhaustivo como jugador de enlace entre la defensa y el ataque, al que respondió plenamente el zaragocista[12]. Por parte[13] del Plus Ultra, el héroe fue Benjamín, tercer[14] portero del equipo, que se lució extraordinariamente en formidables paradas durante el bombardeo a que le sometieron los seleccionados[15].

El público se dejó llevar[16] de la pasión, aplaudiendo o abucheando las jugadas que observaba, con tal algarabía que Balmanya estimó oportuno[17] dirigirse a los espectadores mediante un altavoz para advertirles que, si no se reportaban[18], ordenaría que fuera[19] desalojado el campo[15].

La Vanguardia Española, Barcelona, 21 October 1966

Investigate the use of prepositions in the passage.

[1] tense, *11(c)*. [2] *bajo*, *19*. [3] *ante*, *9*. [4] *un partido*, *25*. [5] *siguiente*, *13(a)*. [6] *gorrito*, *23*. [7] *de*, *9(c)*. [8] *vistió de rojo*, *9*, *11(c)*. [9] *en forma de*, *9(c)*. [10] why subjunctive? *18(a)*. [11] *sino*, *8*. [12] the name given to footballers of the Zaragoza team. [13] *por*, *10*. [14] why no article? *2(a)*. [15] position, *12*. [16] *dejar*, *20*. [17] 'judged it the right moment'. [18] why indicative? *18(k)*. [19] why subjunctive? *18(b)*.

6 My father was a carpenter

– Yo nací arriba, en un pueblecito de los Andes. Mi padre era carpintero[1] y me mandó a la escuela. Hasta segundo año de primaria era todo lo que había. Y eso que tuve suerte de nacer en el pueblo, porque los niños del campo se quedaban sin escuela. Fuera de su carpintería, mi padre tenía un terrenito al lado del pueblo, y lo cultivaba con la ayuda de algunos indios a los que pagaba en plata[2] o con obritas de carpintería: el cabo[3] de una lampa[4] o un hacha, una mesita, en fin. Desde un extremo del corredor de mi casa veíamos amarillear[5] el trigo, verdear[5] el maíz, azulear[5] las habas en nuestra pequeña tierra. Daba gusto. Con la comida y la carpintería teníamos bastante, considerando nuestra pobreza. A causa de tener algo y también por[6] su carácter[7], mi padre no agachaba la[8] cabeza ante[9] nadie. Su banco de carpintero estaba[10] en el corredor de la casa, dando[11] a la calle. Pasaba el alcalde. "Buenos días, señor", decía mi padre, y se acabó. Pasaba el subprefecto. "Buenos días, señor", y asunto concluido. Pasaba el alférez de gendarmes[12]. "Buenos días, alférez", y nada más. Pasaba el juez y lo mismo[13]. Así era mi padre con los mandones[14].

CIRO ALEGRÍA (Peruvian) Calixto Garmendía

Study the use of the imperfect tense and diminutives in this passage.

[1] Why *ser* and no article? *2(a)ii*. [2] *plata*, Latin American word for 'money'. [3] 'handle'. [4] *lampa*, Peruvian word for a 'spade'. [5] *11(a)* and *21(b)*. [6] *para* and *por, 10*. [7] spelling, *26*. [8] *2(c)*. [9] *9(e)*. [10] why *estar? 19*. [11] *20(b)*. [12] 'chief' (of police). [13] *5*. [14] 'bosses'.

7 Cortés prepares to return to Spain (a)

Dispuesto[1] el viaje, envió a su mayordomo, Pedro Ruiz de Esquivel, con barras de oro para que fletase[2] dos navíos en Veracruz[3]. Esquivel se embarcó en la laguna con seis remeros indios y un negro. Pocos días después apareció el cadáver del mayordomo, sin que se supiese[2] ni[4] se intentase[2] averiguar la causa de aquella muerte misteriosa, que unos atribuían a venganza y otros a robo.

Los dos navíos que habían llegado a Veracruz y en los que hizo Cortés la travesía, le llevaron la noticia de la muerte de Martín, su padre, colaborador y agente. Enlutado, y, más que enlutado, atribulado por la pérdida[5] del hombre con quien tanto se identificaba en la vida, abandonó la costa que había pisado como conquistador[6] nueve años antes. Iba con

7

él su inseparable Sandoval[7], en quien ya veía un deudo[8] y no un compañero de armas. "Hijo Sandoval", solía[9] decirle. Después de Sandoval, Andrés de Tapia gozaba de[10] la predilección de Cortés, y este capitán fue también a España en aquel viaje.

CARLOS PEREYRA (Mexican) Hernán Cortés

Study the past participles in the passage.

[1] *dispuesto, 13.* [2] why subjunctive? *18(f).* [3] Veracruz: a seaport, founded by Cortés in 1519. [4] negatives, *16.* [5] *la pérdida:* note accent, *26.* [6] *como conquistador,* as a conqueror. [7] position, *12(a).* [8] *deudo, 25.* [9] *soler, 20(q).* [10] *gozar, 11(b).*

8 Cortés prepares to return to Spain (b)

A la corte no podía dirigirse sin dineros. Los llevó, pero, además, se proveyó[1] de joyas y curiosidades, tales como aceite, bálsamo cuajado, ámbar líquido, aves raras y dos tigres. El cacique tlaxcalteca[2] D. Luis de Vargas, hijo de Xicoténcatl, el Viejo, encabezaba una comitiva de jóvenes de la misma nación. Iban algunos caciques mexicanos y el indispensable séquito de albinos, corcovados, bailadores, jugadores de palos con los pies y jugadores de pelota de hule, novedad asombrosa[3].

Cortés anticipaba que recibiría homenajes como triunfador[4] y que debería[5] contestar cargos[6] como acusado.[4] Contaba para lo uno y para lo otro con[7] grandes admiradores que eran[8] poderosos padrinos, entre los que estaba[8] el duque de Béjar. No desdeñaba a los enemigos mortales por[9] torpes o pequeños. Sin ser vanaglorioso, su sentido práctico eliminaba las acusaciones netamente calumniosas, que no tenían por qué preocuparle. Casi todas las recriminaciones partían de la desmesurada grandeza del hombre. Decíase[10] que Cortés, absolutamente necesario por[9] su autoridad para[9] conservar unidos a los españoles y sometidos a los indios, había consumado una deserción ausentándose[11] de México[12] y yendo[11] a perderse en las regiones pantanosas de la selva

CARLOS PEREYRA (Mexican) Hernán Cortés

Study tenses and the use of *para* and *por*

[1] *se proveyó, 11(b).* [2] *tlaxcalteca,* adj. from Tlaxcala, the name of a Mexican district and the home of the powerful tribe overcome by

8

Cortés a few months before entering Mexico City, November 1519.
³ Note the position of the verb in this long sentence, *12(a)*. ⁴ *como*,
'as a' 6. ⁵ *deber*, *20(c)*. ⁶ *contestar*, *11(b)*. ⁷ *contar con*, *11(b)*. ⁸ *ser*, *19*.
⁹ *para* and *por*, *10*. ¹⁰ *decíase*, *4*. ¹¹ *gerundio*, *14(d)*. ¹² *Méjico* in
Castilian Spanish.

9 Cortés arrives in Spain

La leyenda tendió sus brazos a Cortés. Según ella, el conquistador de
México desembarcó en Palos y fue alojado en el convento[1] de La Rábida.
Allí se vieron Cortés y su primo Pizarro, bajo el mismo techo en que
hablaron Colón y fray Juan Pérez. Todavía se extreman las exigencias
de la fantasía[2], haciendo testigo[3] de aquel coloquio entre el conquistador
de México, que acababa su carrera, y el del Perú[4], que iniciaba la suya,
nada menos que a Juan de Rada, capitán[5] del séquito de Cortés y alma
de la conjuración que años más tarde privó de la vida a Pizarro en la
ciudad de los Reyes.

No contenta con esto, la leyenda dejó a Sandoval en la villa de Palos[6].
Lo alojaba un cordonero de jarcia[7]. Sintiéndose súbitamente atacado
de un mal que se lo llevaba por horas, Sandoval pidió que llamasen[8] a
Cortés, el cual conferenciaba[9] con Pizarro. El malvado cordonero tuvo
maña[10] para que los acompañantes de Sandoval llevasen el recado y él,
mientras tanto, a la vista del moribundo, se apropió[11] trece barras de oro
que el bravo capitán tenía en su alcoba. El ladrón escapó a toda prisa y
pudo[12] cruzar la frontera de Portugal. Cuando Cortés acudió al lado de su
amigo, éste ya no pensaba en[13] el oro robado, sino[14] en hacer su testa-
mento y en prepararse para morir cristianamente. El amado jefe le
confortaba[15] y le ofrecía que sería su albacea.

Con esta nueva tribulación, Cortés partió de Palos, abrazó a su madre
en Mérida y se arrodilló en el monasterio de Guadalupe.

CARLOS PEREYRA (Mexican) *Hernán Cortés*

¹ *convento*, monastery. ² position, *12*. ³ who is the *testigo*? ⁴ *el Perú*
(article needed). ⁵ why no article? *2(a)*. ⁶ *Palos* the seaport in Andalucía
where Columbus sailed from in 1492. ⁷ 'a sail-maker' (subject of the
verb). ⁸ why subjunctive? ⁹ tense, *11(c)*. ¹⁰ *tener maña*, to contrive.
¹¹ *apropiarse*, *11(b)*. ¹² *poder*, *20(m)*. ¹³ *pensar en*, *11(b)*. ¹⁴ *sino*, *8*.
¹⁵ *confortar*, *26*.

10 The generation gap

– Yo no vuelvo más allá.

Ernesto Dascal miró a su hijo con la severidad acostumbrada. Hundió el tenedor en la loma[1] de picadillo y arroz blanco y lo extrajo colmado; se lo llevó a la boca[2] y masticó con lentitud con los[2] ojos fijos en el sudoroso[3] vaso de agua mientras sus[2] sienes se movían al ritmo de la[2] mandíbula.

– Aquello no vale la pena[4], papá – dijo Luis y vio cómo engordaba[5] una vena que atravesaba la frente[6] de su padre. El viejo calculaba su próxima explosión. Luis temía que un día una embolia[7] lo abatiese[8] por[9] aquella costumbre de discutir durante las comidas. Ernesto Dascal tiró violentamente el tenedor sobre el plato.

– Haz lo que te dé[10] la gana con tu vida, siempre has sido un anormal[11].

– Un anormal no, papá, es que no aguanto aquello[12].

– Sí, un anormal, un anormal. Un hombre que no tiene capacidad para ganarse la vida[13], que no sabe enfrentarse a nada. ¿Tú sabes lo que yo he tenido que pasar para[9] llegar aquí?

Dascal temió que su padre comenzase[8] de nuevo la extensa narración de sus privaciones y sacrificios.

– A mí no me importa lo que seas[14], óyelo bien, no me importa; lo único[15] que exijo es que seas[16] el primero. Si quieres ser zapatero, allá tú, pero tienes que ser el mejor zapatero del[17] mundo. Por lo menos[15], el mejor zapatero de[17] Cuba.

LISANDRO OTERO (Cuban) *La situación*

[1] 'pile'. [2] *2(c)*. [3] cf. *sudar*. [4] *20(s)ii*. [5] cf. *gordo*. [6] *1(a)vi*. [7] 'blood clot'. [8] why subjunctive? *18(c)*. [9] *para* and *por*, *10*. [10] *20(b)* and *18(g)*. [11] 'abnormal'. [12] 'I can't take that'. [13] *24*. [14] 'what you are' (what you may be). [15] *5*. [16] why subjunctive? *18(b) iii*. [17] *9(c) ii*.

11 An early morning scene

– ¡Vamos, vamos! ¡Date prisa, que llegamos tarde! ¡Vamos, Bele!

– ¡En seguida estoy! ¡Espérame, que ya voy![1] Un minutín[2].

Eran las ocho de la mañana. El cielo estaba[3] gris panza de burra[4]. En la calle había poca luz. Las casas y las aceras parecían grises, más grises que nunca. Pasaban coches de tarde en tarde[5]. Motocarros de reparto[6] rompían con estridencia[7] el silencio de la calle tranquila y señorial[8]. Pronto volvía la calma[9]. Desde las ventanas de la casa de Bele se podía[10] ver la luz de la panadería[9], titilando en la penumbra matinal, con los cierres aún[11] a medio echar[12]. Se[13] veían dos carros de basura[9] que estaban cargando. Eran[14] como todos: altos y rectangulares, protegidos los laterales con planchas de madera que pudieran provenir[15] de cajones[2]. Entre los dos palos de delante un pobre pollino, a veces una triste mula escuálida, también pardos y grises, esperaban con paciencia[7]. Mientras llegaba el fin de la carga comían alfalfa[16] del saco que colgaba de su testuz[17]. Con medio morro[18] metido dentro y sus orejas de cuero tenían[9] una expresión a la vez[20] estúpida y resignada.

JUAN ANTONIO PAYNO *El curso*

Note the use of the imperfect tense – the tense of description – in this passage.

[1] Note the use of *ir*, correct from the speaker's point of view. In English 'I'm coming'. [2] refer to *23*. [3] *estar, 19*. [4] *gris panza de burra, 3(d)*. [5] *de tarde en tarde*, from time to time, *9(c)*. [6] 'motor-cycle delivery vehicles.' [7] *con estridencia, 6(d)*. [8] 'dignified'. [9] order of words, *12*. [10] *poder, 20(m)*. [11] *aún = todavía, 26*. [12] *a medio echar, 3, 11*. [13] *se, 4*. [14] *ser, 19*. [15] 'which might have come from'. [16] *alfalfa*, a type of grass fodder. [17] why singular? *2(c)*. [18] *morro*, muzzle. [19] what is the subject of this verb? [20] *a la vez, 9(a)*.

12 Bele

Por la calle se veía a algunas mujeres – criadas de servicio muchas – con la leche para el desayuno. En la esquina había una churrera[1]: la ancha caja de zinc estaba acostada[2] sobre las tijeras de pino blanco. Poco más allá, un bar abría sus cierres de hierro[3] y el camarero barría la acera. De algunos portales salían niñas, con uniformes azul marino[4] y carteras en la mano, camino[5] del colegio.

En el último piso de una casa de ladrillo rosa[4], grande, con balcones de hierro, Bele se afanaba[6] por[7] los pasillos alfombrados. Era[8] menuda, que quiere decir[9] baja y esbelta. Al andar llevaba una cadencia suave, semi-rígida, como[10] de alambre tierno. Aun[11] parada se notaba bullir[12] esa cadencia, vitalidad de mozuela[13] de dieciséis años. Los ojos oscilaban entre la chispa de alegría y la caricia coqueta. Coqueta, coquetuela hasta en la melenilla[13] sin gracia, castaño claro. Nariz respingoncilla[13] y barbilla[13] firme. Siempre corría por los pasillos a la mañana, buscando cosas. Ahora era el libro de Filosofía, luego la pluma, más tarde la cinta de la cabeza.

JUAN ANTONIO PAYNO *El curso*

Notice the use of adjectives and diminutives in this passage.

[1] *churrera:* a woman seller of *churros,* a kind of doughnut, very popular in Spain. [2] *acostada, 13.* [3] *cierre de hierro,* an iron blind used as a protection for business premises. [4] *azul marino, 3(d).* [5] *camino de, 24.* [6] *afanarse, 11(b).* [7] *por, 10.* [8] *ser, 19.* [9] *querer, 20(o).* [10] 'as if', *6(e).* [11] *aun, 26.* [12] why infinitive? *11(a).* [13] diminutives, *23.*

13 Bele and her sister Gabriela

Cuando ya llegaba a la puerta, donde su hermana Gabriela esperaba golpeando el suelo con el talón[1], volvió de pronto un poco azarada[2]. Corrió de puntillas[3] para no despertar a los demás[4] y subió a su cuarto. Del resto de la casa a su cuarto había una escalerilla[5] de caracol en hierro. Daba[6] a una habitación cuadradilla[5] pintada de azul. Allí había un sofá de dos asientos, algo hundidos ya por los brincos que año tras[7] año habían dado en él[6]. Pegadas a la pared, dos pequeñas librerías iguales, atestadas de libros de estudio, manoseados y medio rotos, bolígrafos inservibles, cuadernos con hojas a medio arrancar[8] y novelitas[5] de las que se ha dado[6] en llamar "rosas". (Cosa de confundir lo[9] rosado y lo[9] cretino.) Al lado de las librerías se abría una puerta[10]. Daba[6] a un cuarto con dos camas que ahora estaban revueltas. De una silla medio colgaba un pijama de chiquilla[5]. Por todo ello corrió Bele atropelladamente[10]. Cogió algo de la mesa de noche y volvió escaleras abajo, dejando la luz encendida[11] y la puerta abierta. Salió corriendo[12] del piso. Gabriela andaba ya cerca del portal. Cuando la alcanzó, Bele abrió la cartera de mano y metió lo que había recogido. Era[13] la foto de un chico estupendo.

JUAN ANTONIO PAYNO *El curso*

[1] article, *2(c).* [2] 'confused'. [3] 'on tiptoe'. [4] *demás, 3(g).* [5] diminutives, *23.* [6] *dar, 20(b).* [7] *tras, 9.* [8] infinitive, *11(a).* [9] *lo, 5.* [10] order of words, *12.* [11] *encendida, 13(b).* [12] *Salió corriendo, 14.* [13] tense, *11(c).*

14 The end of a siesta

Afuera de la ruinosa casa de campo medio escondida entre el denso follaje de los fresnos, cantaban los pájaros. La melodía se alzaba con un rumor de flautas que estremecía las ramas inmóviles por[1] la modorra[2] de la tarde otoñal. Dentro, de vez en vez, se escuchaba[3] la torpe y desafinada[4] escala de una corneta militar. Cesaba la orquesta. El aire se llenaba con los cuerpos negros de millares de pájaros; subían como en enjambre huyendo de la corneta, se dispersaban en abanico y volvían a los árboles reanudando sus trinos.

En la puerta hacían guardia dos soldaditos[5] inmóviles. El otoño cubría de hojas amarillas el camino. Bajo el puentecillo[5] de piedra, cerca del agua, lavaban sus ropas unas mujerucas[5].

El acre olor del estiércol invadía el patio del cuartel improvisado. Un coronel con la guerrera desabrochada, salió al corredor llamando con voces irritadas:

– ¡Capitán Ramírez! ¡Capitán Ramírez!

El capitán Ramírez llegó corriendo[6] del fondo. Golpeó los tacones de sus botas haciendo el saludo militar al mismo tiempo que arqueaba exageradamente el pecho:

– A las órdenes, mi coronel.

– Pero, ¿dónde diablos se mete usted siempre? ¿Ha olvidado las órdenes que se le dieron?

– No, mi coronel, no las he olvidado, pero . . .

– No hay peros que valgan[7]. A las cinco debería usted haber salido con el pelotón de ejecución y son las cinco y diez.

– Mi coronel – imploró Ramírez mirando angustiado al superior – estoy formando el pelotón. Hubo necesidad de despertar a los soldados.

FERNANDO BENÍTEZ (Mexican) *Otoño*

In this passage study the order of words, the use of tenses and examples of diminutives.

[1] *por, 16.* [2] 'drowsiness'. [3] *se escuchaba, 11(d).* [4] 'out of tune'. [5] diminutives, etc. *23.* [6] *gerundio, 14.* [7] why subjunctive? *18(g).*

15 The condemned man is led away

Los zapatos golpearon las piedras del patio rítmicamente; el compás[1] tomó un aire hueco al cruzar el puente y después se apagó en el blando polvo del camino.

No habían recorrido largo trecho cuando el reo pidió un cigarrillo. El capitán bajó la espada y se palpó los[2] bolsillos. Sacó un paquete y se lo tendió sin detenerse. El preso lo tomó, prendió un fósforo defendiendo la llama con las[2] manos.

– Perdone, – dijo con voz segura arrojando el fósforo apagado – ¿no es usted Ramírez? ¿Luis Ramírez o Ramírez Luis como decía el maestro al pasar lista³ en la clase?

– Sí, soy Ramírez – respondió molesto el jefe de la escolta. – Luis Ramírez. El capitán Ramírez – insistió cargando el acento sobre la jerarquía.

– ¿No se acuerda usted de mí?

– No, no me acuerdo.

– Soy Pablo Trejo, su compañero de colegio.

Ramírez torció el gesto. Aquel reconocimiento era de una inoportunidad absoluta.

El reo continuó hablando en tono indiferente:

– Conocí a su madre. Isabel se llamaba. Se pasaba la vida sentada en el balcón tras las cortinillas de encaje que descorría para seguir nuestros juegos. Tenía los² cabellos rubios, los² ojos azules y era pálida, casi transparente, como los jarrones de alabastro que adornaban la escalera de su casa. ¿Se acuerda usted de ellos?

La primera flecha había dado en el blanco⁴. Ante Ramírez se levantó la imagen de su madre. Vigilándolos en el balcón se apagó dulcemente su vida.

FERNANDO BENÍTEZ (Mexican) *Otoño*

Study the use of the tenses in this passage.

¹ *el compás*, the step (military). ² why the article? *2(c)*. ³ *pasar lista*, to call the roll. ⁴ *dar en el blanco*, to hit the target.

16 Doubtful duck (a)

Un cazador de ocasión¹, observador y filósofo por temperamento, de espíritu analítico y sagaz, a quien yo mucho quería, mató en sus andanzas cinegéticas² uno de esos patos negros de¹ cuerpo aplastado y cabeza de¹ víbora, que suelen³ verse como⁴ pegados en las grandes piedras de nuestros arroyos y a los que nadie molesta por ser⁵ pato hediondo.

Cuando⁶ nuestro hombre llegó con su pato a la linda casa en donde se hospedaba, fue recibido con ruidosa hilaridad; la gente reía a carcajadas⁷, alguien disculpaba el error del cazador, pero las mujeres, sobre todo, se apretaban la nariz y mirábanse a los lados, como⁴ dispuestas a huir.

– ¡Puf⁸, el pato hediondo!

– ¡Solamente a usted se[9] le puede ocurrir[10] matar un pato hediondo!

– ¡Dios mío[8], qué disparate[8]!

– ¿Y para qué[11] lo trae?

– Para que lo comamos[12] en el almuerzo – dijo el cazador.

Todas las manos se dirigieron hacia él y una exclamación, mezcla[13] de terror y asco, hizo[14] vibrar el aire. Hubo arcadas[15] y escupidas[16].

– Pero díganme[17] con calma[18], señoras y señores, ¿han probado alguna vez un pato hediondo?

– ¿Nosotras? ¡Sólo que[19] estuviéramos locas de remate[20]!

– ¿Y ustedes, caballeros?

– ¡No, hombre! ¡Cómo quiere . . .!

– Pues entonces probémoslo[17], y en último caso que me lo preparen[21] para mí: experimentaremos – dijo el cazador.

La cocinera se apoderó[22] del pato.

MARTÍN GIL (Argentine) *Una novena en la sierra*

[1] *de ocasión*, *9(c)*. [2] 'hunting (or shooting) expeditions'. [3] *soler*, *20(q)*. [4] *como*, as if, *6(e)*. [5] *por ser*, *10*, *11(a)*. [6] Study the tenses in this paragraph, *11(c)*. [7] *reír a carcajadas*, *24*. [8] 'Phew', *22*. [9] *se*, *9*. [10] spelling, *26*. [11] ¿*para qué*? *10*, *15*. [12] why subjunctive? *18(f)*. [13] why no article? *2(a)*. [14] *hacer*, *20(j)*. [15] 'retchings'. [16] *escupidas* from *escupir*. [17] imperatives, *17*. [18] adverbs, *6*, *9(b)*. [19] 'only if'. [20] 'hopelessly'. [21] *18(a)*. [22] *apoderarse*, *11(b)*.

17 Doubtful duck (b)

Cuando en medio[1] del almuerzo apareció la sirviente con el pobre animal tendido de lomo[2] sobre una gran[3] fuente de porcelana floreada, engalanado con brillante lechuga, discos de tomates rojos y redondelas de huevo, las canillas tiesas y envueltas en papel picado parodiando calzones, el pescuezo en forma[1] de interrogante y las alas contraídas y rígidas, un profundo silencio reinó[4] en el comedor. Sin embargo, en todas las caras relampagueaban[4] risas ocultas, comprimidas, prontas a estallar como bombas al primer contacto.

– Vamos a ver, traigan[5] para[6] aquí ese animal – dijo el interesado, haciendo[7] crujir el trinchante contra la chaira.

– Quien se anime[8] a comer esto, que avise[9] – agregó; y la hoja reluciente del cuchillo se hundió silenciosa[10] en el cuerpo del pato, buscando con afán sus coyunturas.

– La verdad es que no se siente ningún mal olor – replicó la señora dueña de la casa, con cierta[11] indecisión, pero alcanzando el plato para que la sirvieran[12].

Sea[13] por imitación o[13] por[14] lo que se quiera[15], el hecho es que todos siguieron el ejemplo de la valiente dama y probaron el pato.

– ¡Delicioso! – exclamó la señora, en plena lucha[16] con un muslo.

– ¡Espléndido! ¡Riquísimo! – dijeron todos en coro.

– Pero ¿quién habrá[4] sido el bruto que se le ocurrió[17] llamarle pato hediondo? – refunfuñó el viejo abuelo, chupeteando un ala con fruición y haciendo chasquir su labio caído y embadurnado de[18] aceite.

MARTÍN GIL (Argentine) *Una novena en la sierra*

[1] why no article? *2(a)*, *9(d)*. [2] *de lomo*, on its back. [3] *gran*, *3(h)*. [4] tense, *11(c)*. [5] imperative, *17*. [6] *para*, *10*. [7] *hacer*, *20(j)*. [8] why subjunctive *18(g)*. [9] why subjunctive? *18(a)*, *17*. [10] *silenciosa*, *6(b)*. [11] why no article? *2(a)*. [12] why subjunctive? *18(f)*. [13] *Sea . . .o*, *8*. [14] *por*, *10*. [15] why subjunctive? *18(g)*. [16] *en plena lucha*, *9(d)*. [17] *se*, *4*. [18] past participle and *de*, *13*.

18 Segovia

– Éste es el momento, Raquel; asómese a la ventanilla . . .

Quedaba atrás el hermoso panorama[1] de Segovia, sobre un altozano, entre un macizo de verdura, descollando las esbeltas siluetas[2] del Alcázar y la Catedral, todo visto a través de los arcos del acueducto[2], que describían en el aire diáfano sus graciosas curvas y que, a aquella distancia, más que[3] una labor de titanes parecía un finísimo encaje formado por las milagrosas manos de las hadas.

Las mulas seguían caminando[4] a galope[5]. A nuestra derecha, lejanas, se dibujaban las azules líneas de la sierra[6]; íbamos dejando[4] atrás trotadores borriquillos[7], en los que caminaban a mujeriegas[8] los más variados tipos segovianos. Esos tipos extraños que ha sabido sorprender el pincel[6] de Zuloaga[9]. Las mujeres con los rojos manteos sobre la cabeza; los hombres con sus acartonadas monteras[10], sus capas larguísimas, sus abarcas[11] de cuero y sus medias azules. Lucía el sol esplendoroso en un cielo purísimo, sin una sola nube. Llegaban a nuestros oídos[12], con intervalos, los gritos de nuestro cochero[6] que animaba a las mulas con rotundas interjecciones y restallar[13] de la fusta en el aire.

FRANCISCO DE COSSÍO *El estilete de oro*

¹ *el panorama*, *1(a)*. ² spelling, *26*. ³ *más que*, rather than. ⁴ *gerundio*, *14(c)*
⁵ *a galope*, *9(a)*. ⁶ order of words, *12*. ⁷ diminutives, *23*. ⁸ *a mujeriegas*,
9(a). ⁹ *Zuloaga*, Basque painter 1870–1945 who specialized in depicting
regional types. ¹⁰ *acartonada*, old and stiff (like cardboard); *montera*,
headgear (used also for a bull-fighter's cap). ¹¹ *abarcas*, rustic sandals.
¹² *oídos* not *orejas*. What is the difference? ¹³ infinitive as a noun, *11(a)*.

19 Down the steps to the crypt

Fernando Sandoval empuñó la linterna eléctrica, la misma que había
utilizado la noche anterior para¹ su excursión misteriosa y, cogiendo
debajo del brazo el tubo de hojadelata² donde se encerraba el plano del
castillo, bajamos a la cripta. Yo, sin que supiera³ por qué, iba presa
de un miedo inexplicable. Una serie de sombríos pensamientos desfilaban
tétricamente por mi imaginación y, por más empeño que ponía⁴, me era
imposible descifrarlos. Era como si pensase⁵ en un idioma⁶ desconocido.
Sin embargo, a pesar de no llegar⁷ a conocer el significado de mis pensamientos, palpitaba en el fondo de mi conciencia⁸ un presentimiento
terrible⁹. No había duda; tenía miedo de bajar a la cripta. Hasta estuve¹⁰
por proponer a mi amigo el aplazamiento de nuestras investigaciones.

– Ten cuidado, no te mates¹¹ – dijo éste al dar yo un resbalón¹² en uno
de los escalones –. Hay que bajar con lentitud, porque con la humedad
está esta escalera de lo más resbaladiza.

– No te apures¹¹ – repliqué yo –. Ya llevo cuidado por la cuenta que
me tiene.

Sandoval abría en aquel momento la puerta de la cripta. Entonces
observé¹⁰ un detalle que me llenó¹⁰ de inquietud.

FRANCISCO DE COSSÍO *El estilete de oro*

¹ *para*, *10*. ² *hojadelata* (*hojalata*), tin-plate. ³ why subjunctive? *18(f)*.
⁴ why indicative? *18(g)*. ⁵ why subjunctive? *18(k)*. ⁶ *el idioma*, *1(a)*.
⁷ why infinitive? *11(a)*. ⁸ *conciencia*, *26*. ⁹ order of words, *12*. ¹⁰ tense,
11(c), *10*. ¹¹ imperatives, *17*. ¹² *dar un resbalón*, to slip.

20 1. 2. X. in the hospital pools (a)

– Es un caso difícil el de la¹ señora de Giménez, ¿eh?

– Sí que lo² es, Hortensia, sí que lo es.

– Ya me he dado cuenta. De primera división.

– ¿Qué dice usted?

– Que es un caso de primera división. Es una clasificación que hago yo de los casos según el equipo que juega. Y aquí el equipo es de primera división.

– ¿El equipo?

– ¡Naturalmente! ¡El equipo de médicos! ¿No es medicina de equipo lo que está usted haciendo? A esta señora, por ejemplo, la[3] han visto el internista[4], el ginecólogo, el analista, el radiólogo, el oculista[4], el anatomopatólogo . . . Y si la operan caerá en manos[5] del anestesista[4] del cirujano, del transfusor . . . Indudablemente es un caso de primera división.

– Es muy poco digno de usted tomar en broma[6] cosas tan serias. A este paso[7] acabará haciendo quinielas[8] con los enfermos: enfermo salvado, un uno; fallecido, un dos; y si queda estropeado, una equis[9].

SANTIAGO LORÉN *Diálogos con mi enfermera*

[1] article, *1(g)*. [2] *lo, 5(d)*. [3] *la, 4.* [4] gender, *1(b)*. [5] *en manos de, 2(a), 9(d)*. [6] 'to take as a joke'. [7] 'at this rate'. [8] *quinielas*, pools (football, pelota, etc.). [9] *una equis*, 'x' *1(a)*.

21 1. 2. X. in the hospital pools (b)

– ¡No tendría gracia[1]!. Acertaría[2] siempre los catorce resultados[3]. Pero no es que tome[4] en broma nada. Únicamente que, a veces, me parece demasiada[5] gente para[6] una sola enfermedad.

– En eso consiste precisamente su error: en pensar que es demasiada gente para una sola enfermedad, cuando, en realidad, toda esa "gente" no se ocupa[7] de una enfermedad sino[8] de un enfermo.

– Bueno. ¿Y qué diferencia hay?

– Enorme. Para que la comprendiera[9] tendría que darle un curso de Historia de la Medicina, sobre todo en lo que se refiere al cambio sufrido desde el concepto organicista, localista, del siglo pasado hasta la concepción totalista de nuestros días, en que se considera[10] al enfermo como un ente total e indivisible. No hay ningún proceso ni[11] afección, por simple y aislado que parezca[12], que no tenga[13] repercusión sobre todos los sistemas[14] de nuestra economía. Por eso es necesario, a veces, tanto especialista[15] para[6] lo que parece un solo conflicto.

SANTIAGO LORÉN *Diálogos con mi enfermera*

¹ 'it wouldn't be funny'. ² *acertar*, to hit the mark, guess correctly.
³ spelling. ⁴ why subjunctive? *18(i)*. ⁵ *demasiada*, *3(g)*. ⁶ *para*, *10*.
⁷ *ocuparse de*, *11(b)*. ⁸ *sino*, *8*. ⁹ why subjunctive? *18(f)*. ¹⁰ *se*, *4*.
¹¹ negatives, *16*. ¹² why subjunctive? *18(h)*. ¹³ why subjunctive?
¹⁴ *el sistema*, *1(a)*, *26*. ¹⁵ translate as plural.

22 The telegram

El sábado, día señalado para el retorno de los Rengel¹, el viejo se levantó
optimista como de costumbre. Los nietos se precipitaron a saludarlo:

– ¡Yo primero!
– ¡Yo primero!

Eran dos bellos rapaces de pocos años.

– Abuelito – dijo el mayor – han traído esto. – Y le alcanzó² un telegrama que rezaba³ "urgente". Pero el millonario no encontraba sus
lentes⁴ de lectura y se metió el despacho⁵ al bolsillo.

– Abuelo – agregó el otro – ahora verás lo que yo encontré.

Y nervioso, impaciente, lo llevó al patio colonial, donde el sol invadía
ya la vasta superficie.

En una esquina, sobre un montón de paja, yacía un llamito⁶ blanco,
muy pequeño, casi un recién nacido. Tenía las orejas enhiestas⁷, la piel
suavísima, sin la más leve mancha. Gemía de hambre. Los chicos le
dieron leche y se calmó. Luego alzó los ojos oscuros, aterciopelados
hacia el viejo, y su mirada inocente lo ofuscó. ¿Qué sería?

Un recuerdo lejano desde un tiempo olvidado, hirió como un rayo
su mente.

El millonario subió precipitadamente la escalera de piedra, pidió
sus lentes de lectura, y sostenido por los brazos amorosos de Leonora
leyó el telegrama: "Anoche estréllose contra cordillera avión procedente
del oeste. Viajaban hermanos Rengel. No hay sobrevivientes. Prepare
familia. – Lloyd."

FERNANDO DÍEZ DE MEDINA (Bolivian) *El llamo blanco*

¹ *Rengel*: why singular? *1(b)*. ² *alcanzar*, Bolivian for *entregar*, to hand
over. ³ *rezar = decir*. ⁴ *lentes de lectura*, reading glasses. ⁵ *el despacho =
el telegrama*. ⁶ 'a baby llama'. ⁷ *enhiesto*, erect.

23 A perilous Mexican dance (a)

Por entre[1] la multitud ya apiñada se abrieron paso[2] los que iban a tomar parte en la danza. El primero en[3] subir fue un joven que lucía, atados en la[4] cabeza y en las[4] manos, unos pañuelos de vivos colores. Vestía[5] calzón y camisa de manta muy blanca. Subió a grandes zancadas[6], apoyándose en las vueltas del cable que se enredaba al mástil como enorme culebra. Al llegar[7] a la cúspide, se sentó en el banco, esperando que subieran[8] los demás[9] partícipes en la danza.

El segundo en[3] llegar fue el de la chirimía[10] y el tambor. Después tres jóvenes ocuparon los lados del cuadrado, no sin antes atarse a la[4] cintura los extremos de los cables enrollados en el carrete del cual pendían sus improvisados e inseguros asientos.

Tambor y chirimía comenzaron a sonar. Las miradas de toda la multitud estaban puestas en el que, sentado en la parte más alta, ya hacía intento[11] de levantarse. Cuando se alzó, la música se antojaba más fuerte, tan grande era el silencio que reinaba abajo[12]. El hombre comenzó a danzar, dando saltos[13] sobre una superficie en la que apenas si[14] cabían[15] las plantas de sus pies. Según la música, se inclinaba hacia los cuatro puntos cardinales, pasaba los pañuelos que tenía en las manos por sobre las cabezas de sus camaradas, como si al hacerlo les dijera[16] un secreto y, luego, saltaba tan alto que a cada vez se[17] pensaba en la muerte. De vez en cuando emitía un alarido que era[18] contestado por los que estaban también en la altura.

GREGORIO LÓPEZ Y FUENTES (Mexican) *El indio*

Study the use of tenses in this passage.

[1] *por entre*, through. [2] *abrise paso*, *11(b)*. [3] *en*, *9(d)*. [4] definite article, *2(c)*. [5] tense, *11(c)*, *11(b)*. [6] 'in great strides', *9(a)*. [7] *al* and infinitive, *11(a)*. [8] why subjunctive? *18(c)*. [9] *demás*, *3*. [10] *chirimía*, flageolet. [11] cf. *intentar*, *25*. [12] *abajo*, *9(i)*. [13] *dar saltos*, *20(b)*. [14] *apenas si*, hardly. [15] *cabían*, *20(a)*. [16] why subjunctive? *18(k)*. [17] *se*, *4*. [18] *ser* and *estar*, *19*.

24 A perilous Mexican dance (b)

Al terminar la danza, el de la cúspide volvió a sentarse en el pequeño banco. El de la chirimía y el tambor comenzó a bajar por la escalera hecha con las vueltas del cable. Y el sitio que el otro dejó libre fue ocupado por el bailarín, quien se ató el lazo libre a la[1] cintura. Cuando volvió a sonar la música, los cuatro hombres se lanzaron al vacío. El carrete comenzó a dar vueltas y los lazos comenzaron a desenrollarse. A medida que giraban[2], los círculos iban haciéndose[3] más grandes. Los voladores, con la[1] cabeza hacia abajo y con los brazos abiertos como las alas de un pájaro, parecían[2] la reencarnación del viejo anhelo de volar. De vez en[4] cuando lanzaban gritos como las águilas, a los que respondía la multitud entusiasmada[5]. La música era rápida como el giro de los voladores. El objeto de éstos, en los casos fatales, es el de atrapar en la caída al que, a la hora de la danza, se expone en lo[6] más alto.

Cuando estuvieron[2] en tierra fueron[2] agasajados con un trago de aguardiente[7] e invitados a[8] comer, pues[9] entre los rituales para el volador figura, en primer lugar[10], el ayuno.

Pasadas[11] algunas horas, el volador fue tan sólo una de las diversiones en la fiesta, sin duda la más espectacular.

GREGORIO LÓPEZ Y FUENTES (Mexican) *El indio*

[1] article, *2(c)*. [2] tense, *11(c)*. [3] *gerundio, 14, 21(b)*. [4] *en, 9(d)*.
[5] *entusiasmada, 26*. [6] *lo, 5*. [7] (colourless) 'brandy'. [8] *invitados a, 11(b)*.
[9] *pues*, since. [10] *en primer lugar, 9*. [11] past participle, *13*.

25 The deserted village

Los funcionarios del pueblo, después de haber avisado a la superioridad lo[1] sucedido, organizaron la expedición violentamente[2], pues la respuesta fue ordenando que se castigara[3] a los culpables. La columna fue integrada por los policías, por algunos de los vecinos más resueltos y que se prestaron de buena gana, así como[4] por el profesor de la localidad y por el secretario del presidente municipal. Éste, montado en su mejor caballo, encabezaba la pequeña tropa.

En un sitio adecuado, la expedición se dividió en tres grupos, bajo la advertencia de que, al pisar sus sombras[5], todos deberían[6] hallarse en las afueras de la ranchería. Se trataba de[7] cerrar todos los caminos, algo así como si hubieran[8] querido ponerle puertas al monte.

Los que avanzaron[9] por los sitios más escabrosos dejaron sus cabalgaduras y siguieron a pie. Todos llevaban listas sus armas, como que[10] las órdenes del presidente municipal eran muy enérgicas: fuego a los que huyeran[11] y exterminio en caso de resistencia. La mayoría lamentaba el mal estado de los caminos, culpando a los naturales[12] de no haber mejorado en[13] tantos años sus vías de comunicación. Por[14] primera vez el presidente municipal pisaba aquellos lugares, percatándose de la miseria en que vivían aquellos a quienes iba a perseguir.

Dadas[15] las señales convenidas con un cuerno a falta de[16] corneta, los grupos entraron[9] a la ranchería sin que habitante alguno[17] pasara[18] por los callejones o al menos se asomara[18] a[19] las puertas. Las casas permanecían cerradas. Ningún indicio revelador de la presencia de los naturales.

GREGORIO LÓPEZ Y FUENTES (Mexican) *El indio*

[1] *lo*, 5. [2] *violentamente*, here, 'forcefully'. [3] why subjunctive? *18(b)*. [4] 'as well as'. [5] 'with the sun behind them'. [6] *deber*, *20(c)*. [7] *tratarse de*, *24*. [8] why subjunctive? *18(k)*. [9] tense, *11(c)*. [10] *como que*, since. [11] why subjunctive? *18(g)*. [12] 'natives'. [13] *en*, *9(d)*. [14] *por*, *10*. [15] past participle, *13*. [16] *a falta de*, *20(g)*. [17] negatives, *16*. [18] why subjunctive? *18(f)*. [19] *asomarse a*, *11(b)*.

26 Private lessons

Vivía[1] en un hotel de primera clase, sola, naturalmente. Su origen era[2] alemán, aunque ella había[3] nacido en Francia. Era una mujer muy solitaria. Que diera[4] clases de francés no me parecía extraño. Pero que viviese[4] en ese hotel, rodeada de comodidad, no alcanzaba a comprenderlo[5]. Era una mujer alta, anormalmente alta, de[6] cara grande y surcada, muy blanca a causa de los polvos abundantes que ponían aún[7] más en evidencia el estrago de su belleza. Todo en ella propendía a lo[5] aumentativo, a la grandeza, a una expresión desmesurada de su propia personalidad. Así, viéndola de[6] pie, imponía por su volumen: como si fuera[8] más alta de lo que[9] en realidad era. Vestía[10] con mucha ropa, muchos paños de lana, como si su enemigo declarado fuese[8] el frío. Nuestro encuentro regularizado duró un mes. Cada vez que se trataba de[11] la lección explícita, pronunciación y explicaciones, su actitud guardaba por completo la apariencia profesional y en ella regían la norma, el interés vivo y la paciencia requeridos al acto de enseñar. Pero cuando se motivaba, como por azar[12], un paréntesis en el transcurso de la hora de clase, podía[13] yo darme[14] cuenta de que la pobre mujer se transformaba. Luego volvía a la pronunciación como[15] cayendo de una nube.

CARLOS EDMUNDO DE ORY *Una exhibición peligrosa*

[1] tense, *11(g)*. [2] *ser*, *19*. [3] why indicative? *18(f)*. [4] why subjunctive? *18(i)* and *(j)*. [5] *lo*, *5*. [6] *de*, *9(c)*. [7] *aún* or *aun*? *26*. [8] why subjunctive? *18(k)*. [9] *de lo que*, *17*. [10] *vestía*, *11(b)*. [11] *tratarse de*, *24*. [12] *como por azar*, as if by chance. [13] *poder*, *20(m)*. [14] *dar*, *20(b)*. [15] *como*, as if, *6(e)*.

27 A ghost in the forest

Esa noche me tocaba[1] entregar la guardia[2] al sargento, que roncaba sonoramente, a[3] veinte pasos de mí[4], echado[5] entre las pajas, sobre el poncho, y con la[6] cabeza apoyada[5] en la mochila[7].

A[8] la luz de la fogata, que manteníamos encendida[5] para ahuyentar las fieras, miré mi reloj y vi que era la hora[9]. La noche era[10] tibia y serena y las estrellas palpitaban en un cielo infinitamente profundo y lejano.

Me iba a levantar para despertar al[11] sargento Chala, cuando advertí una sombra que se aproximaba por la otra parte del fuego.

Empuñé mi pistola y me incorporé de un salto.

– ¡No se mueva, mi teniente![12] ¡Soy yo[13], Tipor, el guía!

– ¡Ah! ¿Por qué estás[14] despierto, indio, cuando te toca[1] dormir? Mañana amanecerás[15] cansado y se te caerán[16] los[6] ojos en la marcha y erraremos el camino.

– Hace cuatro días que mis ojos no se cierran[17], ni[18] de día ni de noche[19] – me contestó –. Y ya no volveré a cerrarlos nunca más . . . nunca más[18].

Se arrimó al tronco seco donde yo estaba[14] sentado[5], un inmenso[20] quebracho[21] derrumbado por el huracán[20] o por el rayo o por el hacha[22] de los exploradores cien años atrás[23]; y notando que mis[6] manos no habían soltado la pistola, y leyendo en mis ojos que desconfiaba de él, me dijo con una voz que me penetró como una corriente de aire helado:

– ¡He visto la sombra de un muerto! . . . ¡La sombra de mi padre, que murió aquí, en Otumpa, a manos de[24] un hijo!

HUGO WAST (Argentine) *Sangre en el umbral*

Study the use of tenses and participles in this passage *11(c)*

[1] *tocar*, *24*. [2] gender, *1(a)*. [3] *a*, required before an expression of distance, *9(a)*. [4] *mí*, *27(c)*. [5] why past participle? *13(b)*. [6] *la*, *2(c)*. [7] 'haversack'. [8] *a*, *9(a)*. [10] why *ser*? *19*. [11] why *al*? *2(d)*. [12] why *mi*? *2(d)ii*. [13] *Soy yo*, it is I. [14] why *estar*? *19*. [15] 'you will wake up'. [16] 'you will fall asleep'. [17] tense? *11(c)*. [18] negatives, *16*. [19] *9(c)*. [20] *26*. [21] name of a South American tree. [22] *2(b)*. [23] 'before'. [24] *9(a)vi*.

28 Trouble with the neighbours

Dolores fue a la cocina, vació la bolsa de la plaza y se dispuso a[1] preparar la comida. Encendió el gas; apenas si[2] daba una llamita[3] trémula. "No nos faltaba[4] ahora más que esto", pensó.

Sentóse en un escaño, abatida. De cuando en cuando miraba a la llamita azul del gas, que en vez de crecer disminuía.

Se oyó abrir[5] con el llavín la puerta. Era Lucía.

– Buenas[6], señora.

– ¿Ve usted eso? – le dijo, refiriéndose al gas.

– Pues lo que nos faltaba[4]; que después de la abundancia de comida de que disfrutamos[7], nos quiten[8] el gas . . .

Seguía sentada, sin levantarse, Dolores. Se encontraba floja y mareada.

– ¿Tenemos astillas?

– Ahí queda medio cajón, pero hay que hacerlas.

– Parta unas pocas; pondremos unos huevos fritos . . . ¿Trajo el litro de aceite?

– Sí.

La asistenta[9] se fue al cuarto de al lado[10] y empezó a hacer astillas. Retembló el suelo, sacudido por los hachazos[11] y se desquijeraron[12] las tablas[13] en largas esquirlas[14].

En el piso de abajo empezaron a golpear con el mango del escobón en el techo en señal de protesta. Pero Lucía seguía dándole al hacha. El ruido era[15] infernal; las ventanas del patio empezaron a florecer y a erizarse de gritos de protesta.

– ¡A hacer astillas, a la calle; que ésta es una casa de vecindad! – gruñó[16] la señora del principal derecha[17].

JUAN ANTONIO DE ZUNZUNEGUI *Mis páginas preferidas*

[1] *a*, 9(*a*). [2] *apenas si*, hardly. [3] diminutives, 23. [4] *faltar*, 20(*g*). [5] why infinitive? 11(*a*). [6] *tardes*, is sometimes omitted, as here. [7] *disfrutar*, 11(*b*). [8] why subjunctive? 18(*i*). [9] *asistenta*, helper. [10] *de al lado*, next. [11] *hachazos*, blows with a hatchet. [12] *desquijerar*, (here) to split. [13] *las tablas*, boards (from the *cajón!*). [14] *esquirlas*, splinters (here) of wood. [15] *ser*, 19. [16] *gruñó*, from *gruñir*, to growl, grumble. [17] 'first floor on the right'.

29 The origins of Columbus (a)

Según Bernardini-Sjoestedt, Colón habría pertenecido, eso sí[1], a una familia de navegantes[2]; hubo en ella algunos hombres famosos, de lo cual se alabaría él repetidamente, aunque con palabras vagas, rodeadas siempre de misterio; en algún momento se alabaría incluso de no ser el primer almirante[2] que había en su familia. No obstante, estos navegantes se dedicaron en su mayoría al corso[3], según la práctica de la época y también el futuro descubridor debió[4] tomar parte en algunas de aquellas expediciones.

Es, en efecto, casi seguro que Colón navegó como[5] corsario desde muy joven, al parecer desde los catorce años. Tal vez lo hizo a las órdenes de algún pariente[6] o, como dice, de su propio padre. En estas correrías debieron de[7] entrar en conflicto con las autoridades de Génova[8] y hasta de la propia isla, y así se explicaría, siempre según este biógrafo, el interés de Colón en mantener el misterio[2], en dejar siempre envuelta en sombras la cuestión[2] de su familia y de su patria, en la necesidad de ocultar esta parte de ella, para no perjudicar[2] a los suyos y, sobre todo, al esplendor de su gloria naciente[9].

SEBASTIÁN JUAN ARBÓ *La Vanguardia Española*, 22 October 1966

Study the use of tenses in these passages.

[1] *eso sí*, 'certainly'.   [2] spelling, *26*.   [3] 'privateering'.   [4] *deber*, *20(c)*.   [5] *como*, *6(e)vi*.   [6] *pariente*, *25*.   [7] *debieron*, must have, *20(c)*.   [8] *Génova*, Genoa.   [9] present participle, *13*.

30 The origins of Columbus (b)

Se ha escrito mucho, como sabemos, sobre este punto de la vida de Colón; es casi seguro que continuará escribiéndose[1], dado el empeño de algunos fanáticos en probar[2] lo que es y lo que no es, en demostrar lo[3] discutible y lo indiscutible; pero sea lo que fuere[4], esta biografía de Bernardini-Sjoestedt habrá de ser tenida[5] en cuenta. De aquí en adelante, cuando se hable[6] de la patria del descubridor, de sus antecesores, de sus ideas, no podrá dejarse[7] de contar con este estudio, sin duda el más interesante que se[1] ha escrito hasta[8] hoy sobre aquella vida, y el más profundo.

Quizá la versión llegue[9] a aclararse del todo o a oscurecerse aún[10] con nuevas pruebas, como se[1] ha aclarado y se ha oscurecido en tantas ocasiones. De momento, pocas tesis se[1] han presentado, a mi juicio, defendidas con mejores razones, con argumentos más convincentes[11], que hayan[12] arrojado sobre estas cuestiones una luz más clara; de tal modo, que casi me atrevería a predecir, a partir de aquí, que la tesis del origen corso del almirante ha de quedar establecida definitivamente, y al lado de ella la falsedad de su origen judío, y no ya de judíos conversos procedentes de las Baleares, como quiere Madariaga[13], sino[14] ni siquiera[15] judíos.

SEBASTIÁN JUAN ARBÓ *La Vanguardia Española* 22 October 1966

[1] *Se*, *4(b)*. [2] why infinitive? *11(a)*. [3] *lo*, *5*. [4] 'be that as it may'. [5] take, *21(i)xv*. [6] why subjunctive? *18(e)*. [7] *dejar*, *20(d)*. [8] *hasta*, *9(a)*. [9] why subjunctive? *18(a)*. [10] *aún*, *26(b)*. [11] spelling, *26*. [12] why subjunctive? *18(g)*. [13] Madariaga, Salvador de: well-known Spanish writer and diplomat (1876–). [14] *sino*, *8*. [15] negatives, *16*.

31 Caribbean snobbery

Jazz en el tocadiscos de la terraza[1]; variante cool. El viento norte es débil al cruzar el jardín, porque la casona[2] de piedra gris protege de las ráfagas moderadas. Queda un frío seco, extranjero. La noche es morada, de nublazón[2]. Los criados con guantes blancos de alinear la plata[3] la porcelana sobre la larga[4] mesa de cristal[5].

   – ¿Por qué estabas aquí? – pregunta Dascal.

   – ¿Dónde?

   – Aquí, detrás del seto, apartada.

   – Estaba fatigada – dice María del Carmen.

   – Fatigada ¿de qué?

   – Las voces, la gente . . .

   – Se supone que eso no debe fatigarte. Se supone que debes estar acostumbrada.

   – Y sin embargo me fatiga.

   – A veces esto puede ser desagradable – dice Dascal.

   – A veces, pero no siempre.

   – Hay que pertenecer . . .

   – Estaba ahí, oyéndolos a todos y de pronto sentí un gran cansancio, como si estuviera haciendo lo[6] mismo desde hace mil años.

   – Pero tú perteneces.

   – ¿A qué?

– A eso, a ellos. Yo no . . .

– Yo no . . . No voy a Varadero durante las regatas ni el domingo al Contri Clob. No tengo un convertible ni hago remos; ningún deporte. No compro mi ropa en Mieres. No conozco los teatros de Broduei ni puedo conversar sobre los últimos pleis. Mi padre no juega golf y mi madre no juega bridch. No tengo aire acondicionado en mi cuarto ni cuenta abierta[7] en ningún restaurante: no firmo en El Carmelo.

– No te he preguntado nada de eso. Eres muy acomplejado.

– Tú eres socia del Bilmor, estudias filosofía en la Universidad de Villanueva y perteneces al equipo de sof-bol.[8]

– ¿Cómo sabes eso?

– Leo el Libro de Oro de Álvarez de Cañas y las memorias de fin de curso. Son mis lecturas[4] favoritas. Los leo todas las noches antes de acostarme. En vez de rezar[9] hago eso. Todo el mundo debería[10] hacer lo mismo.

LISANDRO OTERO (Cuban) La situación

Study in this passage:

    a. the use of *ser* and *estar*
    b. the use of americanisms
    c. negative expressions

[1] 'flat part of a roof'. [2] augmentative, (23). [3] 'silver'. [4] *25*. [5] 'crystal', *26*.
[6] *5*. [7] 'charge account'. [8] 'soft-ball' (baseball played with a rubber ball).
[9] *11(a)*. [10] *debería, 20(c)*.

32 The birth of a book (a)

Tal vez es un augurio malo empezar[1] así, pero sin este doble signo previo jamás se habría podido[2] escribir esta historia.

Éramos tres buenos amigos y los tres éramos poetas. A ninguno de los tres nos gustaban[3] los poemas[4] de los otros dos, pero nos resignábamos a oírlos cuando no había[5] otro remedio. Cultivábamos la amistad como una de las formas más eficaces de la insinceridad. Hace de esto más de[6] veinte años.

Pasamos dieciocho días inolvidables junto al mar, sin más preocupación que la de llegar a veinte. El dinero se nos[7] acabó dos veces: una a los diez y otra a los trece. El dinero se nos[7] acababa siempre antes que[8] el amor. Ahora, a veces, nos sucede[9] lo[10] contrario. Alifafes[11] de la madurez.

En el tren, de regreso de nuestras ya inolvidables vacaciones improvisadas, uno de nosotros dijo:

– De todo lo que nos ha pasado, con un poco de inventiva y de sal[12], se podría[2] escribir un libro.

Otro añadió:

– Cuanto[13] mejor fueran la inventiva y la sal, mejor[13] sería el libro. La vida es siempre lo de menos[14].

Y el tercero terminó la idea:

– Y así, a fuerza de[15] inventiva y de sal, podríamos escribir el libro sin habernos tomado el trabajo de vivir estos días. La[16] realidad es despreciable y pasajera. Sólo el[16] arte perdura.

NOEL CLARASÓ Tres poetas junto al mar

[1] infinitive, *11(a)*. [2] *poder*, *20(m)*. [3] *gustar*, *20(h)*. [4] gender, *1*. [5] tense, *11(c)*. [6] *más de*, before numerals. [7] *nos*, to indicate owner of money. [8] *antes que* (conjunction, because verb is understood). [9] *suceder*, *25*. [10] *lo*, *5*. [11] 'ailments'. [12] *sal*, wit. [13] correlatives, *8*. [14] *lo de menos*, *5, 24*. [15] *a fuerza de*, by dint of. [16] article should not be translated.

33 The birth of a book (b)

– Sin embargo, hemos pasado tres semanas buenas, gracias a la realidad.

– Tres semanas escasas[1].

– Pero ahora ellas influirán en nuestras vidas hasta el fin, gracias al recuerdo.

– Y gracias al arte influirán en las vidas ajenas[2]. Nuestras obras serán leídas[3] . . .

– Y traducidas a cuarenta y seis idiomas; uno menos que el[4] Quijote.

Estábamos[5] los tres apesadumbrados y con el[4] alma rota[3] en nuestro viaje de regreso del mar a la ciudad. La flor invertida del sol, la gasa desgarrada de los atardeceres húmedos, el sabor amargo del sudor ocioso, la vela blanca – ala y pañuelo del mar – y la presencia en el paisaje interior de las muchachas tomadas del sol, de la juventud y de la novelería que nos habían amado, todo quedaba lejos, convertido en recuerdo, en uno de los elementos, ya moldeables a placer, de nuestra vida pasada.

NOEL CLARASÓ Tres poetas junto al mar

34 Quality rather than quantity

– Mis dos amigos me han hablado tanto de ti[1], que ya sólo falta[2] que yo te hable[3] de mí para conocernos a fondo.

Con estas palabras Santos se presentó[4] a Albertina en la playa. No quiso esperar que se la presentáramos nosotros. Albertina nos presentó a Rosario y a otras dos[5] amigas: Cuqui y Tola. Rosario, por su gracia, parecía hermana gemela de Albertina, pero tenía el[6] cabello negro, la[6] boca más grande y la nariz más aplastada. No era[7] más guapa, pero tal vez más expresiva, sí. Ubaldo dijo de ella, después, cuando ya la amaba, que era expresión pura. Sin embargo, en principio, a todos nos gustó más Albertina por[8] un no sé qué[9] indefinible, una rara atracción sexual que emanaba de toda su[6] persona, de sus[6] gestos, de su[6] voz y hasta de sus[6] palabras.

Santos se mostró muy expresivo y asiduo con ella. Acaparó toda su atención y le recitó algunos poemas[10] en voz baja[11]. Santos se equivocaba al juzgar a la humanidad en general y uno de sus errores graves era éste: creía que todo el mundo, hombres y mujeres, eran sensibles[12] a sus poemas inéditos.

Ubaldo, desde el principio, se quedó con Rosario y yo tuve que conformarme con Cuqui y Tola. Eran dos, pero las dos, sumadas, valían menos que una sola de las otras. Aquel día comprendí que en eso de[13] la mujer es mejor la calidad[14] que la cantidad[14].

NOEL CLARASÓ *Tres poetas junto al mar*

[1] *ti*, why is there no accent? cf. *mí*? [2] *faltar*, *20(g)*. [3] why subjunctive? *18(i)*. [4] *presentar*, *25*. [5] notice the position of *otras*. [6] article, *2*. [7] *ser*, *19*. [8] *por*, *10*. [9] 'something'. [10] gender, *1*. [11] *en voz baja*, *9(d)*. [12] *sensibles*, *25*. [13] 'in the matter of'. [14] spelling, *26*.

35 The tragedy of speed

En el jardín la nieve continuaba[1] enharinando[2] la ciudad, disfrazándola de payaso[3] para divertir al vecindario a[4] la mañana siguiente. Tomás y Carmen montaron en el coche cuyos treinta caballos se pusieron en seguida al galope.

– No corras[5] tanto – rogó[6] la Princesa, viendo que la aguja del velocímetro se aproximaba[7] con rapidez a las tres cifras.

– Tengo que llegar – murmuró angustiado el Ceniciento, pisando a fondo[8] el acelerador[9].

Y se aferraba al volante, esforzándose en[10] mantener el automóvil en el centro de la carretera. Las nubes empezaron a ponerse[11] paliduchas[12], síntoma[13] de que el sol estaba saliendo detrás de ellas. Los copos se adherían al cristal del parabrisas, luchando por cubrir las dos pequeñas medias lunas que defendían tenazmente los bracitos[12] limpiadores[14].

– No corras, por favor – repetía la Princesa como una jaculatoria.

– No tengas miedo[5] – se jactó Tomás con una risita estúpida – . Conduzco maravillosamen . . .

La última sílaba[9] se estrelló, al mismo tiempo que el coche, contra un árbol robusto de la cuneta. El esqueleto metálico de la hermosa carroza color de calabaza[15] se partió por varios[16] sitios con crujidos horribles. Bajo la capa torácica del capote, aplastada por el choque, el corazón del motor dejó de latir. Y la sangre del automóvil, espesa y negruzca, brotó por las heridas del cárter[17], manchando la nieve.

ÁLVARO DE LAIGLESIA *Dios le ampare, imbécil*

[1] *continuar* + *gerundio*, *14*. [2] *enharinar*, cf. *la harina*, flour. [3] *disfrazar de payaso*, to disguise as a clown. [4] *a*, on. [5] imperatives, *17*. [6] *rogar*, *21(a)*. [7] *aproximarse a*, *11(b)*. [8] *a fondo*, to the full. [9] spelling, *26*. [10] *esforzarse en*, *11(b)*. [11] become, *21(b)*. [12] diminutives, etc., *23*. [13] gender, *1*. [14] order of words, *12*. [15] *calabaza*, *3*. [16] *varios*, *25*. [17] 'oil sump'.

36 The horse my grandfather gave me

Caminábamos y caminábamos hablando no más de la tierra. Yo era el nieto consentido[1] de mi abuelo. Casi desde que nací me sacó a sus andanzas de todos los días; primero, abrazándome; luego, en la cabeza de la silla; después, a enancas[2]. Si no el mero día de mi nacimiento, sí a la siguiente semana, o a lo sumo[3] antes de cumplir un mes de nacido. Si no puedo decir que nací a caballo, sí me crié a caballo, y a caballo crecí. El mismo día que yo nació un potrillo[4] de la yegua más fina, y lo apartó mi abuelo para mí[5]; lo cuidó tanto como[6] a mí, como si fuéramos[7] gemelos, o todavía más: una sola persona. Cuando fue tiempo, mi abuelo, en persona, lo amansó; mandó hacer una sillita de montar[8]:

especial para el nieto[5]; me trepó en el que llamaba mi *tocayo*[9], lo tomaba de la rienda y me paseaba, primero alrededor del patio, después por los caminos del Llano; y el día que cumplí años[10].

– Toma la rienda – me dijo –, ya es tiempo que lo manejes[11] solo.

Me regaló curata[12], soguilla[13] y espuelas hechas a mi tamaño. Pronto no fue necesario que me subiera[11] en peso[14]; yo mismo arrimaba el caballo a un batiente y trepaba al brinco; en igual forma ensillaba y desensillaba al *tocayo*. El Tocayo se le quedó, por nombre. Un alazán[15] muy noble, de veras[16] bonito, que nos entendíamos como si de cierto fuéramos[7] una sola persona del mismo genio, de idénticos pareceres y sentimientos.

AGUSTÍN YÁÑEZ (Mexican) Las tierras flacas

---

[1] 'spoilt'. [2] 'behind'. [3] *5(g)*. [4] diminutive of *potro*, colt. [5] *por* and *para*. [6] *8*. [7] why subjunctive? *18(k)*. [8] 'saddle'. [9] 'namesake'. [10] 'on my birthday'. [11] why subjunctive? *18(i)*. [12] Mexican word for 'whip'. [13] 'halter'. [14] *subir en peso*, to be lifted up. [15] 'a sorrel horse'. [16] *9(c)iv*.

37 The haughty prisoner

– Que traigan[1] a Conce Maille – ordenó Huacachino una vez que todos terminaron de beber.

Y, repentinamente, maniatado y conducido por cuatro mozos corpulentos, apareció ante[2] el tribunal un indio de edad incalculable, alto, fornido, ceñudo y que parecía desdeñar las injurias[3] y amenazas de la muchedumbre. En esa actitud, con la ropa ensangrentada[4] y desgarrada por las manos de sus perseguidores y las dentelladas[5] de los perros ganaderos[6], el indio más parecía la estatua de la rebeldía que la del abatimiento[7]. Eran tal la regularidad de sus facciones de indio puro, la gallardía de su cuerpo, la altivez de su mirada, su porte señorial[8], que, a pesar de sus ojos sanguinolentos, fluía de su persona una gran simpatía, la simpatía que despiertan los hombres que poseen la hermosura y la fuerza.

– ¡Suéltenlo[1]! – exclamó la misma voz que había ordenado traerlo.

Una vez libre, Maille se cruzó de brazos, irguió la desnuda y revuelta cabeza, desparramó sobre el consejo una mirada sutilmente[9] desdeñosa y esperó.

– José Ponciano te acusa de que el miércoles pasado le robaste su vaca y que has ido a vendérsela a los de Obas. ¿Tú qué dices?

– ¡Verdad! Pero Ponciano me robó el año pasado un toro. Estamos pagados.

– ¿Por qué entonces no te quejaste?

– Porque yo no necesito de que nadie[10] me haga[11] justicia. Yo mismo sé hacérmela.

ENRIQUE LÓPEZ ALBÚJAR (Peruvian) *Ushanan-Jampi*

Study the use of pronouns in this passage.

[1] *18(a).* [2] *9(e).* [3] *25.* [4] *ensangrentada* from *sangre.* [5] 'bites'. [6] *ganaderos*, adj. from *ganado*, cattle. [7] 'humiliation'. [8] 'his noble bearing'. [9] *sutilmente.* [10] negation, *16.* [11] why subjunctive? *18(b).*

38 Letter-writing in a quiet café

"Alma mía lejana," escribió.

Alzó un poco la[1] cabeza, con el extremo de la pluma apoyado[2] en el[1] mentón. Era[3] tarde ya, y el café estaba[3] casi desierto.

Sus[4] ojos fijáronse en los panzudos[5] recipientes de café, bajo los cuales danzaban, para calentar el líquido aromado, unas llamitas azules. Oyó, en el silencio del quiosco[6], la canción que canta el agua que hierve sorda y continuamente[7]; una canción animosa y confortable[8] que recuerda el tibio[9] lecho y las puertas que detienen al viento gruñidor[10], y las ventanas donde repiquetea[11] el granizo, y cierto ponche dulzón y agradable que, al regresar a la casa en las noches de invierno, espera sobre una lamparilla de alcohol, que tiene también una llamita azul, hermana de aquéllas[12].

Jacinto dejó[13] de pensar en su carta y sonrió, como si hubiese[14] entendido la tierna evocación hogareña[15] de las marmitas del café solitario. Cuando volvió a encorvarse sobre el papel, habían huído las expresiones de congoja. Se advertía[16] feliz y con un ya olvidado placer de reposo. La carta fue breve y la dictó el cerebro más que el corazón.

WENCESLAO FERNÁNDEZ FLÓREZ *Ha entrado un ladrón*

[1] *la*, *2(c).* [2] why past participle? *13(b).* [3] *ser* and *estar*, *19.* [4] *sus*, *2(c).* [5] *panzudos*, adj. from *panza*, belly, paunch. [6] 'kiosk'. [7] *sorda*, *6(a).* [8] spelling, *26.* [9] *tibio*, warm. [10] *gruñidor*, adj. from *gruñir.* [11] 'rattle'. [12] 'the other little flames'. [13] *dejar*, *20(d).* [14] why subjunctive? *18(k).* [15] *hogareño*, adj. from *hogar.* [16] 'he noticed he was'.

39 Spain and the Americas (a)

A veces, ante la magnitud de sus convulsiones, solemos decir con orgullo: son hispanos, reaccionan como nosotros; llevan nuestra sangre; y al hablar así hemos hecho una afirmación que quiere ser definitiva y que impide el paso a toda futura investigación, pero en realidad lo único que logramos fue montar una base falsa y soltar una estupidez mayúscula.

Si los mineros de Bolivia van a la huelga o los campesinos de El Cuzco invaden las tierras inexplotadas queriendo apoderarse de ellas, no han reaccionado como hispánicos, porque ni una gota tienen de nuestra sangre ni un ápice de nuestra manera de pensar, pero sí es posible que parte de nuestra sangre esté interviniendo, aquella parte que ha perdido la paciencia de inmediato, sin tener en cuenta que los mineros o los campesinos, antes de hacer tal cosa, habían sido pacientes durante años y aun siglos.

No pretendo con esto acusar a unos y defender a otros; lo único que deseo es mostrar lo más claramente posible por qué los países de América, de las mil Américas, son tan complejos que no pueden ajustarse a moldes.

Todas las razas, todos los sentimientos, todas las formas de pensar intervienen en la formación de la personalidad de cada una de las veinte repúblicas y, por tanto, atribuirnos la compleja maternidad de ellas es cometer un grave error.

ALBERTO VÁZQUEZ-FIGUEROA *Las mil Américas*

40 Spain and the Americas (b)

Hay allí un cincuenta, quizás un sesenta por ciento de hispanismo, pero si nos obstinamos en no advertir el resto, si no le damos la importancia que tiene a lo que falta, nunca, nunca, en forma alguna podremos comprender, ni aun remotamente, a las mil Américas.

Quien pasee por las calles de Santiago de Chile, se sentirá en España, y lo mismo le ocurre a quien vaya al San Juan Viejo o a algunos barrios de Ciudad de Méjico, La Habana o Buenos Aires; pero si esa misma persona sube a los poblados de los Andes, se adentra en la espesura de la Amazonia o asiste a una ceremonia vudú en la Dominicana, comprenderá sin más palabras que, aunque marcamos profundamente nuestra huella allí donde pisamos, quedó mucho terreno, mucho, por el que no cruzó siquiera nuestra sombra.

No debe echársenos en cara; nos faltó tiempo y gente; era muy largo el camino y resulta corta siempre la vida de los conquistadores. Además y a mi entender, tal vez en eso debe centrarse precisamente nuestro orgullo: tanto les dimos que no les dimos todo y les dejamos lo suficiente de sí mismos como para que formasen su propio diferente y complejo espíritu.

Ahora, lo que debemos intentar es comprender ese espíritu, distinguir cuántos hay y a qué causas responde cada uno, y qué es lo que les une o les separa del nuestro.

ALBERTO VÁZQUEZ-FIGUEROA *Las mil Américas*

41 Reflections

Juan asegura cuando hay ocasión que soy muy inteligente. Demasiado inteligente para mujer, y harto más para una mujer de la vida, dice. A mí, la verdad, lo que me parece es que soy guapísima, y al fin y al cabo esto es lo que me interesa. Presumo de ello, porque puedo, y de nada más.

Sin embargo, tal vez no ande descaminado el hombre, porque en todas las historias de personas que fueron célebres siempre hallé cosas raras, vidas alborotadas por la inquietud y una como locura oculta que les hacía acertar muchas veces cuando los demás erraban. Yo no sé si habré acertado o no en mi corta mas ajetreada existencia, pero creo que hice muy bien en escaparme con los gitanos, porque pasé con ellos los meses mejores de mi vida. Tanto, que muchas veces sueño con aquellas carreteras polvorientas de Andalucía y con la aventura extraordinaria que me traían todas las jornadas. Por cierto que no hace muchos días, yendo de paseo en el coche de Juan, con el que tengo alguna confianza, me apeteció recobrar aquello y se me antojó andar un rato descalza por la carretera.

Llovía mansamente, la tierra echaba todo su olor y las cunetas estaban encharcadas. A mí, que soy de tierras polvorientas y secas, me sacan de quicio estos días así, grises, templados y húmedos. Por eso me empeñé en bajarme del coche y en andar un par de kilómetros sola y descalza por allí, para sentir en mis pies otra vez la buena tierra.

DARÍO FERNÁNDEZ FLÓREZ *Lola, espejo oscuro*

42 Life's complications

Comprendo que todo esto va saliendo sin orden ni concierto y me temo que cuanto más adelante mi historia, más desordenada va a parecer. Preocupada, hablé de ello con Juan que, como ya se sabe, es el culpable de haberme metido en este fregado, y le dije que yo me sentía incapaz de poner aquí las cosas en su sitio y que, a la vez, quisiera esforzarme en que todo aparentara un fiel remedo de lo ocurrido. Pero que, al ocurrir, las cosas ocurren mezcladas, embarulladas, y no como se leen en los libros. Hablamos un poco de las complicaciones de mi vida y le confesé que no sabía cómo seguir.

Se rió mucho de mis dudas y de verme metida en estos graves problemas. Y me aconsejó que escribiera las cosas como me vinieran a las mientes y como me diera la gana según el humor del momento. Porque la vida tampoco suele tener ni orden ni concierto y aun cuando esta historia mía habrá de salirme muy distinta de la realidad, que nunca puede copiarse, lo mejor será que la escriba lo más naturalmente posible.

DARÍO FERNÁNDEZ FLÓREZ *Lola, espejo oscuro*

43 Savings (a)

El mejor procedimiento para ahorrar, conocido hasta la fecha, es el ahorro.

¿Qué es necesario para ahorrar? Muy poco: voluntad, perseverancia, fortaleza de espíritu, ánimo sereno, paciencia, dominio de sí mismo, carácter reflexivo, laboriosidad, honradez, cultura moral, desprecio a las pompas y vanidades, modestia, sobriedad, rectitud de juicio, firmeza, prudencia, espíritu de sacrificio, tenacidad, buena salud y energía. ¡Con qué pequeño esfuerzo puede el hombre alcanzar la soñada meta de la felicidad!

Los enemigos del ahorro son: la indolencia, la ociosidad, los vicios y los placeres. La ociosidad es hija de la indolencia, y los vicios son hijos de la ociosidad, o sea que la indolencia es la abuela de los vicios. Los placeres son primos de los vicios y, por tanto, sobrinos de la ociosidad.

El hombre que no sabe refrenar sus instintos y no puede resistir al funesto deseo de beber una copa de licor o de fumar un cigarrillo, ¡desgraciado! ¡Jamás – entiéndase bien – jamás podrá ahorrar! Ya lo sabe, y luego no podrá llamarse a engaño.

De la copa de licor pasará a la de sidra achampanada; de la sidra achampanada al coñac, y del coñac al terrible ajenjo, azote de la Humanidad. Se empieza en la barra de un bar, y ya en la pendiente, de escalón en escalón, se acaba todos los días en el café, donde las malas compañías de ociosos e indolentes arrastran al hombre débil, que termina tomando taxis. Y de ahí a la miseria, a la delincuencia y al presidio.

"CERO" *Reflexiones sobre el ahorro*

44 Savings (b)

Sin embargo, ¡qué contraste el del hombre seguro de sí mismo, que practica la virtud del ahorro! El virtuoso del ahorro trabaja con alegría, sin que su ánimo decaiga un instante. Cuando otro cualquiera necesita fumar, él canta alegres canciones e himnos a la laboriosidad y la economía, sedante del sistema nervioso mejor que el tabaco. Si desea tomar café, extrae de su bolsillo dos pesetas, que echa en una hucha, y después mete también veinticinco céntimos, de propina. Por último, se limpia con una servilleta que lleva siempre para estos casos.

En su hogar, todo es felicidad y alegría. Rodeado de su prudente esposa y de sus sensatos hijos, en vez de malgastar su dinero en cines, meriendas y demás inútiles dispendios, siempre encuentra diversiones honestas y saludables. Ora caracterizado con una graciosa barba postiza, recita trozos de *Bertoldo, Bertoldino y Cacaseno*, ya imita el tambor con una cacerola, o bien, agarrados de las manos, cantan bellas canciones regionales. La educación de sus pequeños hijos la hace a base de sabias máximas, como:

> *De bienestar es un chorro*
> *la práctica del ahorro*

O también:

> *Alcanzará dicha mucha*
> *el joven que tenga hucha*

Sin echar en saco roto la que dice:

> *El que su dinero ahorra*
> *podrá comprarse una gorra*

"CERO" *Reflexiones sobre el ahorro*

45 Mexican teacher

El maestro había surgido de una familia sumamente pobre y sus estudios los siguió con grandes esfuerzos. Relataba que viviendo en alguna de las barriadas del norte de la ciudad, acabó por acostumbrarse a ir a pie hasta San Jacinto, lo que hizo por muchos años. En ocasiones, el relato amargo de sus afanes por alcanzar el coronamiento de sus estudios se teñía con los tonos suaves del humorismo, para evocar aquella aventura en que sufrió el suplicio de caminatas diarias a lo largo de una semana, ahormando unos zapatos que le quedaban un tanto estrechos.

No fue de esos profesores que atormentan a sus alumnos con conocimientos tan abstrusos o extemporáneos que no solamente ninguno entiende, sino que, además, debido a la cantidad, resulta que ni siquiera serían capaces de deglutirlos muy poco a poco. Nunca dejó tareas fuera de las horas de clase y jamás le oímos incitar a sus alumnos por los caminos del juicio peyorativo o las expresiones duras. Menos aún, supimos que recurriera a esos castigos que van desde el palmetazo hasta el coscorrón o el confinamiento en el cuarto oscuro, destinado a la guarda de los útiles del aseo. Empleaba el consejo y la persuasión como los caminos más accesibles para conducir, orientar, pulir y perfeccionar al auditorio infantil que vivía pendiente del milagro de sus palabras.

– Es preferible aprender poco – gustaba de repetir –, pero saber bien lo poco que se ha aprendido, que saber mucho mal aprendido.

ANTONIO ARMENDÁRIZ (Mexican) Semblanzas

46 Arrival by plane

El avión emerge de las nubes como un puro entre las barbas de un señor. Abajo, en las plisadas faldas de los montes Titicanos, repta cual verdoso reptil el río Agüitafresca. Pegada a él, lo mismo que la novia chacha al novio soldado, duerme su siesta importada por Colón la indolente ciudad de Patacuán. Una de las hélices afeita el rabo a un cóndor altanero. Otra de las hélices, al mismo tiempo, rapa la hierba de la coronilla de un picacho precolombino. Y otra de las hélices, para no ser menos, pela una patata.

La geografía se mece a nuestros pies haciéndonos pensar en las colinas atenienses – olas petrificadas de la cultura con altivas crestas de espuma marmórea –. También pensamos en los amoratados viñedos de la Itálica famosa, pues tenemos más sed que un esbelto dromedario saudita.

El avión – ángel mecánico con blanca sangre de octanos – se posa en
el aeropuerto, lamiendo con fruición la tierra incaica.
– ¡Chachipulca machicuana! – nos saluda el alcalde de la ciudad,
saludo ancestral en lengua pachuquí que significa: ¡Ya están aquí esos
pelmazos!

ÁLVARO DE LAIGLESIA *Dios le ampare, imbécil*

47 Don Fadrique's dance (a)

Por desgracia, en la primera visita que hizo don Diego a una hidalga
viuda que tenía dos hijas doncellas, se habló del niño Fadrique y de lo
crecido que estaba y del talento que tenía para bailar el bolero.
– Ahora – dijo don Diego – baila el chico peor que el año pasado,
porque está en la edad del pavo: edad insufrible, entre la palmeta y el
barbero. Ya ustedes sabrán que en esa edad se ponen los chicos muy
empalagosos, porque empiezan a presumir de hombres y no lo son.
Sin embargo, ya que ustedes se empeñan, el chico lucirá su habilidad.
Las señoras, que habían mostrado deseos de ver a don Fadrique
bailar, repitieron sus instancias, y una de las doncellas tomó una
guitarra y se puso a tocar para que don Fadrique bailase.
– Baila, Fadrique – dijo don Diego, no bien empezó la música.
Repugnancia invencible al baile en aquella ocasión se apoderó de su
alma. Veía una contrariedad monstruosa, algo de lo que llaman ahora
una antinomia, entre el bolero y la casaca. Es de advertir que en aquel
día don Fadrique llevaba casaca por primera vez; estrenaba la prenda,
si puede calificarse de estreno el aprovechamiento del arreglo o refundición de un vestido, usado primero por el padre y después por el
mayorazgo, a quien se le había quedado estrecho y corto.

JUAN VALERA *El comendador Mendoza*

48 Don Fadrique's dance (b)

– Baila, Fadrique – repitió don Diego, bastante amostazado.
Don Diego, cuyo traje de campo y camino, al uso de la tierra, estaba
en muy buen estado, no se había puesto casaca como su hijo. Don Diego
iba todo de estezado, con botas y espuelas y en la mano llevaba el
látigo con que castigaba al caballo y a los podencos de una jauría
numerosa que tenía para cazar.

– Baila, Fadrique – exclamó don Diego por tercera vez, notándose ya en su voz cierta alteración, causada por la cólera y la sorpresa.

Era tan elevado el concepto que tenía don Diego de la autoridad paterna, que se maravillaba de aquella rebeldía.

– Déjele usted, señor de Mendoza – dijo la hidalga viuda –. El niño está cansado del camino y no quiere bailar.

– Ha de bailar ahora.

– Déjele usted, otra vez le veremos – dijo la que tocaba la guitarra.

– Ha de bailar ahora – repitió don Diego –. Baila, Fadrique.

– Yo no bailo con casaca – respondió éste al cabo.

Aquí fue Troya. Don Diego prescindió de las señoras y de todo.

– ¡Rebelde! ¡Mal hijo! – gritó –. Te enviaré a los Toribios; baila o te desuello.

Y empezó a latigazos con don Fadrique.

JUAN VALERA El comendador Mendoza

49 Don Fadrique's dance (c)

La señorita de la guitarra paró un instante la música, pero don Diego la miró de modo tan terrible que ella tuvo miedo de que la hiciese tocar, como quería hacer bailar a su hijo, y siguió tocando el bolero.

Don Fadrique, después de recibir ocho o diez latigazos, bailó lo mejor que supo.

Al pronto se le saltaron las lágrimas; pero después, considerando que había sido su padre quien le había pegado y ofreciéndose a su fantasía de un modo cómico toda la escena y viéndose él mismo bailar a latigazos y con casaca, se rió, a pesar del dolor físico, y bailó con inspiración y entusiasmo.

Las señoras aplaudieron a rabiar.

– Bien, bien – dijo don Diego –. ¡Por vida del diablo! ¿Te he hecho mal, hijo mío?

– No, padre – dijo don Fadrique –. Está visto, yo necesitaba hoy de doble acompañamiento para bailar.

– Hombre, disimula. ¿Por qué eres tonto? ¿Qué repugnancia podías tener, si la casaca te va que ni pintada y el bolero clásico y de buena escuela es un baile muy señor? Estas damas me perdonarán. ¿No es verdad? Yo soy algo vivo de genio.

Así terminó el lance del bolero.

JUAN VALERA El comendador Mendoza

50 Bathing delights, dangers and disasters (a)

Se miraban en torno, circunspectos, recelosos del agua ennegrecida.
Llegaba el ruido de la gente cercana y la música.
– No está nada fría, ¿verdad?
– Está la mar de apetitosa.
Daba un poco de luna en lo alto de los árboles y llegaba de abajo
el sosegado palabreo de las voces ocultas en lo negro del soto anochecido.
Música limpia, de cristal, sonaba un poco más abajo, al ras del agua
inmóvil del embalse. Sobre el espejo negro lucían ráfagas rasantes de
luna y de bombillas. Aquí en lo oscuro, sentían correr el río por la piel
de sus cuerpos, como un flúido y enorme y silencioso animal acariciante.
Estaban sumergidos hasta el tórax en su lisa carrera. Paulina se había
cogido a la cintura de su novio.
– ¡Qué gusto de sentir el agua como te pasa por el cuerpo!
– ¿Lo ves? No querías bañarte.
– Me está sabiendo más rico que el de esta mañana.
Sebas se estremeció.
– Sí, pero ahora ya no es como antes que te estabas todo el rato que
querías. Ahora en seguida se queda uno frío y empieza a hacer tachuelas.

RAFAEL SÁNCHEZ FERLOSIO *El Jarama*

51 Bathing delights, dangers and disasters (b)

Miró Paulina detrás de Sebastián: río arriba, la sombra del puente, los
grandes arcos en tinieblas; ya una raya de luna revelaba el pretil y los
ladrillos. Sebas estaba vuelto en el otro sentido. Sonaba la compuerta,
aguas abajo, junto a las luces de los merenderos. Paulina se volvió.
– Lucita. ¿Qué haces tú sola por ahí? Ven acá con nosotros. ¡Luci!
– Si está ahí, ¿no la ves ahí delante? ¡Lucita!
Calló en un sobresalto repentino.
– ¡¡Lucita!!
Se oía un débil debatirse en el agua, diez, quince metros más allá,
y un hipo angosto como un grito estrangulado, en medio de un jadeo
sofocado en borbollas.
– ¡Se ahoga . . .! ¡¡Lucita se ahoga!! ¡¡Sebastián!! ¡¡Grita, grita . . .!!
Sebas quiso avanzar, pero las uñas de Paulina se clavaban en sus
carnes, sujetándolo.
– ¡Tú, no!, ¡tú, no, Sebastián! – le decía sordamente – ; ¡tú, no; tú,
no; tú, no . . .!

Resonaron los gritos de ambos, pidiendo socorro, una y otra vez, horadantes, acrecentados por el eco del agua. Se aglomeraban sombras en la orilla, con un revuelo de alarma y vocerío.

RAFAEL SÁNCHEZ FERLOSIO El Jarama

52 Bathing delights, dangers and disasters (c)

Ahí cerca, el pequeño remolino de opacas convulsiones, de rotos sonidos laríngeos, se iba alejando lentamente hacia el embalse. Luego sonaron zambullidas; algunas voces preguntaban: "¿Por dónde, por dónde?" Ya se oían las brazadas de tres o cuatro nadadores, y palabras en el agua: "¡Vamos juntos, tú, Rafael, es peligroso acercarse uno solo!" Resonaban muy claras las voces en el río. "¡Por aquí! ¡Más arriba!," les indicaba Sebastián. Llegó la voz de Tito desde la ribera:

– ¡Sebastián! ¡Sebastián!

Había entrado en el agua y venía saltando hacia ellos. Sebas se había desasido de Paulina y ya nadaba al encuentro de los otros. Le gritaba Paulina: "¡Ten cuidado! ¡Ten cuidado, por Dios!"; se cogía la mandíbula con ambas manos. Todos estaban perplejos, en el agua, nadando de acá para allá, mirando a todas partes sobre la negra superficie. "¿Dónde está? ¿No lo veis? ¿Lo veis vosotros?" Tito llegó hasta Paulina y ella se le abrazaba fuertemente.

– ¡Se ahoga Luci! – le dijo.

RAFAEL SÁNCHEZ FERLOSIO El Jarama

53 Bathing delights, dangers and disasters (d)

Él sentía el temblor de Paulina contra todo su cuerpo; miró hacia los nadadores desconcertados que exploraban el río en todas direcciones. "No la encuentran . . .", se veían sus bultos desplazarse a flor de agua. La luna iluminaba el gentío alineado a lo largo de la orilla. "¿No dais con él?"; "Por aquí estaba la última vez que la vimos", era la voz de Sebastián. "¿Es una chica?". "Sí". Estaban ya muy lejos, en la parte de la presa y se distinguían las cabezas sobre el agua, cinco o seis, a la luz de la luna rasante y el reflejo de bombillas que venía del lado de la música. "¡Llévame a tierra, Tito; tengo un miedo terrible, llévame!", se erguía encaramándose hacia Tito, como queriendo despegar del agua; tiritaba. Se vio el brazo y el hombro de uno de los nadadores blanquear un momento, allá abajo, en la mancha de luz. Tito y Paulina se encaminaron hacia la ribera, venciendo con trabajo la resistencia de las aguas. "¡Aquí!", gritó una voz junto a la presa. "¡Aquí está!" Había sentido el cuerpo, topándolo con el brazo, casi a flor de agua.

RAFAEL SÁNCHEZ FERLOSIO El Jarama

54 Sabotage (a)

Pero la cosa se descompuso por completo desde el descarrilamiento del tren en la cuesta de Sayula. De no haber sucedido eso, quizás todavía estuviera vivo Pedro Zamora y tantos otros, y la revuelta hubiera seguido por el buen camino. Pero Pedro Zamora le picó la cresta al gobierno con el descarrilamiento del tren de Sayula.

Todavía veo las luces de las llamaradas que se alzaban allí donde apilaron a los muertos. Los juntaban con palas o los hacían rodar como troncos hasta el fondo de la cuesta, y cuando el montón se hacía grande, lo empapaban con petróleo y le prendían fuego. La jedentina se la llevaba el aire muy lejos, y muchos días después todavía se sentía el olor a muerto chamuscado.

Tantito antes no sabíamos bien a bien lo que iba a suceder. Habíamos regado de cuernos y huesos de vaca un tramo largo de la vía y, por si esto fuera poco, habíamos abierto los rieles allí donde el tren iría a entrar en la curva. Hicimos eso y esperamos.

JUAN RULFO (Mexican) El llano en llamas

55 Sabotage (b)

La madrugada estaba comenzando a dar luz a las cosas. Se veía ya casi claramente a la gente apeñuscada en el techo de los carros. Se oía que algunos cantaban. Eran voces de hombres y de mujeres. Pasaron frente a nosotros todavía medio ensombrecidos por la noche, pero pudimos ver que eran soldados con sus galletas. Esperamos. El tren no se detuvo.

De haber querido lo hubiéramos tiroteado, porque el tren caminaba despacio y jadeaba como si a puros pujidos quisiera subir la cuesta. Hubiéramos podido hasta platicar con ellos un rato. Pero las cosas eran de otro modo.

Ellos empezaron a darse cuenta de lo que les pasaba cuando sintieron bambolearse los carros, cimbrarse el tren como si alguien lo estuviera sacudiendo. Luego la máquina se vino para atrás, arrastrada y fuera de la vía por los carros pesados y llenos de gente. Daba unos silbatazos roncos

y tristes y muy largos. Pero nadie la ayudaba. Seguía hacia atrás arrastrada por aquel tren al que no se le veía fin, hasta que le faltó tierra y
yéndose de lado cayó al fondo de la barranca. Entonces los carros la
siguieron, uno tras otro, a toda prisa, tumbándose cada uno en su lugar
allá abajo. Después todo se quedó en silencio como si todos, hasta
nosotros, nos hubiéramos muerto.

Así pasó aquello.

JUAN RULFO (Mexican) *El llano en llamas*

56 Sabotage (c)

Cuando los vivos comenzaron a salir de entre las astillas de los carros,
nosotros nos retiramos de allí, acalambrados de miedo.

Estuvimos escondidos varios días; pero los federales nos fueron a
sacar de nuestro escondite. Ya no nos dieron paz; ni siquiera para
mascar un pedazo de cecina en paz. Hicieron que se nos acabaran las
horas de dormir y de comer, y que los días y noches fueran iguales para
nosotros. Quisimos llegar al cañón Tozín; pero el gobierno llegó
primero que nosotros. Faldeamos el volcán. Subimos a los montes más
altos y allí, en ese lugar que le dicen el Camino de Dios, encontramos
otra vez al gobierno tirando a matar. Sentíamos cómo bajaban las balas
sobre nosotros, en rachas apretadas, calentando el aire que nos rodeaba.
Y hasta las piedras detrás de las que nos escondíamos se hacían trizas
una tras otra como si fueran terrones. Después supimos que eran
ametralladoras aquellas carabinas con que disparaban ahora sobre
nosotros y que dejaban hecho una coladera el cuerpo de uno; pero
entonces creímos que eran muchos soldados, por miles, y todo lo que
queríamos era correr de ellos.

JUAN RULFO (Mexican) *El llano en llamas*

57 A fantastic memory

Locke, en el siglo XVII, postuló (y reprobó) un idioma imposible en el
que cada cosa individual, cada piedra, cada pájaro y cada rama tuviera
un nombre propio; Funes proyectó alguna vez un idioma análogo, pero
lo desechó por parecerle demasiado general, demasiado ambiguo. En
efecto, Funes no sólo recordaba cada hoja de cada árbol de cada monte,
sino cada una de las veces que la había percibido o imaginado. Resolvió
reducir cada una de sus jornadas pretéritas a unos setenta mil recuerdos,
que definiría luego por cifras. Lo disuadieron dos consideraciones: la
conciencia de que la tarea era interminable, la conciencia de que era

inútil. Pensó que en la hora de la muerte no habría acabado aún de clasificar todos los recuerdos de la niñez.

Los dos proyectos que he indicado (un vocabulario infinito para la serie natural de los números, un inútil catálogo mental de todas las imágenes del recuerdo) son insensatos, pero revelan cierta balbuciente grandeza. Nos dejan vislumbrar o inferir el vertiginoso mundo de Funes. Éste, no lo olvidemos, era casi incapaz de ideas generales, platónicas. No sólo le costaba comprender que el símbolo genérico *perro* abarcara tantos individuos dispares de diversos tamaños y diversa forma; le molestaba que el perro de las tres y catorce (visto de perfil) tuviera el mismo nombre que el perro de las tres y cuarto (visto de frente).

JORGE LUIS BORGES (Argentine) Ficciones

58 Preparations for a double wedding (a)

La Alicita y su tía andaban muy atareadas con los preparativos de la boda. Habían pensado casarse las dos el mismo día; se ahorran muchos cuartos y, además, casarse así las dos de golpe, era de mucho efecto.

La Alicita y su tía estaban radiantes de alegría, tan radiantes, que tenían que tomar píldoras para poder dormir.

– Trastornos neurovegetativos – les había dicho el médico a las dos –, la emoción, algo muy explicable, muy explicable.

La Alicita y su tía estaban amables y sonrientes con las vecinas. Las vecinas, cuando vieron que la cosa ya no tenía arreglo y que se casaban de verdad, también empezaron a estar amables y sonrientes con Alicita y su tía.

– Nada, nada, que sean ustedes muy felices es lo que hace falta.

– Gracias, gracias, que Dios la oiga . . .

CAMILO JOSÉ CELA El molino de viento

59 Preparations for a double wedding (b)

La Alicita y su tía andaban todo el día de compras y yendo y viniendo a la modista y a la sombrerera.

– Yo quiero que os caséis las dos de blanco – les había dicho la abuela, cuando ya los novios entraban en la casa y las cosas tomaron estado oficial –; no se casa una más que una vez en la vida, y ese día hay que echar las campanas a vuelo. Además, el blanco es símbolo de pureza, y vosotras, ya que sois puras gracias a Dios, debéis pregonarlo bien alto para honra de vuestros maridos. En estos tiempos de costumbres licenciosas, conviene distinguir para que la gente se entere.

La Alicita se había encargado un traje de *peau d'ange*. A la Pía se lo estaban haciendo de *crêpe satin*. Las vestía Suzanne, una señora muy habilidosa que se había hecho una buena clientela teniendo cuidado de arrastrar las erres. Suzanne era de La Carolina, provincia de Jaén.

CAMILO JOSÉ CELA El molino de viento

60 After the assassination of Eduardo Dato

– Anda, ve, te espera el viejo.

– Hasta luego, Lobo.

– Anda, corre. Comprendo que tienes prisa.

Y se quedó con un aire muy sufrido.

Don Vicente se había detenido a esperarme después de haber andado un poco.

– ¿Qué te ha pasado?

– Nada, creí que había olvidado la bufanda.

Excusa absurda, obvia. Pero don Vicente no me atendía. Caminaba aprisa y yo tenía que forzar el paso, sin saber bien si íbamos a la funeraria o la iglesia. No me importaba. El inesperado diálogo con Lobo me había dejado mal sabor, pero levanté la cabeza con ánimo y miré a mi alrededor.

La noche estaba fría y agradable y me parecía que el aire me mojaba la cara, y mis zapatos crujían como yo había deseado siempre que me crujiesen unos zapatos, como los de un militar, por más daño que me estuviesen haciendo. Miraba a los transeúntes, miraba las tiendas. Tenía hambre de ver cosas y todas las cosas se me ofrecían y se avenían a trabarse por sí mismas en una vívida escenificación. En el cielo, muy próximas, temblaban las estrellas, aunque yo no las veía más que cuando cruzábamos tramos oscuros, después de dejar atrás las luces de un escaparate o de un café. No era demasiado tarde y en la Calle Mayor y en la Mercería había gente, y la plaza estaba llena de hombres que hablaban en grupos; parados y acalorándose, a pesar del fresco.

La bandera del Ayuntamiento estaba a media asta. Yo oía en todas las bocas el nombre de Dato y frases que necesitaban repetirse infinitas veces para consumir el fuego de su novedad. La moto agresora había sido una "Indian". Mazzantini había tenido un gesto.

Y también frases muy difíciles de entender.

VICENTE SOTO La zancada

61 The reluctant hall porter

– Vamos a buscar un guardián y se los entregaremos. Acompáñeme, maestro Garrido.

Estuve tentado de echarlo al diablo, meterme en mi cuarto y cerrar la puerta; pero, no sé si se lo he dicho: soy un hombre tímido; mis iniciativas, al encontrarse en oposición con otras, quedan siempre en proyecto; no sé discutir ni me gusta imponer mis ideas.

– Bueno; espérese . . .

Entré a mi cuarto, me eché un revolver al bolsillo trasero del pantalón – ignoro por qué motivo hice esto, ya que el arma estaba descargada y tampoco la necesitaría –, me puse el saco, desperté a mi mujer, y después de decirle que iba a salir y que tuviera cuidado con la puerta, me reuní con el maestro Sánchez, quien estaba parado en medio del pasadizo, dominando con su alto y musculoso cuerpo a los dos pobres diablos que allí estaban.

– Vamos, en marcha, y si intenta arrancarse le daré un puntapié que le va a juntar la nariz con los talones.

Al oír esta terminante declaración, el hombre delgado pareció encogerse. En seguida, malhumorado, tironeó de un brazo al borracho, y éste, desprevenido, dio una brusca media vuelta y se fue de punta al suelo. Lo levantamos como quien levanta un barril de vino, mientras gimoteaba, quejándose amargamente de que la policía procediera de ese modo con él, que era un obrero honrado y trabajador.

MANUEL ROJAS (Chilean) *El delincuente*

62 Frogs and toads

Estoy sentado junto a la alcantarilla aguardando a que salgan las ranas. Anoche, mientras estábamos cenando, comenzaron a armar el gran alboroto y no pararon de cantar hasta que amaneció. Mi madrina también dice eso: que la gritería de las ranas le espantó el sueño. Y ahora ella bien quisiera dormir. Por eso me mandó a que me sentara aquí, junto a la alcantarilla, y me pusiera con una tabla en la mano para que cuanta rana saliera a pegar de brincos afuera, la apalcuachara a tablazos . . . Las ranas son verdes de todo a todo, menos en la panza. Los sapos son negros. También los ojos de mi madrina son negros. Las ranas son buenas para hacer de comer con ellas. Los sapos no se comen; pero yo me los he comido también, aunque no se coman, y saben igual que las ranas. Felipa es la que dice que es malo comer sapos. Felipa tiene los ojos verdes como los ojos de los gatos. Ella es la que me da de comer en la cocina cada vez que me toca comer. Ella no quiere que yo perjudique a las ranas.

JUAN RULFO (Mexican) *El llano en llamas*

63 An insatiable appetite

Pero, a todo esto, es mi madrina la que me manda hacer las cosas . . . Yo quiero más a Felipa que a mi madrina. Pero es mi madrina la que saca el dinero de su bolsa para que Felipa compre todo lo de la comedera. Felipa sólo se está en la cocina arreglando la comida de los tres. No hace otra cosa desde que yo la conozco. Lo de lavar los trastes a mí me toca. Lo de acarrear leña para prender el fogón también a mí me toca. Luego es mi madrina la que nos reparte la comida. Después de comer ella, hace con sus manos dos montoncitos, uno para Felipa y otro para mí. Pero a veces Felipa no tiene ganas de comer y entonces son para mí los dos montoncitos. Por eso quiero yo a Felipa, porque yo siempre tengo hambre y no me lleno nunca, ni aun comiéndome la comida de ella. Aunque digan que uno se llena comiendo, yo sé bien que no me lleno por más que coma todo lo que me den. Y Felipa también sabe eso . . . Dicen en la calle que yo estoy loco porque jamás se me acaba el hambre.

JUAN RULFO (Mexican) *El llano en llamas*

64 A threat of divorce

A todo esto, cuando el doctor Albarracín, fuera ya de quicio con los trotes de su mujer, saturado de indignación al verla danzar de huelga en huelga, de mitin en mitin, de zoco en colodro, olfateó los planes de aquella terrible demoledora, se puso como un energúmeno y planteó, por centésima vez, de puertas adentro, la cuestión del divorcio.

– Esto no puede continuar así – la dijo una mañana con voz tonante, irguiendo su fosca personilla, más fiero que nunca el rostro hirsuto, el bigote jaro, el hocico de zorro, los ojuelos grises –. Me estás poniendo en ridículo . . . y yo no lo puedo consentir. Estoy de belenes hasta la punta de los pelos . . . ¡Rediez! Ya no aguanto más.

Y uniendo la acción a la palabra, dio un tremendo puñetazo sobre la mesa, que hizo saltar la vajilla dispuesta para el desayuno.

Doña Belén, harto acostumbrada a los furores del mediquín, estrepitosos y fugaces como la espuma del champán, le oía como quien oye llover. Con su aire marcial y diligente de amazona intrépida y mujer de su casa, pues para todo tenía mimbres, tiempo y humor, puso en la mesa, debajo de las narices de su frenético marido, la cafetera rusa, el azucarero y un sabrosísimo tortel hecho por sus propias manos anarquizantes, que eran como de monja – ¡extraña contradicción! – para toda suerte de reposterías.

– ¡Esto se llama dar gato por liebre! – voceó Albarracín, que entre sus muchas flaquezas tenía la de espiritarse por el buen moka y los torteles de mantequilla –. Creí casarme con una mujer y me encuentro casado con un bandido . . . ¡Voy ahora mismo a pedir el divorcio!

– Toma primero el café – repuso ella con fisga, conociendo los flacos de Albarracín –. No hay nada como el café para estimular las resoluciones heroicas.

RICARDO LEÓN *El hombre nuevo*

65 Class-consciousness

Para Navidad vino Jeromo, hijo de Gregorio. Jeromo era un hombre alto, tan parecido al padre que las escardadoras cuando lo veían de espaldas lo confundían con él. Había ejercido todos los oficios del campo, exactamente como su padre; pues Gregorio sabía que tarde o temprano terminaría como él de aperador de "San Rafael". Sin embargo, había un punto nebuloso y era su matrimonio, que inesperadamente cortaba todos los proyectos de Gregorio. Cuando Encarna hablaba de su hijo, decía con un cierto puntillo de orgullo:

– Mi hijo está casado con una señorita.

Al llegar Jeromo aquella Navidad al cortijo, con botas recién lustradas y traje de paño negro, los gañanes le tenían extraño e inevitable respeto.

Gregorio no entendía aquello; pero empezaba a sospechar que la absurda aventura alejase a Jeromo del único camino respetable: ser aperador de "San Rafael". Encarna todas las noches cuando lo veía escribiéndole cartas, llamándole y contándole cómo iban las cosas en "San Rafael", volvía a decirle como un sonsonete:

– Gregorio, tú no te das cuenta de que nuestro hijo está casado con una señorita.

Y era verdad. Jeromo, el hijo de Gregorio, estaba casado con una señorita. Él mismo contó su historia una noche en "San Rafael", de manera inefable, con ese impudor que tienen las gentes del campo para sus problemas personales.

JOSÉ y JESÚS DE LAS CUEVAS *Historia de una finca*

66 The entertainers (a)

Un hombre de carnes flojas y esqueleto grande y derrumbado camina por la Avenida Mixcoac con un perrito blanco en los brazos. El perrito luce un traje de listones amarillos y azules, con cascabeles alrededor del cuello y en las cuatro patas. Detrás del hombre, camina otro, moreno y más viejo que el hombre grande: carga un cilindro de cartón, una trompeta raspada y una escalerilla. Los dos hombres usan sombreros de fieltro desteñido, camisas sin corbata, pantalón y saco de distinto color y viejísimo uso, y los dos caminan sin ritmo, como si las calles mismas los fueran arrastrando. Pero el hombre grande, aun en su perplejidad, luce cierta seguridad teatral en sus ademanes, en tanto que el más pequeño casi no levanta los pies y se veía más natural tirado en la calle, dejado a un lado, que tratando de caminar con un cansancio tan absoluto, que le luce en los ojos sin brillo, en la boca larga y cerrada, en todas las facciones alargadas como por la mano de un escultor sobre una pasta gris y sin resistencia. Caminan al lado de tendajones mixtos y cines de barrio, entre tranvías amarillos y postes de luz, caminan como dos figuras de un carnaval perpetuo que no se detiene a celebrarse a sí mismo, que va corriendo en pos de la consumación de su propia alegría decretada. Vienen desde la Colonia Portales, de donde salieron muy temprano, deteniéndose al mediodía en General Anaya, y más tarde en la Noche Buena. Las casas son iguales, la gente igual. Sólo el cansancio les obliga a detenerse y entonces comienzan a trabajar.

CARLOS FUENTES (Mexican) *La región más transparente*

67 The entertainers (b)

El hombre grande se detiene, se quita el sombrero y de su bolsa saca un cucurucho rojo. El hombre pequeño y cansado toca la corneta con un gemido desigual entre el aire y el metal, y el grande lo acompaña con un tararará sin letra desde su voz cascada. Algunas criadas se asoman a las azoteas de las pequeñas casas, de un gris polvoso. Ixca Cienfuegos, antes de entrar en una de ellas, se detiene para observar cómo el perrito camina sobre el cilindro rodante. El hombre grande se quita el cucurucho y saluda a las criadas. "Les presento al gran perrito Josué, de largo historial en los grandes circos internacionales que han visitado esta tierra donde la providencia ha dejado más dones que hojas tiene un laurel: ¡México!", resopla el hombre grande mientras el pequeño continúa berreando la corneta raspada y ahora, con lentitud, coloca en el centro de la calle mal pavimentada la escalera y el animal sube con rapidez y se queda sentado en el descanso, gimiendo y asustado. "Y ahora véanlo bajar, señoras y señores. Es el gran perrito Josué, del circo Barnum, que ha dado la vuelta al mundo." El perrito gime y sus cascabeles se agitan en un temblor imperceptible. El hombre grande truena los dedos y por fin toma al animal del cuello y lo obliga a descender mientras la trompeta alcanza un crescendo roto. El traje ajironado y los cascabeles brillan en el crepúsculo. Las criadas se han retirado. El hombre grande pasea su cucurucho ante ventanas cerradas. El pequeño se ha sentado en la banqueta con la cara más oscura que la próxima noche.

CARLOS FUENTES (Mexican) La región más transparente

68 Tigre Juan (a)

Era Tigre Juan un hombre alto y sobremanera enjuto. Siempre se le veía en su puesto del aire. Apenas dormía. Levantábase con el alba y salía al campo a recoger hierbas de virtud medicinal. De vuelta a las siete de la mañana, erguía en la plaza su tinglado y no se retiraba de allí hasta las siete de la tarde, que se encerraba en casa a elaborar menjurjes y pildorillas. Al posar en la vecina iglesia de San Isidoro el Angelus meridiano, una criada viejísima, tuerta y con jeta de bruja, la Güeya de apodo, le traía al puesto un humeante pote de barro vidriado, que Tigre Juan colocaba entre las rodillas y de él comía despaciosamente, con cuchara de boj. A las nueve de la noche solía tomar, en pie, un refrigerio frugal, y en concluyendo, luego que el sobrino le leía por encima un diario de Madrid, iba a jugar naipes, no más de dos horas, a la tienda de una señora conocida.

RAMÓN PÉREZ DE AYALA Tigre Juan

69 Tigre Juan (b)

Como Tigre Juan era epítome de habilidades y centón de conocimientos, acudían a su puesto gentes las más heterogéneas e inesperadas: estudiantes, a empeñar libros a principio de curso y a comprarlos en vísperas de examen; señoras grávidas en busca de nodriza; criadas de servir, a que las escribiese un mensaje para el cortejo ausente; solteronas en vinagre, que no se ahitaban de leer folletines; sacerdotes obesos y reumáticos, por probar eso de la homeopatía; cobradores de banco, a recoger las letras ultramarinas que Tigre Juan había negociado;

labriegos solapados, en consulta de toda laya, así en lo tocante a la salud como a litigios y pleitos que sin cesar entre sí traían, y, finalmente, la parroquia de su negocio de granos.

Teníasele en reputación de rico y avaricioso, si bien se le alababa el rasgo liberal de dar carrera a un sobrino pobre. La claridad y honradez de su vida desde que años atrás, lo menos veinte, había plantado su tenderete en la plaza, eran proverbiales. Con todo, inspiraba a los convecinos invencible y no oculto recelo, quizás a causa de sus orígenes misteriosos, tal vez por su traza hosca y su carácter insociable, que le habían valido el alias de Tigre Juan.

RAMÓN PÉREZ DE AYALA *Tigre Juan*

70 Tigre Juan (c)

Su verdadera filiación era Juan Guerra Madrigal, pareja nada compatible de apellidos que, como perro y gato, sorprende ver juntos y concordes. No obstante el apodo, algunos amigos, de los muy contados y no menos leales que tenía, propalaban a todos los vientos que, en el fondo, era un bragazas. Es lo cierto que, inopinadamente, le acometían arrechuchos de frenesí, los cuales, con el discurrir de los años, iban espaciándose y amenguaban de intensidad. Aunque no se le conocía sino por el mote, no era raro que al dirigirse a él le llamasen don Juan, por urbanidad y y deferencia a su edad, ya madura. Pero jamás se supo de este don Juan trapicheo alguno, ni siquiera se le sorprendió mirando a una mujer con ansia o insinuación. Sin embargo, a pesar de sus cuarenta y cinco años y de su temerosa y huraña catadura, o quizás por esto mismo, despertaba en no pocas mujeres una especie de curiosidad invencible, mezcla de simpatía y atracción; que es propio de la naturaleza femenina inclinarse hacia lo fuera de lo común y perecerse por lo temible o misterioso.

RAMÓN PÉREZ DE AYALA *Tigre Juan*

Section Two

Passages for Translation from English into Spanish

Year after year the reports of examiners say practically the same things: the work of the average candidate is frequently ruined by carelessness and elementary inaccuracies. Errors abound, even at this stage, in genders, concords, *ser* and *estar*, *para* and *por*, common irregular verbs, the use of tenses and of the subjunctive mood.

These English prose passages, if translated with the help of the footnotes, should go far to reduce in the future the number of the apparently ineradicable mistakes mentioned above. To supply 'A' Level practice, a fair proportion of the passages are purposely devoid of any help. It is unwise to rely always on notes and vocabularies, and practice without them is essential.

Candidates would be well advised to:

1. Read through all the passage first.
2. Translate the passage mentally.
3. Write a rough copy of the difficult sections if time is available.
4. Correct this as you write the final copy neatly and legibly.
5. Read and check everything thoroughly; look out, in particular, for errors due to carelessness including those mentioned already.

Under normal conditions it is still a good idea to produce a first copy without using a vocabulary, grammar or footnotes. Then after checking it carefully, re-check it and correct with all help available. Finally write the finished version legibly and accurately.

Passages for Translation from English into Spanish

1 In a Madrid restaurant

During my holiday in Madrid I was fortunate[1] to find a little restaurant for my evening meal where the food was[2] both inexpensive and good. Here, after spending[3] the day in one of the famous museums, I could[4] sit at an outside[5] table, giving me a view[6] of the park, and settle down[7] to a leisurely[8] meal with wine and soup and cheese and fruit.

Soon I began to recognize the other regular customers as I suppose they did me. Among them was a group of students who occupied a table every evening. But I was most interested[9] in a delightful[10] young couple who spoke English with a faint[11] accent.

'What part of England do you think we come[12] from?' they asked with a smile, after we had talked one night.

I had no idea. All I could[4] suppose[13] was that they came[12] from London.

They laughed loudly, and said, 'But we have never been in England in our lives[14]! We both come from Denmark[15].'

[1] use *tener la suerte*. [2] why *ser*? *19*. [3] use the infinitive *pasar*. Why? *11(a)*. [4] *poder*, *20(m)*. [5] use *al aire libre*. [6] say *con vista al parque*. [7] use *disponerse*. [8] use *con toda calma*. [9] use active voice, *11(d)*. [10] don't forget agreement, *3(b)*. [11] *un poco de acento*. [12] use *ser*, *19*. [13] use *suponer*. [14] *en la vida*. [15] say 'We are Danish', *27(d)*.

2 Never sleep when on duty!

I returned quickly to the police station eager[1] to tell all[2] I had discovered[3]. I ran up[4] the stairs, hastened along[5] the corridor to the office I knew so well, knocked impatiently on the door and, receiving[6] no reply, opened it and entered.

As I did so, the words I was about to speak[7] died away[8]. There was[9] the stern police sergeant, Alonso, lying[10] back in his chair, his[11] eyes closed, his[11] feet resting on another[12] chair, his great body[13] breathing gently[14] and deeply. He appeared to be fast asleep[15].

I stood[16] watching him till I suddenly realized I was being looked at[17] through half-closed eyes[18]. With a start[19] Alonso woke up.

'Don't think I was sleeping, young man,' he said. 'A Spanish policeman never sleeps on duty[20].'

'No sir,' I said.

We looked at each other. A moment later, he began to smile and so did I.

After telling him briefly what I knew about the crime, and receiving his thanks, I asked simply[21]: 'What do you want me to do[22] now?'

[1] *deseoso*. [2] *5(g)*. [3] past participle? *13(b)*. [4] say 'I went running', *14(e)*. [5] use *apresurarse por*. [6] *al no recibir*, *11(a)*. [7] *pronunciar*. [8] use *morir en la garganta*. [9] *ser* or *estar*? *19*. [10] use past participle, *13(b)*. [11] *2(c)*. [12] *2(a)*. [13] *su cuerpo grandote*. [14] two adverbs *6(a)*. [15] *dormir a pierna suelta*, *24*. [16] say 'I remained'. [17] avoid passive, *11(d)*. [18] *por los párpados entreabiertos*. [19] *dando un respingo*. [20] say 'when he is on duty', *19(b)*. [21] *sencillamente*, *25*. [22] subjunctive? *18(b)*.

3 Turkish spies

Aunt Dot and I had[1] a very good evening on the lake and we caught quite a number of[2] fishes. The two spies turned up, and landed on the island, spying all about it[3] and peering[4] into the little ruined church, where probably messages had been hidden[5] for them[6], and it was a pity we had not found[7] them first[8]. They crouched behind[9] a wall while they put the documents in their[10] pockets; at least I supposed this was what they were doing, but aunt Dot said that when they reappeared they were chewing something, and that they were probably eating the documents up. All this spying was very interesting to us, as we had so often heard[11] of it but without knowing[12] that it was so common in Turkey.

'I wonder how much they are paid[13],' said aunt Dot, 'and how often.'

'And who by,' I said.

ROSE MACAULAY *The Towers of Trebizond*

[1] use *pasar*. [2] *bastantes peces*. [3] use *escudriñar*. [4] use *asomarse*, *11(b)*. [5] avoid passive by using 'there were'. [6] *por* or *para*? *10*. [7] why subjunctive? *18(c)* and *(i)*. [8] *antes*, *9(e)*. [9] use *agapazarse*. [10] *2(c)*. [11] insert 'speak', *11(a)iii*. [12] *sin saber*, *11(a)*. [13] use *cobrar*, to receive in payment.

4 The peacocks

Any time[1] he was[2] out of work and lonely[3] he thought of[4] the peacocks.

When he was[2] a little boy in the country he used to go for a walk with his father every Sunday afternoon, and sometimes they used to walk so far that they would find themselves at last way up in the hills, tired from so much walking[5] but happy, hardly talking, just standing there, letting[6] the cold wind blow on them and feeling[7] the long shadows of evening fall around them[8]. Then on the way back his father would[9] stop at[10] Mrs[11] Dawkins' big white house at the bottom of the hill and say good evening to old Mrs Dawkins who was[2] English and very rich but kindhearted. Then he would[12] go with his father and look[13] at Mrs Dawkins' peacocks.

There were a lot of them[14]. His father used to stand[9] in the near-darkness[15] and make a funny sound with his[16] mouth and the peacocks would[12] scream and run out[17] of the bushes and look at the man and the little boy.

They were[2] very beautiful.

F. D. WELLER The Peacocks

Revise the use of the imperfect tense (*11(c)*) and soler (*20(q)*).

[1] *Siempre que.* [2] *ser* or *estar*? [3] *a solas*, *9(a)iv.* [4] preposition? *21(j).* [5] *andar.* [6] *dejar*, *20(d).* [7] use *observar* + infinitive, *11(a)iii.* [8] *en torno suyo.* [9] use *soler*, *20(q).* [10] preposition? *9(d).* [11] *2(d).* [12] tense? Is a conditional needed? [13] say 'to look'. [14] omit 'of them' and say 'There were many'. [15] *la semioscuridad.* [16] *2(c).* [17] say 'come running out', *14(e).*

5 The last train to Valencia

Late that afternoon Don Luis found a way to leave Aranjuez. By accident[1] he met the postman, Señor Felipe, who was amazed that he had not gone[2] south.

'I really did not believe you would still be[3] here,' said Felipe. 'Everyone is leaving[4] or has gone. Don't you know that the *comandante* has been ordered[5] to turn[6] the town over to the Fascists tonight?'

Don Luis nodded, 'I'm trying to go to Valencia,' he said. 'It is not as easy as[7] you think.'

'We're leaving in[8] an hour,' Felipe said, 'my wife and I.' There's a train at[8] the station. It will be the last one[8] going south. I'll come for you. You certainly shouldn't[9] stay behind[10] even[11] though you are who you are, Don Luis. No one will recognize you. Soldiers always get drunk[12] when they occupy[13] a town.'

At seven in the evening the postman and his thin, pale-faced wife[14], carrying[15] bundles and suitcases, came for[16] Don Luis. The latter carried no baggage because he had not thought of[17] packing any[18]. The three made their way to the station, skirting around the edge of the village[19].

JAMES NORMAN The Fell of Dark

[1] *por*, *10*. [2] subjunctive? *18(c)*. [3] subjunctive? *18(d)*. [4] *gerundio*, *14(c)*.
[5] avoid the passive voice, *11(d)*. [6] subjunctive? *18(b)*. [7] 'as . . . as', *8*.
[8] preposition? *9(d)*. [9] *deber*, *20(c)*. [10] *atrás*. [11] *aun* or *aún*? *26*. [12] to get
drunk, *21(c)*. [13] infinitive? *11(a)*. [14] *de*? *9(c)*. [15] participles, *13*. [16] use
venir a buscar. [17] think, *21(j)*. [18] negatives, *16*. [19] use *bordeando el pueblo
por las afueras*.

6 An unusual arrival

'How[1] far away is it?'

  'Fifteen[1] miles.'

  'Is there a bus?'

  'There is not.'

  'Is there a taxi or a car I can[2] hire in the village?'

  'There is not.'

  'Then how am I to get there?'

  'You might[3] hire a horse hereabouts[4],' someone suggested after a silence.

  'I can't[5] ride a horse,' she said in exasperation, 'and in any case there's my luggage.'

They stared at her with quiet, dreamy[6] curiosity. She had been told[7] that the local people were[8] friendly, but these big slow men, while not exactly hostile[9], entirely lacked[10] the responsiveness of civilization[11]. They had looked at her a little strangely when she told them where[12] she was going. Perhaps[13] that was[8] it.

She saw now that it was foolish and even discourteous not to have announced[14] her exact time of arrival. It had seemed more exciting, more romantic and somehow less alarming to come at her own pace. But now that the dusty little train which had brought her from Greytown Junction had coughed away[15] among the rocks, leaving her in this silence a spectacle[16] for these men, she felt[17] helpless and almost frightened.

IRIS MURDOCH The Unicorn

[1] Begin with *a* to introduce an expression of distance *9(a)*. [2] subjunctive?
18(g). [3] *poder*, *20(m)*. [4] *por estos alrededores*, [5] *21(e)*. [6] use *somnolienta*.
[7] avoid the passive, *11(d)*. [8] *ser* or *estar*, *19*. [9] *aunque nada hostiles*.
[10] use *carecer de*, *11(b)*. [11] say 'civilized reactions'. [12] why *adonde*? [13] use
acaso and subjunctive, *18(a)*. [14] *11 (a)*. [15] *se hubo alejado tosiendo*, *14*.
[16] *para servir de espectáculo a*, *20(p)*. [17] why *se sintió*? *11(a)* and *(c)*.

7 Sheltering from a Caribbean hurricane

We dug a narrow shelf into the hillside. It was like a trench except that the sides were[1] one above the other. The ground sloped before us down to a river. There was a large grove of trees[2] behind us on the left. When we all got into[3] the trench with the dogs it was unbearably hot[4]. The mules stayed near. We had taken the rifles and shot-guns from them, and three bottles of rum. There wasn't room for[5] anything else in the trench. I didn't think we would have to wait long. While we were waiting I scrambled out[6] and went to my mule and took my plastic wash-bag[7] from the saddle-bag[8] and put my cigarettes into the waterproof plastic. I went back into the trench and held the bag open for the other packets of cigarettes. The mule tried to put its[9] head into the trench and we had to slap[10] the coarse, bony face before [11] it would go away.

JOHN HEARNE *Only One Blow of the Wind*

[1] *Ser* or *estar*? *19*. [2] *un gran boscaje*. [3] use *meterse*. [4] say 'the heat was unbearable' (why *ser*?). [5] *por* or *para*? *10*. [6] use *salir a gatas*, *9(a)iv*. [7] *la bolsa de aseo de plástico*. [8] order of words? *12*. [9] *2(c)*. [10] *palmotear*. [11] say 'till it went away'.

8 The beginnings of Uruguay

The first white man to set foot on[1] what is now Uruguayan soil was[2] Spain's chief navigator Juan Díaz de Solís, who discovered the great estuary later named Río de la Plata and landed about 100 miles[3] east of present-day[4] Montevideo in 1516[5]. He[6] claimed the territory for[7] the Spanish Crown, but his explorations came to a tragic end when he was killed by[8] the warlike Charrúa Indians. Solís was followed[9] by two other[5] great navigators[10] in the service of[11] Spain who were searching for an ocean passage to the Orient: the Portuguese explorer Ferdinand Magellan, who anchored[2] briefly in the River Plate in 1519, but continued southward to discover[12] the strait[10] which bears his name; and Sebastian Cabot, who arrived in 1527 and built[13] the first fort on the banks of[14] the Uruguay River.

[1] use *pisar*. [2] tense? *11(c)*. [3] *a* before distance, *9(a)*. [4] use *actual*, *25*. [5] order of words, *12*. [6] repeat the proper noun; why? [7] *por* or *para*? *10*. [8] *a manos de*, *9(a)*. [9] avoid passive, *11(d)*. [10] spelling, *26*. [11] *al servicio de*, *9(a)*. [12] say 'where he would discover'. [13] use *hacer construir*, *20(j)*. [14] *a orillas de*, *9(a)*.

9 The Banda Oriental

The fierce resistance of the Charrúas and failure to find[1] the anticipated precious metals discouraged the early explorers and settlers. The first settlement, San Salvador, in what is now Argentina, disappeared, and it was not until after the missionaries had pacified the Indians that permanent communities were established[2]. Nova Colonia do Sacramento (now Colonia) was founded in 1680 by the Portuguese as an outpost against Spanish penetration from Buenos Aires on the opposite shore of the Río de la Plata. Almost half[3] a century later the Spaniards founded Montevideo as a stronghold against the huge Portuguese colony of Brazil. Thus the Banda Oriental, as the region east of the Uruguay River was called, became[4] a battleground over which the Spaniards and the Portuguese and later, the Argentines and Brazilians, struggled[5] for supremacy until 1828. After the Portuguese were[5] expelled from Colonia in 1777, the Banda Oriental became part of Spain's new Vice-royalty[6] of the Río de la Plata.

[1] *el no encontrar*, *11(a)*. [2] say 'permanent communities were only established when the missionaries . . .'. [3] *medio*, *2(a)*. [4] became, *21(b)*. [5] tense? *11(c)*. [6] *virreinato*.

10 Don Juan

No wonder Dolores sighs[1] as she watches Don Juan disappear round[2] the corner. He is the hero of Seville – a wicked playboy, whose exploits have been described with bated breath[3] in all the patios with many a whispered confidence and giggling[4], when Father and Mother were not looking. Don Juan makes no class distinction; Pepita the maid knows him as well as the Condesa de Santa Cruz living in the palace yonder[5]. Don Juan is part[6] of the symbolism[7] of Andalusia: he is the vagabond in love, the tempter who arrives at the gate and behaves like the wicked goblin in the fairy stories. Very often he comes armed with[8] a guitar and then he is even more dangerous, for he had added the magic of the Pied Piper to his sinister, Oriental powers of seduction. For Don Juan Tenorio is the descendant[7] of countless Moorish ancestors. He is, as a famous author has pointed out[9], a symbol[7] of the Oriental way of looking at life as opposed to[10] the Occidental.

WALTER STARKIE *Don Gypsy*

[1] Why subjunctive after *no es de extrañar*? [2] *gerundio, 14.* [3] *en voz baja.*
[4] use diminutive of *risa, 23.* [5] *de más allá, 9(c).* [6] say 'forms part of'.
[7] spelling, *26.* [8] *de, 13(b).* [9] order of words? *12.* [10] *a diferencia de.*

11 The bullfighting business

On the fringe of Madrid thousands are being attracted to see 96 fighting bulls[1] calmly grazing[2] in well-protected enclosures. But during the next two weeks all of them are fated to die in the Madrid arena.

Daily bullfights are the highlight in the programme[3] of entertainments arranged to commemorate[4] the festivals of San Isidro, the[5] patron saint of Spain's capital[6].

Millions of pesetas will be paid to 23 of Spain's leading matadors engaged to show their skill with the cape and in killing the 96 bulls with one sword thrust, if possible, when the 'moment of truth' arrives[7].

The famous Madrid bullring holds[8] around 23,000, so that when the last of the 16 bullfights takes place[9] on May 29th, some 368,000 spectators will have been present. All tickets have been sold and speculators who have cornered many tickets are making huge profits, especially with[10] the tourists.

The Evening Standard, 19 May 1966

[1] *toros de lidia.* [2] use a relative clause. [3] *del programa.* Why? *9(c)* and *1(a).* [4] spelling, *26.* [5] article? *2(a).* [6] gender? *1(a)vi.* [7] say *a la hora de la verdad.* [8] *caber, 20(a).* [9] subjunctive? *18(e).* [10] *a costa de.*

12 The Maine family (a)

This Captain[1] Charles Maine and his wife, Señora Maine[2], were blessed with a son[3], Alphonso Charles Maine. This son they made both[4] English and Spanish, sending him to Eton College[5] and to Oxford University to be educated, and bringing him back to Spain, to make a good hidalgo of him when his education was completed[6].

The young gentleman returned to his parents at Cadiz with an even wider education than[7] they had expected or intended, for he brought back with him[8] an English wife; and in the famous old town of Cadiz where there was already a considerable English colony, this Alphonso Charles Maine, and Mary his wife, settled down[9]. To them was born[10] a son, Miguel Charles Maine, who had at least one distinction[11]. He was my father.

P. C. WREN *Spanish Maine*

[1] rank, *2(d)*. [2] is *la* required? *2(a)*. [3] say 'received the blessing of a son'. [4] correlatives, *8*. [5] say 'sending him to study at Eton College'. [6] say 'at the end of his studies'. [7] comparatives, *7*. [8] pronouns, *4*. [9] order of words, *12*. [10] say 'they had a son'. [11] say 'who distinguished himself in one thing at least'.

13 The Maine family (b)

My father, intensely Anglophile – in some ways more English than the English, although a Spaniard – had me taught English from the cradle[1]. I grew up bi-lingual, reading as much English literature as Spanish[2].

Fortune frowned not[3] on my birth, in one way; but in another it did, for my parents spoilt me. My troubles began in the nursery[4].

I was educated at the best school in[5] Cadiz, my mother refusing to part with me, when my father wanted[6] to send me to England. How different might[7] my life have been, had he had his way[8]; for, from school, I went to Cadiz University instead of to that of Oxford, and thus never left my home and the influence – or lack of influence – of my mother and her family.

I grew up an extremely dissipated young man.

I admit it.

Not that I was a loafer[9], a waster, mark you. Far from it. I had too much energy for[10] that. I was indefatigable, both[2] at work and play.

P. C. WREN *Spanish Maine*

[1] *desde mi más tierna infancia.* [2] correlatives, *8*. [3] say 'smiled'. [4] *en la cuna.* [5] preposition, *9(c)*. [6] tense, *11(c)*. [7] *poder*, *20(m)*. [8] subjunctive? *18(k)*. [9] *no es que fuera un gandul.* [10] *para* or *por?*, *10*.

14 A new tenant

Two or three people, hearing sounds of a quarrel[1] in the patio, came out of their rooms and listened.

'It's the new lodger,' said a woman. 'She's having a row[2] with the porter who brought her[3] things.'

It was a tenement house[4] of two storeys, built round a patio, in a back street of La Macarena, which is the roughest quarter[5] in[6] Seville. The rooms were let[7] to working men and the small functionaries[8] with whom Spain is overrun[9], postmen, policemen, or tram-conductors, and the place swarmed[10] with children. There were twenty families there. They squabbled[11] and made it up[12]; they chattered their heads off[13]: they helped one another when help was needed; for the Andalusians are good-natured[14] people, and on the whole they got on well enough together[15]. One room had been[16] for some time unlet. A woman had taken it that morning, and an hour later had brought her bits and pieces[17], carrying as much as she could herself, a *gallego* – the Galicians are[18] the general porters of Spain – laden with the rest.

But the quarrel was growing more[19] violent, and the two women above, on the first floor, anxious not to miss[20] a word, leant over[21] the balcony.

W. SOMERSET MAUGHAM *The Mother*

[1] *una riña.* [2] use *reñir.* [3] *2(c).* [4] *una casa de vecindad.* [5] *el barrio de peor vivir.* [6] preposition? *9(c)ii.* [7] use reflexive to avoid passive, *11(d)* [8] *funcionarios.* [9] say 'who abound in Spain'. [10] *los chiquillos pululaban* [11] say 'they had quarrels'. [12] use *hacer las paces.* [13] use *charlar por los codos, 24.* [14] *de buen carácter.* [15] *se llevan bastante bien.* [16] tense? *11(c)* [17] *sus trastos y cosas.* [18] use *soler, 20(q).* [19] use *cada vez más, 24.* [20] say 'to lose'. [21] use *asomarse, 11(b).*

15 Inter Caetera

The Magnificent Lord Cristóbal Colón (whom we always call Christopher Columbus)[1] sighted Watling Island in[2] the Bahamas on 11 October 1492. Thence he went on[3] to discover the West Indian island of Cuba and Hispaniola (Haiti). On his return[4] to Spain in 1493, he informed King[5] Ferdinand that he had reached the outlying parts of eastern Asia, somewhere in the neighbourhood of Japan or China. He did not know that the continent of America lay between what he had discovered and what he thought he had discovered.

The two kingdoms of the Iberian peninsula, Spain and Portugal, were exploring in opposite directions. When Columbus discovered the West Indies, the Portuguese were navigating as far as the Cape of Good Hope in a methodical attempt to reach the East Indies. To avoid disputes in the future the two countries asked the Borgia Pope, Alexander VI, to demarcate[6] their spheres of interest. Taking a pen he drew a line down the middle of the Atlantic and in a Bill called Inter Caetera declared the Portuguese[7] to have exclusive rights to all lands they already possessed or might[8] discover eastward of it and the Spaniards a similar right to what Columbus had discovered in the West Indies and to what subsequently they might[8] come upon beyond those islands.

MAURICE COLLIS Cortés and Montezuma

[1] omit the words in the brackets. [2] preposition? *9*. [3] use conditional tense. [4] infinitive, *11(a)*. [5] titles and rank, *2(d)*. [6] subjunctive? *18(b)*. [7] small 'p'. Why? [8] *poder, 20(m)*.

16 A dangerous beach for bathing

'Hey, you!'

She started back[1] and sat down, already exhausted. A man was approaching.

She sat upon the beach until the man was near to her, and then got up and threw a towel round her shoulders[2]. The voice[3] from the sea and the stones was so loud that it was difficult to hear[4] what he said. He seemed[5] to be a local man[6].

'You mustn't[7] go swimming in that sea.'

Almost in tears now, Marian said, exasperated and determined[8] to misunderstand him, 'Why not? Is this a private[9] beach? I come from Gaze Castle'.

'You mustn't go swimming here,' said the man as if he had not heard[10] her. Perhaps he had not. 'You'll be drowned directly.'

'I won't be[11]!' said Marian. 'I can swim[12] very well.' But she knew with a premonition of deeper fear that she was[13] defeated.

'Two Germans were drowned[14] last week,' said the man. 'Swimming near Blackport they were. We're watching for their bodies[15] yet.'

IRIS MURDOCH The Unicorn

[1] Inició el regreso. [2] say 'on the shoulders', *2(c)*. [3] say 'noise'. [4] *11(a)i*. [5] *parecer, 11(b)*. [6] *un lugareño*. [7] *deber, 20(c)*. [8] say 'resolved', *13(b)*. [9] *particular, 25*. [10] subjunctive? *18(k)*. [11] *De ninguna manera*. [12] *21(e)*. [13] *ser* or *estar? 19*. [14] avoid the passive by using reflexive, *11(d)*. [15] *los cadáveres*.

17 Don Roberto in prison

Though badly battered[1] about the shoulders and arms, Burns passed away time by singing[2] snatches out of *The Mikado* throughout the night, whilst his companion, with only the help of his handkerchief, tried to stem the flow of[3] blood which still oozed out of his wound.

In the morning they saw go past their cell men with bandaged heads[4], who, the night before, had had nothing wrong with them.

Towards noon, when Don Roberto's mother was allowed to visit the prisoners, she took with her[5] a basket filled with food and drink. Sorely distressed, she found her son sitting on the edge of his bunk, his mop[6] of hair covered with congealed blood.

Having kissed him and John Burns, whom she thanked for the brave manner in which he had defended her son[7], she produced the food which the two hungry men accepted with joy. Noticing that his mother was[8] still very distressed, Don Roberto said with a laugh: 'The condemned men ate heartily,' whereupon the three laughed together[9]. Presently he was allowed to go into the yard where, at a pump[10], he washed his head.

A. F. TSCHIFFELY *Don Roberto*

[1] *magullado*. [2] *gerundio, 14*. [3] omit 'flow of'. [4] singular or plural? *1(c)*. [5] *consigo, 4*. [6] use *greña*. [7] 'having defended her son so bravely'. [8] use *seguir*. [9] say 'which made'. [10] use *una fuente*.

18 Bolívar in Jamaica

Bolívar meanwhile was in Jamaica, waiting for the opportunity of going on with the war of independence. It was not that he never knew when he was beaten[1]. He knew only too well. He had been beaten twice, thoroughly, and should have been[2] utterly discredited. But one of his greatest qualities was that he was always ready to try again. From Jamaica (6 September 1815) he wrote a long letter to an English correspondent[3] who had asked[4] his opinion on the future of Spanish American peoples. The inquirer is supposed to have been the Duke of Manchester, at that time governor of Jamaica, a man of wide human sympathy and considerable political intelligence.

Bolívar must have[2] realized by this time[5] that there were two main types of Englishmen influential in foreign policy and foreign relations: the types represented respectively by Canning and Byron. If[6] Canning did great things for[7] British power and influence and trade – and, with these objects in view, materially discouraged Spain from persisting[8] in the reconquest of South America – Byron did as much or more to establish Britain in the eyes of all nations[9] as the great paladin of justice[10] and liberty[10].

J. B. TREND *Bolívar and the Independence of Spanish America*

[1] use *darse por vencido*, *18(i)*. [2] *deber*, *20(c)*. [3] *25*. [4] ask, *21(a)*. [5] *para entonces*. [6] *si*, *18(k)*. [7] why *por*, *10*. [8] subjunctive or infinitive? *18(b)*. [9] say 'that Britain should appear'. [10] insert the article.

19 Bolívar's Angostura speech

Bolívar began his speech at Angostura with a historical summary. The origins of their present[1] situation, he said, could be found in the records of Spanish rule in America, in the Laws of the Indies, in the acts of the various Viceroys and Spanish governors. The Church, too, had played its part[2] in maintaining the colonies in bondage to the mother country; and all of these causes should[3] be considered in attempting to account for the brusque action of the Republican Government in proclaiming its independence of Spain, and for the ferocity of the supporters of Spain in opposing it[4]. The separation of South America from the Spanish monarchy resembled nothing so much as the Roman Empire falling to pieces at the beginning of the Dark Ages. The dismembered parts of the Empire formed independent peoples: but in Europe those people returned to a certain extent to their original condition, while in Venezuela they had left hardly[5] a vestige of what they were before the Spaniards came. The present[1] inhabitants of Venezuela were neither Europeans nor Indians, but[6] an intermediate race between the two.

J. B. TREND *Bolivar and the Independence of Spanish America*

[1] present, *25*. [2] play, *21(f)*, *24*. [3] *deber*, *20(b)*. [4] what does 'it' refer to? [5] *apenas si*. [6] *sino*, *8*.

20 The Saint in Mexico

The Saint lighted a cigarette, and put[1] his lighter away very quietly. He glanced at Consuelo for[2] a moment as[3] she sat[4] down slowly on the other wooden chair at the table, and then he looked at Ned Yarn again[5].

'I'm sorry,' he said. 'How long ago did that happen?'

'Almost as soon as I got here.' The other gave a kind of short two-toned grunt[6] that might[7] have been meant for a laugh[8]. 'How much did she tell you about all this?'

'As much as[9] she knows, I think.'

'I can figure what else she thinks. And what everybody else thinks. But you know as[10] much now as I knew when I came down here with Tiltman. That's the truth, so help me[11].'

'I hope you'll tell¹² me the rest.'

Yarn sipped¹³ his drink, and put it down without a grimace, as if he was¹⁴ completely inured to the vile taste.

'We flew here from Tijuana, and I thought it was all on the level¹⁵. A chance to make some big money legitimately – that is, if we weren't bothered¹⁴ about bribing a few Mexicans not to watch us¹⁶ too closely.'

LESLIE CHARTERIS *Señor Saint*

¹ put, *21(g)*. ² *por* or *para*? *10*. ³ use *mientras*, *6*. ⁴ tense, *11(c)*. ⁵ use *volver a*, *11(b)*. ⁶ *gruñido en dos tonos*. ⁷ *poder*, *20(m)*. ⁸ say 'could be interpreted as', *18(g)*. ⁹ say 'everything'. ¹⁰ *tanto como*, *8*. ¹¹ say 'I swear that's the truth'. ¹² subjunctive? *18(c)*. ¹³ use *sorber del vaso*. ¹⁴ subjunctive? *18(k)*. ¹⁵ say 'in order'. ¹⁶ say 'so that they should not watch us too much', *18(f)*.

21 The beauty of Lisbon

It would be hard, indeed, to exaggerate¹ the beauty of Lisbon² in the heat of³ August and early⁴ September. A city where, although the trams run late and early and motor traffic never ceases, you are woken⁵ by a cock crowing in some hidden backyard or corner of a garden, and standing at the window you look down at the bank of geraniums⁶ in front of the house opposite and they are glowing, in incandescence⁷, like blind flowers, for the dawn has not reached to them; the palm trees are but shadows of themselves, and looking up over the roofs the morning just touches, that moment, on the white walls of a castle, high up, the Castelo de São Jorge, like a celestial city in a cloudless sky.

SACHEVERELL SITWELL *Portugal and Madeira*

¹ *26* and *11(a)i*. ² *Lisboa*. ³ *bajo los calores de*. ⁴ *9(a)v*. ⁵ use indefinite *uno* and avoid the passive, *11(d)*. ⁶ *macizos de geranios*. ⁷ *incandescentes*.

22 Jamaica is saved from the French

Firing from the cover of stout walls at targets largely in the open¹, the Jamaicans decimated² the enemy ranks. To add to the misery³ of the French, another detachment of the Jamaican forces had pushed up from the Bay and was hitting⁴ them on a flank. They were⁵ effectively stopped. It was⁵ the end of the invasion. They retreated⁵ to the beach.

On their way back, they set fire to the small town of Carlisle, and then boarded their ships again[6]. Next morning, they ran up their sails[7] and turned their prows[8] for sea and San Domingo[9].

It was[5] the end of the most serious attempt at capture[10] that Jamaica had undergone since the British occupation began in 1655. Behind them, the town[11] smoked[5] and Jamaican dead were gathered[12] for burial: several scores[13] of them, black and white Jamaicans. But weary soldiers, planters, and armed slaves (freed for the duration of the emergency) grinned a little self-consciously[14] at each other and slapped[15] their muskets contentedly.

V. S. REID Anniversary at Carlisle Bay

[1] <i>en su mayoría sin protección.</i> [2] use <i>diezmar.</i> [3] <i>el infortunio.</i> [4] say 'attacking', <i>26.</i> [5] tense? <i>11(c).</i> [6] use <i>volver a, 11(b).</i> [7] use <i>izar las velas.</i> [8] use <i>hacer proa al mar.</i> [9] the correct form in Spanish is <i>Santo Domingo, 3(f).</i> [10] <i>de captura.</i> [11] word order, <i>12(a)ii.</i> [12] avoid the passive, <i>11(d)iv.</i> [13] use <i>decenas.</i> [14] <i>un tanto embarazados.</i> [15] use <i>dar palmadas.</i>

23 The body on the beach

The same eyes which had only just finished looking sulkily at the streets, the sea, the church and the mountain looked at all these things again; but this time with expressions of wonder and respect, for lying on the shore with his feet in the water, as peaceful as an upturned boat and as naked as a bone, there was a man no one had ever seen before.

At first it was only a rumour.

'There's a man asleep on the shore!'

'There's a man sleeping on the beach – he must have been in the sea!'

'He must be from the ship! He must have swum ashore in the night!'

Like a rumour the story rose; then dropped when it changed a little. The man was dead.

CHAPMAN MORTIMER Mediterráneo

24 The greatness of Spain

'Well, we annexed Portugal, at a loss[1] of possibly a few hundred casualties. Our claim is doubtful, but the spoils are ours[2]. That actually[3] means that for all commercial purposes, Ana, we own the world. Look at the map[4]. We now possess the two best fleets in the world. England has some good sailors, but we have two experienced and organized fleets. Pirates allowed for, we now control not only[5] our own great western possessions, but also through Portugal the Indian Ocean[6]. Our sailors and missionaries are everywhere. Our wealth is uncharted[7]. This situation has been growing on us for some time, until it became fixed and inevitable. Luck caused it in the beginning, but it has been secured[8] by the plain bravery and imaginative perseverance of our ordinary people, our sailors and soldiers and missionaries. So you'd think, wouldn't you, that there might[9] be some sign in our national life, our home life, of this extraordinary economic strength? You'd think there might be roads and merchant ships and schools, and new houses and better shops and better wages, and more to eat and more ordinary human hope and decency? Yet there isn't[10].'

KATE O'BRIEN That Lady

[1] spelling, <i>26</i>. [2] article? <i>2</i>. [3] say 'in reality', <i>25</i>. [4] gender, <i>1</i>. [5] correlatives, <i>8</i>. [6] <i>Océano Índico</i>. [7] say 'countless'. [8] avoid passive voice, <i>11(d)</i>. [9] <i>poder</i>, <i>20(m)</i>. [10] say 'there is none of this'.

25 A hazardous venture

The time was now close for Cortés[1] to march[2]. He had so regulated his legal position that if he achieved[3] a conquest it would be his[4], not Velázquez's. And he had made a conquest more possible[5]; it had been impossible when he was not fully master[6]. He had discovered, moreover[7], that not only were the Totonacs longing to throw off Montezuma's rule, but also other peoples between the sea and the capital. If he directed[3] his march through their territory, the operation would become[10] less hazardous. It remained, however, a desperate venture as far as his information went[11]. With no reserve of arms and ammunition except what he carried[12], with no provisions beyond what the country might[13] provide, and no hope of Spanish reinforcements to take the place of casualties[14], he was setting out in the face of an army hundreds of times larger than his own[15] and armed nearly as well as the seven-eighths of it[16] which had no horses, muskets or[17] crossbows.

MAURICE COLLIS Cortés and Montezuma

[1] <i>faltar</i>, <i>20(g)</i>. [2] use <i>ponerse en camino</i>. [3] subjunctive? <i>18(k)</i>. [4] article? <i>2</i>. [5] use <i>realizable</i>, to avoid the repetition of <i>posible</i>. [6] say 'without him as

absolute master it would have been impossible'. [7] order of words, *12*.
[8] correlatives, *8*. [9] capital, *25*. [10] become, *21(b)*. [11] say 'to judge by the information which he relied upon'. [12] say 'they carried with them', *4*.
[13] *poder*, *20(m)*. [14] *las bajas*. [15] omit 'his own'. [16] change to 'of his own'.
[17] negatives *16*.

26 Philip II (a)

The death of Philip II (13 September 1598) was announced by the Venetian Ambassador to his Government in words which sum up the man and his reign with no little penetration: 'His majesty expired at El Escorial this morning at daybreak, after having received all the sacraments of the Church with every sign of devoutness, piety and religion. . . . He was a Prince who fought with gold rather than with steel, by his brain rather than by arms. He acquired more by sitting still, by negotiation, by diplomacy, than his father did by armies and by war. . . . Profoundly religious, he loved peace and quiet. He displayed great calmness and remained unmoved in good or bad fortune alike. . . . On great occasions . . . he never counted the cost; he was no close reckoner, but lavished gold without a thought; but in small matters, he was more parsimonious than became his station. . . . In short, he left a glorious memory of his royal name, which may serve as an example, not only unto his posterity and his successors, but unto strangers as well.'

R. TREVOR DAVIES *The Golden Century of Spain*

27 Philip II (b)

The reign of Phillip II has been very variously estimated. Historical tradition in northern Europe makes[1] it an unmitigated failure. And there is much to be said for[2] this conclusion. The loss[3] of the northern Netherlands, the failure of the Invincible Armada, and the economic impoverishment of Spain[4] during his latter years strongly support it. On the other hand, the Spanish tradition that[5] Philip the Wise (*el Prudente*) was a great king and his reign the culminating[6] glory of Spanish history, is by no means unfounded. The acquisition of Portugal and her vast colonial empire, the destruction of the hitherto invincible sea power of Turkey at Lepanto[7], the centralization of the Peninsula by[8] the assimilation of Aragon into his system[9], the half-success of keeping France Catholic and of retaining the southern Netherlands[10] –

these are achievements that mitigate the most adverse judgement of Philip's statesmanship[11]. The growth, moreover[7], of literature, art and science[12] in many forms under[13] Philip II gave Spain for a time the cultural and intellectual hegemony of the world.

R. TREVOR DAVIES *The Golden Century of Spain*

[1] say 'considers'. [2] say 'to justify'. [3] spelling, *26*. [4] say 'the impoverishment of Spain's economy'. [5] *de que*. [6] use the verb *culminar*. [7] order of words, *12*. [8] use *mediante*. [9] omit 'into his system'. [10] *Países Bajos*. [11] *como estadista*, *6*. [12] article required before these abstract nouns. [13] say 'during the reign of'.

28 Montezuma's death

Bernal says that during this colloquy on the wall the soldiers guarding Montezuma lowered their shields as there seemed no danger. Suddenly a volley of stones was flung at him. Who the slingers were, whether they were aiming at him or not, whether they were ordered to sling or did so on their own initiative, is not known, though many guesses have been made. Three of the stones hit Montezuma, one of them on the head. He was carried to his apartments. It did not seem at first that he was mortally wounded. But he was suffering from severe shock, not only the physical shock of the wound but the psychic shock of his own misery. Bernal says that he refused food and would not let them dress his wounds. The next day it was evident that he was sinking. The *Padre de la Merced* made great efforts to convert him to Christianity, efforts which were followed with anxiety by the Spaniards, who, as they loved him, wished to save him from eternal damnation. But these ministrations were unavailing.

MAURICE COLLIS *Cortés and Montezuma*

29 At the bullfight

I went[1] early, for it amused me to see[2] the people gradually filling the vast arena[3]. The cheaper seats in the sun were already packed, and it was a curious effect that the countless fans made[4], like the fluttering[5] of a host[6] of butterflies, as[7] men and women restlessly fanned themselves. In the shade, where I was sitting, the places were taken[8] more slowly, but even there, an hour before the fight began, one had to look rather carefully for a seat[9]. Presently a man stopped in front of me and with a pleasant smile asked if I could make room for him[10]. When he had[11] settled down I took[11] a sidelong glance[12] at him and noticed that he was well-dressed, in English clothes, and looked like[13] a gentleman. He had beautiful hands, small but resolute, with thin, long fingers. Wanting a cigarette, I took out my case[14] and thought it would be polite to offer him one. He accepted[15]. He had evidently seen that I was a foreigner for he thanked me in French.

'You are English?' he went on.

'Yes.'

'How is it you haven't run away from the heat?'

I explained that I had come on purpose to see the Feast of Corpus Christi[16].

'After all, it's something you must come to Seville for.'

W. SOMERSET MAUGHAM *The Point of Honour*

[1] Insert 'there'. [2] *11(a)*. [3] *el anfiteatro*. [4] say 'the effect of countless fans, etc. was curious', and consider the word order. [5] *el aleteo*. [6] *una legión*. [7] *según*. [8] avoid the passive by using the reflexive, *11(d)*. [9] say 'it was difficult to find an empty seat'. [10] *hacerle sitio*. [11] tense, *11(c)*. [12] *mirar de soslayo, 24*. [13] *20(r)*. [14] *la pitillera, 2(c)*. [15] insert 'it'. [16] *del Corpus* (omit *Christi*).

30 The blonde artist (a)

Pepe Parra then told me the whole story.

Stina had come to Ronda to paint. And so she set out early in the morning after her arrival and descended into the gorge to sketch[1] the Moorish bridge. But hardly had she set up[2] her easel and immersed herself in her work, when crowds of youths gathered round and began to jeer and point at her[3]. They were not[4] wicked little boys. Oh no! They were merely primitive[5] and ignorant. One could not be too hard on them[6] for expressing in too lively a manner[7] their surprise at seeing a fair-haired goddess sketching as if she was[8] a man – and dressed, too, in such strange masculine garments. For Stina, when she went out sketching, wore[9] rough[10], blue slacks, overall[11] and a broad-brimmed Tuscan straw hat. At first she made allowance[12] for native ebullience and high spirits[13], but soon matters[14] became more serious, for the youths were not satisfied with[15] jostling her and upsetting her easel and paint-box, but[16] they actually threw stones and clods of earth at her. She retreated in dismay.

WALTER STARKIE Don Gypsy

[1] say 'to make a sketch of'. [2] use *montar*. [3] use *señalar con el dedo*. [4] *No se trataba de.* [5] use *rústico*. [6] *No podía tomárseles muy a mal.* [7] *que expresaran con demasiados aspavientos.* [8] subjunctive? *18(k)*. [9] use *soler llevar*. [10] *de tela burda.* [11] *mandilón.* [12] use *atribuir.* [13] *la ruidosa alegría.* [14] use *la cosa.* [15] *a los chicos no les bastaba con.* [16] *sino que.* Why? *8(b)*.

31 The blonde artist (b)

But being[1] a girl of energetic character[2], she went straight off to the mayor of Ronda and lodged a vigorous complaint. The mayor then ordered two civil guards to accompany the young lady on her sketching expeditions[3]. When she pitched[4] her easel in some picturesque spot they stood[4], one each side leaning on their rifles, ready for[5] any attack. There they remained[4], like soldiers ready to defend the statue of the *Virgen del Carmen*. Stina enjoyed[4] the novelty of painting under police protection and she tried to make herself very agreeable to the two civil guards. One of them was fat and low-sized: she did not pay[6] much attention to him. But the other was tall and thin with romantic dark eyes and a handsome profile[7]. The guard did not need much encouragement: he had fallen in love with her at first sight. His first plan was[4] to get rid[8] of his companion by saying that he would mount guard himself alone. Hour after[9] hour he stood motionless, leaning[10] on his gun and gazing ecstatically[11] at the blonde Valkyrie[12].

WALTER STARKIE Don Gypsy

[1] use *por ser.* [2] spelling, *26.* [3] say 'when she went out to paint'. [4] tense? *11(c).* [5] say 'ready to repel'. [6] use *prestar, 24.* [7] spelling, *26.* [8] use *deshacerse de.* [9] preposition, *9(g).* [10] participles, *13(b).* [11] use an adjective, *6(b).* [12] *la valkiria.*

32 Antoñito (a)

'Ay-yy!' said the dark-skinned young man watching the ship. 'What a row!' And the bell in the yellow church tower went on ringing.

Peal followed peal out into the peaceful air, and worried by this faraway clamour Antonio Santiago Gómez began to imagine that the noisy bell could not be ringing like that for nothing.

'What's that for?' he said, and forgetting about the ship he listened. Then, although he knew that he was only talking to himself, he answered after a while.

'It's nothing to worry about, Antoñito. It's only a bell.'

'I wasn't worrying,' he said, 'I only wondered.'

He was alone on the mountainside and he could see neither the town nor the church; but the bell had reminded him that they were there somewhere below him and he began to feel melancholy, so he looked at the ship again.

CHAPMAN MORTIMER *Mediterráneo*

33 Antoñito (b)

This time, however, he could imagine nothing that would make[1] him laugh.

'It must be a big ship,' he thought. 'I wonder where it could have come from?'

'Never mind the ship[2], Antonio. Tell me something.'

'What?'

'Where have you come from?'

He did not answer. He was alone. The mountain was as empty as the air.

'Tell me, Antoñito.'

Silence.

'Antoñito – I want to know. I'll go on asking you till you tell me[3]. I like to hear you say it. Where have you come from?'

'From Mora de Ebro,' he replied, impatiently.

'That is a lie! It's the same old lie. You have never been in Mora.'

He shrugged his shoulders[4].

'Then why ask?' he said.

CHAPMAN MORTIMER *Mediterráneo*

Use the familiar *tú* here.

[1] make, *20(j)*, *18(g)*. [2] *Déjate de barco*. [3] subjunctive? *18(f)*. [4] verbs, *11(b)*, *24*.

34 Juanito and Mary

Juanito opened the café door and they went out together and along the narrow street into the Alameda. They hurried through the dusk into a square where the black sports car was parked. They drove in it away from Altorno, at a great speed, out on to the road towards France. It was dark now, but the moon was up and brilliant. Mary caught sight of the sea here and there, and of little silver bays and fishing villages, as they zigzagged eastward. Soon the car climbed, took hairpin bends, passed through long woods, and by roaring waterfalls.

'This is my country,' said Juanito. 'This is the good Basque country of my people.'

'You seem to know it well.'

'I know it well.'

'I lost my postcard today. My postcard of the Holy Angels.'

'I'll get you another. How did you lose it?'

'It blew out of my window.'

He laughed.

'I was in despair, Juanito.'

He drove more slowly over the stony track. Mary studied his gentle face.

'You're good at finding people,' she said. 'This is the third time.'

'If you intend to find anyone in a given area, and have an ounce of brain, you'll find her,' he said proudly. 'Didn't you know I'd be looking for you today?'

'Juanito – how could I know?'

KATE O'BRIEN *Mary Lavelle*

35 An unexpected gift

As they were toiling up a sharp incline, a shout brought their hearts into their mouths[1]. Looking back, they saw two mountaineers rushing to intercept them, from a neighbouring hill. No time for any consultation, or[2] do more than cock their guns and sit quite meekly waiting for the[3] worst. On came the natives, bounding from stone to[4] stone till they appeared on the track and blocked[5] the travellers way.

It seemed[6] the desperadoes wanted the travellers to stop until a little boy brought down[7] some Indian corn and milk, for it appeared it was the custom of these hills never to let a well-dressed Moor pass without some little offering[8]. Of course, a poor man, or anyone to whom maize and milk would have been a great service, passed[9] unnoticed, as[10] in other lands. Don Roberto promised[11] to accept whatever gift these two men had to offer, and, in due course, a boy appeared, carrying a wooden bowl, from which he drank, and then passed it to his followers, after having said: *El Ham du Lillah* (Praise be to God), the usual grace. The tribesmen would accept no money, but asked Don Roberto to say a word for them, about their taxes, which were paid[13] to their liege lord. Promising[14] that he would do this, the little party once more proceeded.

A. F. TSCHIFFELY *Don Roberto*

Revise subjunctives. No hints given below.

[1] use *helar la sangre*. [2] or, *16*. [3] *lo, 5*. [4] *en*. [5] use *cerrar el paso*. [6] *Era como si*. [7] say 'came down with'. [8] say 'without offering some refreshment'. [9] tense? *11(c)*. [10] say 'as occurs in'. *26*. [11] verbs, *11(b)*. [12] *querer, 20(o)*. [13] say 'which they would have to pay'. [14] insert 'them'.

36 The talisman

Accordingly, she hung about my neck[1] the tiny gold case, shaped like a book, which contained these priceless treasures as well as portraits of her mother and father. She bade me wear[2] it for ever. When out[3] of her presence, it would remind me of her; and whether[3] far from her or[4] near, it would be my sure shield against any and every danger. Not that, as she explained, she would[5] ever invoke the aid of the Prophet and pray to Allah, but[4] still – well, there could be no harm, could there, in keeping[6] and wearing the most sacred thing that ever came out[7] of Mecca? Of course she was a true Christian now, and it was really only the fragment of the Cross that was the true invaluable talisman, she said. This was to be[8] her wedding-gift to me, and perhaps I would value it because, all her life, she had worn it next her heart?

That night in my tent, wakeful, distraught, more wretchedly miserable than ever before in all my life, weary beyond words[9], though unable to sleep, I idly examined the trinket, and, playing with it, opened it. What I saw was[10] a pair of miniatures, portraits of a woman and a man, the former presumably covering the hair of the Beard of the Prophet, the latter the splinter of the True Cross[11].

P. C. WREN *Spanish Maine*

[1] article, *2(c)ii*. [2] subjunctive? *18(b)*. [3] insert 'I was', *18(e)*. [4] correlatives, *8*. [5] subjunctive? *18(i)*. [6] say 'that she should keep and that she should

wear', *18(i)*. [7] *que hubiese salido jamás de La Meca*. [8] say 'The case was going to be'. [9] *en un grado indecible*. [10] 'was' is the same tense as 'saw'. [11] *la Santa Cruz*.

37 Trebizond

When we saw Trebizond lying there in its splendid bay, the sea in front and the hills behind, the cliffs and the ravines which held[1] the ancient citadel, and the white Turkish town lying along the front[2] and climbing up the hill, it was like seeing an old dream change its shape, as dreams do[3], becoming something else, for this did not seem[4] the capital[5] of the last Byzantine[6] empire, but[7] a picturesque Turkish port and town with a black beach littered[8] with building materials[9], and small houses and mosques climbing the hill and ugly buildings along the quay. The citadel, the ruins of the Comnenus palace, would be somewhere on one of the heights, buried in brambled thickets[10] and trees; a great cliff, grown[8] with tangled shrub,[11] divided the city into two parts. Expecting[12] the majestic, brooding[13] ghost of a fallen empire, we saw, in a magnificent stagey setting,[14] an untidy Turkish port. The ghost would be brooding[15] on the woody cliffs and ravines, haunting the citadel and palace, scornfully taking no notice of the town that Trebizond now was[16], with the last Greeks expelled by the Father of the Turks twenty years back[17].

ROSE MACAULAY *The Towers of Trebizond*

Revise *(13)* and *(14)*.

[1] say 'surrounded'. [2] say 'shore'. [3] use *soler, 20(q)*. [4] insert 'to be'. [5] gender, *1(a)*. [6] *bizantino*. [7] *8*. [8] say 'covered'. [9] *materiales de construcción*. [10] *espesuras de zarzas*. [11] *matas entrelazadas*. [12] insert 'to see'. [13] *adusto*. [14] *un escenario magnífico*. [15] use *cavilar*. [16] *la ciudad de Trebisonda actual, 25*. [17] say 'twenty years after the last Greeks were expelled by the Father of the Turks'.

38 Farewell to humanity

It was 10 p.m. when we started. The cars under the street lamps bulged with packages enclosed in nets. They looked like two large and dusty widows returning from market. A few idlers hung around us, for three days we should not see strangers again, for three days I should see only the familiar faces of my present companions: I looked wistfully at the porter of the Allenby Hotel: what a gulf, I felt, separated him from his colleague at Baghdad. I leant forward and lovingly pressed a note into his hand. It was my farewell to humanity. The car hooted at that, and then jerked off and out under the Damascus Gate: it then swerved to the right, past the Gate of Herod and the Tower of the Storks. The great walls loomed square above us against the stars. We began to descend: a few olive trees flashed into the circle of the headlights and flicked back again into the dark: a village street illumined suddenly, an open door showing a deal table and a lamp, the hurried barking of dogs.

HAROLD NICOLSON *Miriam Codd*

39 The fugitives

If they could have had the start originally planned, the fugitives might have reached the Sierra de Lucena and taken refuge in the fastnesses of the Granada Mountains before their pursuers had been long on the road. As it was, they could not hope to reach the pass without a fight; and even if this were at first successful, it would be hard to shake off pursuit[1]. For it would not do merely to gain the mountains; they must[2] disappear long enough to find their way undetected[3] to the coast – Almería or Cartagena – and with luck secure passage for Italy. To be penned in the mountains would be fatal as it would give the Inquisition time to cut off their escape by sea. After that, with a price on their heads and the province raised[4] against them, their ultimate capture was inevitable.

Warned by a shout from Pedro, whose quick ears[5] had picked up the sound of approaching, though still distant[6], horsemen, Don Francisco dropped back for conference. Like a veteran captain, he had his plans ready for the event and now communicated them to Pedro, García, and Soler.

'Look, you. I remember a trail to the right[7] not more than five furlongs[8] from here. We used it in the Moorish wars. It's impossible for a woman, but fair enough[9] for men. Am I wrong, *señor*?'

'No,' agreed Soler, 'but it's better for goats. It leads west to Priego and hits[10] the road to Puente Genil.'

SAMUEL SHELLABARGER *Captain from Castille*

Revise *poder* (*20(m)*) subjunctive (*19*) tenses (*11(c)*) *para* and *por* (*10*). No hints are given below on these.

[1] say 'to get rid of'. [2] use *'tener que'*. [3] say 'without being discovered'.
[4] use *en pie*. [5] *oído* or *orejas*? [6] use *en la distancia* after the verb.
[7] why should *a* be inserted? 9(*a*). [8] five furlongs = 1 kilometre.
[9] *puede servir*. [10] *cruzar*.

40 Gold talks

Fray Bartolomé de Olmedo, whose priestly rank gave him immunity, carried with him these letters and a rich supply of gold to grease the palms of key people among the invaders.

'My son,' he told Pedro on the eve of departing, 'if by management or bribery I can prevent bloodshed among friends, nay, among kinsmen, it will be a good work, and therefore I am undertaking it.' He sighed but added, 'Would that it were possible to do this by preaching the simple gospel of peace and good will; but in this world, we must sometimes use the ways of the world to do God service.'

Sauntering together, he and de Vargas had come to the apartment in Cortés' quarters which was used as a chapel, and they now stood within the doorway. The altar light and a few votive candles faintly illumined the long, low room.

'Yes,' said Pedro, 'and meanwhile it's good news that Captain Velázquez de León is on our side and is marching to Cholula. We'd have made a poor front without him. The General doesn't expect to avoid a fight for all your parleying, Father.'

'God send he's wrong!' Olmedo put in.

De Vargas went on, 'What frets me is to see the gold we've sweated and bled for going into the pockets of loons who hadn't the heart to join up with our enterprise and now come for the fruit of it.'

'That is the way of the world, my son.'

SAMUEL SHELLABARGER *Captain from Castille*

41 Not yet!

If she could have torn herself up by the roots[1] Emma would have packed[2] her bags and gone away. But she could not go away. She had taken[3] root. Slowly, imperceptibly, this had happened. Later, perhaps she could and must[4] leave Don Alfonso and Señorita Joaquina, leave the cold Sierra and the hot sun, the wide valley and the white house beneath the immense, brooding[5] sky. But not yet. She was not ready. It was almost as if Daniel had said: 'Not yet, Emma, not yet. You will find your destiny here as I found it[6]. You belong.' Or perhaps, in her sense of belonging, of home-coming, that is what she would have liked him to say, to sanction her[7] own desires. Apart from all else[8] Gracia needed her. Gracia, unless she were prevented, would run headlong[9] to her own unhappiness, for Emma knew instinctively that as far as Gracia was concerned Vicente's only emotion was vanity[10]. It pleased him that this beautiful and rich woman had fallen completely under his spell, it was part of all that went to being[11] a famous matador, a tribute, in its way[12], to his courage and skill, as much a tribute as the applause of the crowd.

SYLVIA SARK The Spanish Dancer

No hints on subjunctive or *poder*.

[1] use *arrancarse de raíz*. [2] use *hacer el equipaje*. [3] use *echar raíces*. [4] use *tener que* (tense?). [5] use *protector*. [6] say 'like mine'. [7] avoid ambiguity. [8] *lo demás, 5.* [9] say 'blindly'. [10] say 'that of vanity'. [11] *todo lo que significaba ser.* [12] *en cierto modo.*

42 Jealousy

There had been a moment, in the restaurant in Barcelona, when Emma had been sure that Van was in love with Jacinta. She had hated the thought then for all that it had implied of disloyalty and treachery and she had come to believe it a momentary hallucination, having no basis in truth. But with Van standing there, the gentle sounds of life about them, the horse plucking at the grass, the flutter of wings above them, a child laughing as he herded goats, Emma knew that another emotion had filled her at the thought. The emotion was jealousy, a quick stab, ignored and disowned as soon as felt.

SYLVIA SARK The Spanish Dancer

43 A silent couple

'And they haven't spoken to each other for[1] more than[2] two years!' The new cook could[3] hardly believe what she heard.

'That's nothing. The old lady's husband is dead now, but she went for eighteen years without speaking a word to him[4]. And they were always together. Even when old Mr G. was dying he asked[5] the nurse who was looking after him to tell[6] his wife that he had always loved her in spite of everything. I know because she told me[7]. And his wife was[8] there at his bedside all the time. They kissed each other, but they didn't say a word. .... As if after not speaking for so long it wasn't[9] worth the trouble! Mrs G. used to say to me: 'The funny thing[10] is that we can't remember[11] how it all began . . .'. I think she really likes to be silent, for[12] she has begun to do the same thing with her son-in-law and that seems to prove it, although her tongue can move fast enough[13] when she is[14] annoyed or talking to the servants. But that's because they'll listen to her and always agree[15]. The master is just like her – they both want everyone to obey[16] them. You can understand it though, can't you, with all that money[17]?'

[1] begin with *hace*, *11(c)*. [2] why *de*? [3] *poder*, *20(m)*. [4] say 'she did not speak to him in eighteen years', *11(c)*. [5] ask, *21(a)*. [6] subjunctive? *18(b)*. [7] insert *lo*, *5*. [8] tense? *11(c)*. [9] subjunctive, *18(k)*. [10] use *lo*, *5*. [11] remember, *11(b)*. [12] say 'and the fact that (*18(j)*) she has begun seems to prove it'. [13] use *saber darle a la lengua*. [14] *ser* or *estar*? [15] use *estar de acuerdo con ella*. [16] subjunctive? *18 (b)*. [17] say 'with all the money they have'.

44 Rumours of war (a)

As everyone withdrew from the windows Lance went up to the bar and ordered:

'A cognac and soda for the *señora*, please, and, for me, I think the best thing to steady the nerves would be one of your iced vodkas.[1]

Outside the crowd swirled and roared in the broad avenue under the dusty acacias. Lance and his wife were marooned for more than an hour, and then, against everyone's advice, they escaped, using the back door of the bar. They had not gone ten yards down the street before, from a recessed doorway, a rifle shot rang out at Jinks' ear. She was unhurt, but Lance hurried her home as quickly as possible to their flat in the Calle de Espalter. On arrival, they found their trusted Spanish maid, Petra, in a state of high excitement. She had been told by Antonio, the porter of the flats, she said, and by several friends, that terrible times were about to begin in Spain. She had never spoken in such a manner before, and the Lances were surprised.

C. E. LUCAS PHILLIPS *The Spanish Pimpernel*

45 Rumours of war (b)

'Señor,' said Petra, 'It is going to be worse than anything else that has happened[1] before[2]. War is going to begin and we are going to be bombed. Mother of God, protect us!'

Lance, who enjoyed times of excitement, chaffed[3] her gently and tried to reassure her.

'Put a smile on your face[4], Petra,' he said, 'and let us have lunch. We're starving[5]. It will all be over in[6] a few days – like all the others[7].'

So he and Jinks thought[8]. But years afterwards, it was[9] that moment which he fixed[9] in his mind as the beginning of the physical and moral collapse that was to plunge[10] Spain into a savage and bloody conflict, a[11] conflict in which he himself was numbered for[12] the firing squads[13].

C. E. LUCAS PHILLIPS *The Spanish Pimpernel*

[1] use *lo, 5.* [2] say 'up to now', *9(h).* [3] use *tomarle el pelo.* [4] simplify to 'smile'. [5] use *estar muerto de hambre.* [6] *dentro de,* within. [7] say 'the other times'. [8] tense, *11(c).* [9] use the same tense for 'was' and 'fixed'. [10] use *sacudir.* [11] why no article? *2(a)i.* [12] say 'destined to appear before'. [13] *el pelotón de fusilamiento.*

46 Stopping the express train (a)

George pushed his chair back from the table. 'I think we've discussed our affairs enough,' he said gruffly. 'Perhaps I ought to be thinking of my train.'

'Yes, of course.' Winslow rang the bell again and told the butler: 'Mr Boswell will be catching the nine-forty. Will you telephone the stationmaster?'

'Very good, your lordship.'

'Why do you have to ask the stationmaster to do this for me?' George asked. 'I can find a seat, or if I can't, it doesn't matter.'

Winslow smiled. 'My dear chap, if I didn't telephone you wouldn't even find a train. The nine-forty's fast from Bristol to London unless I have it stopped for you.

'You mean you can stop an express at that little local station just to pick up one passenger? And in war-time?'

JAMES HILTON *So Well Remembered*

47 Stopping the express train (b)

'Certainly, but it isn't done by favour. It's a legal right dating back to the time the railway was built a hundred years ago. My great-grandfather wouldn't sell land to the company except on that condition, in perpetuity. And I'm extremely glad he did.'

Soon afterwards Lord Winslow shook hands most cordially with George, and the latter was driven to Castle Winslow station in the Rolls-Royce. The station was normally closed at that time of night, but the stationmaster had opened it for the occasion and personally escorted him along the deserted platform.

'First-class, sir?'

'No, third.' George answered grimly.

After that they conversed till the train came in.

JAMES HILTON *So Well Remembered*

48 The photograph

We crowded round to study the photograph, and compare it with the map.

'What's *that*?' asked a Major of Intelligence, pointing.

The object he indicated showed as a pale oval outline, with a shape, judging by the shadows, not unlike the inverted bowl of a spoon. The Chief Constable bent down, peering more closely.

'I can't imagine,' he admitted. 'Looks as if it *might* be some unusual kind of building – only it can't be. I was round by the Abbey ruins myself less than a week ago, and there was no sign of anything there then; besides, that's British Heritage Association property. They don't build, they just prop things up.'

One of the others looked from the photograph to the map, and back again.

'Whatever it is, it's in just about the mathematical centre of the mystery,' he pointed out. 'If it wasn't there a few days ago, it must be something that's landed there.'

JOHN WYNDHAM *The Midwich Cuckoos*

49 The Midwich business

'You live in Midwich?' he inquired, looking from her to me. 'Have you been there long?'

'About a year now,' I told him. 'We'd normally be there now, but——'. I explained how we came to be stranded at The Eagle.

He thought for some moments after I finished, and then seemed to come to a decision. He turned to Janet.

'Mrs Gayford, I wonder if you would excuse me if I were to take your husband along with me? It's this Midwich business that has brought me here. I think he might be able to help us, if he's willing.'

'To find out what's happened, you mean?' Janet asked.

'Well – let's say in connexion with it. What do you think?' he added to me.

'If I can, of course. Though I don't see . . . Who is *us*?' I inquired.

'I'll explain as we go,' he told me, 'I really ought to have been there an hour ago. I'd not drag him off like this, if it weren't important, Mrs Gayford. You'll be all right on your own here?'

Janet assured him that The Eagle was a safe place, and we rose.

JOHN WYNDHAM *The Midwich Cuckoos*

50 Planning an escape (a)

Could he pull this thing off[1] alone? Apart from the obvious need for secrecy[2], he did not want to drag[3] anyone else into such a risky affair. He cast his mind over those whom he knew, but could not see the right[4] man. He wanted a 'sympathetic'[5] person who understood the Spaniards thoroughly.

He lit a pipe, walked over to the window and gazed contemplatively over the bleak rooftops to where, in a light breeze, the Union Jack[6] of the Embassy was flying[7] freely. Away somewhere in the neighbourhood of the Telefónica, Franco's shells were dropping with a crash and tinkle of glass. What was Jinks doing[8] at home in England on this spring day? Was it fair to her to take these risks? What would she say if she knew what he was going to do? In his thoughts he could[9] hear her say, as he knew she would:

'Dagger, whatever you decide to do, I shall back you up[10].'

All these things Lance resolved, he would keep entirely to himself, with one exception – Margery Hill. For one thing, he was anxious to clear[11] the hospital of its refugees, for another he had tremendous faith in her knowledge of the Spanish mind and method, which he had seen so remarkably demonstrated on that last convoy[12] to Alicante. He had no intention whatever of taking her with him on these excursions, but there was no one else he could trust so completely for[13] sound advice and practical help in dealing with Spaniards.

C. E. LUCAS PHILLIPS The Spanish Pimpernel

[1] use *llevar a buen término*. [2] say 'to keep the secret.' [3] use *envolver*.
[4] use *apropiado*. [5] use *afín*. [6] say 'the British flag'. [7] use *ondear*.
[8] tense? *11(c)*. [9] *poder 20(m)*. [10] *estaré de tu lado*. [11] *desembarazar*.
[12] *convoy*. [13] insert 'when he needed'.

51 Planning an escape (b)

Thus, about an hour later, under Lance's stage management, five or six captains and mates, all of whom he had primed for their parts, accompanied him through the dock gates in high spirits. As he had done before, Lance went from place to place with them, greeting all the port officials, guards and police whom he knew, to advertise his presence to the full. Then they went on board the second ship and over lunch discussed their plans together. The sailors entered into the plot with the greatest zest.

As he came out on deck after lunch, Lance noted that the air had become oppressive, as with the threat of imminent rain. That, he reflected, would suit his purpose well. On his orders, Pepe had brought the car right into the docks, alone. It was a thing Lance had never asked him to do before, for it involved a terrible risk for the chauffeur.

C. E. LUCAS PHILLIPS The Spanish Pimpernel

52 Planning an escape (c)

But it was a vital part of the plan he had devised for this special occasion, designed to drop into the Spaniard's minds the idea that the car was to be seen again going in and out. The loyal Pepe did not turn a hair. The big black Chevrolet, wearing the Union Jack, was as familiar a sight outside the docks as Lance's check coat, and Pepe, though stopped by the guards, came through successfully.

Ostensibly, the car had come only to collect Lance after his luncheon party on board, but his real intention was to advertise the fact that he would be coming back later in the afternoon for another party, in a different ship. As he drove away from the ship's side with all the signs of good cheer, he continually stopped the car, therefore, to greet some acquaintance, tell him what a wonderful luncheon he had had and say how much he was looking forward to yet another merry party that evening.

C. E. LUCAS PHILLIPS The Spanish Pimpernel

53 The Armada

Spring passed; May opened and spread its beauty on Pastrana; and they learnt that the Great Armada was to be put to sea, and commanded indeed for good or ill by their unhappy Alonso, Magdalena's husband, who had never directed as much as a sardine-boat in his life, and who would be honestly terrified, Ana knew, of his appalling honour.

It sailed, and with it sailed, as occasional letters told them, many, many that they knew – cousins and friends and neighbours, and Bernardina's son, her only child, in the flag-ship of his new employer, the new Great Admiral.

By the end of September its tale was done – what was left of it was back in Santander, and Ana's unhappy son-in-law was hurrying south to hide himself in Sanlúcar from the anger of the people. Bernardina's son did not come back, and there were many others, friends of Rodrigo's, young men Ana had seen christened, who never returned from the Enterprise against England. Spain, even to two lost, forgotten women-prisoners in Pastrana, writhed in anger and grief, and Ana sometimes thought with bitter embarrassment of the February night when she had laughed so enchantedly at Bernardina's rumour and drunk the health of Medina Sidonia, 'that great sailor.'

KATE O'BRIEN That Lady

54 Class distinction in old Spain

Spaniards are very helpful, kind and intelligent about cars. If they see a woman changing a wheel on the road, they leap from their lorries or their cars and offer help; it is, I suppose, one side of their intense and apparently universal astonishment that a woman should be driving a car at all. All over Spain, except in the more sophisticated cities, my driving-by was greeted with the same cry – a long, shrill cat-call, reminiscent of a pig having its throat cut, usually wordless, but some-times accompanied by '¡Olé, olé! ¡Una señora que conduce!' For Spanish women do not drive cars. I was told this many times, and indeed, observation confirmed it; I saw not a single woman driving all the time I was in Spain. 'Why not?' I sometimes asked. 'It is not the custom here. Spanish ladies live very quietly.' One man, more analytic, explained, 'You see, we Spanish do not live in this century at all, nor in the last, but several hundred years back. We hear that in England women do the things men do, but in Spain it has never been the custom.' This is not true: the peasant women work in the fields and drive donkey carts everywhere; what he meant was *señoras*.

ROSE MACAULAY *Fabled Shore*

55 Sunrise

There was a moment before the sun rose when the little town looked so obviously typical that it was dull; when its walls seemed more bleak than white, and when in the colourless daylight its big yellow church had an air of stupid banality that was discouraging. With the night gone and the ship with it there was nothing to look at but the sky which was empty, or the monstrous hump of the mountain which was always there, or the leaden sea or the harmlessly familiar, dusty streets; and those who rose early turned impulsively away from everything in sight.

'It will be hot today,' they muttered, and though most of them remembered that it was *fiesta* it was a sour moment.

Then the sun came up and glared into the face of the town from the far edge of the sea, and almost immediately the moment passed.

CHAPMAN MORTIMER *Mediterráneo*

56 An unexpected visit

The snow had only just stopped, and in the court below my rooms all sounds were dulled. There were few sounds to hear, for it was early in January, and the college was empty and quiet; I could just make out the footsteps of the porter, as he passed beneath the window on his last round of the night. Now and again his keys clinked, and the clink reached me after the pad of his footsteps had been lost in the snow.

I was comfortable in my armchair, relaxed and content. There was no need to move. I was reading so intently that I did not notice the steps on the staircase, until there came a quick repeated knock on my door, and Jago came in.

'Thank the Lord I've found you,' he said. 'I'm glad you're in.'

He was still wearing his gown, and I guessed that they had sat a long time in the combination room. He apologized for disturbing me. He apologized too much, for a man who was often so easy.

But sometimes he found the first moments of a meeting difficult; that was true with everyone he met, certainly with me, though we liked each other. I had got used to his excessive apologies and over-cordial greetings. He made them that night, though he was excited, though he was grave and tense with the news he brought.

C. P. SNOW *The Masters*

57 Spain and Portugal

The writer on Portugal who has already any knowledge however superficial of the Spaniards and of Spain is confronted immediately by the difficulty of how vastly different are the two countries. It is not a question of those radical differences which divide ourselves from the French so much more effectually than the English Channel, that a railway porter and his equivalent or opposite number at Calais are as unlike each other as a Red Indian and a Chinaman. But the contrasts between Portugal and Spain are divergencies of similarity. They are members of the same family who bear little or no resemblance to each other, and nothing is more confusing than brothers and sisters of the same parents who are not alike. Persons of education from the one country can read a newspaper of the other; but a Spaniard would have to learn Portuguese in order to read a novel by Eça de Queiroz, and the two races cannot meet on common ground in conversation. It could be said, in paradox, that it is mostly where they are alike that they are different.

SACHEVERELL SITWELL *Portugal and Madeira*

58 The Cardinal and the Princess

One evening of late July in 1585 a guard came to the grill outside Ana's rooms and announced to Paca that His Eminence, Cardinal Quiroga, Archbishop of Toledo, was in the court-yard in parley with the governor of the house, and would shortly ascend to visit Her Highness, the Princess of Eboli.

This was indeed good news and a break in loneliness. The Cardinal had only come to see Ana once before in her imprisonment, during 1581, but he wrote often, and though for her sake his letters had to be guarded in phrase he managed through them to make her understand that his concern for her was constant, that he continued to speak his mind to the king, that he sometimes saw Pérez and watched as he could over him, and that one day he would visit her again, and bring her word of the world that had locked her up.

When he stood in the drawing-room and she knelt and kissed his ring she was much moved and could not speak. He murmured the Blessing softly over her bowed head and when she rose he looked first at her and then all about the room shrewdly before he spoke again.

KATE O'BRIEN *That Lady*

59 An early call

When I went into my sitting-room next morning, half-an-hour before my usual time, there was Sir Horace, bright and trim ready for breakfast. He had had less than five hours sleep, but he was as conversational as ever. He referred to common acquaintances, such as Francis Getliffe's brother; he asked questions about the men he had met the night before. He was much taken with Jago. 'There's an unusual man,' said Sir Horace. 'Anyone could see that in five minutes. Remarkable head he's got. Will he be your next Master?'

'I hope so.'

'Brown and Chrystal want him, don't they?'

I said yes.

'Good chaps, those,' Sir Horace paused. 'If they were in industry, they'd drive a hard bargain.'

His intention became masked at once in a loquacious stream about how much his nephew owed to Brown's tutoring. 'I want him to get an honours degree. I don't believe these places ought to be open to the comfortably off, unless the comfortably off can profit by them,' said Sir Horace, surprisingly unless one knew his streak of unorganized radicalism. 'I hope you agree with me? If this boy doesn't get his honours degree, I shall cross off the experiment as a failure. But he'd never have touched it if it hadn't been for Brown. I'll tell you frankly, Mr Eliot, there have been times when I wished the boy didn't require so much help on the examination side.'

C. P. SNOW *The Masters*

60 Modern adventure

Of course there is still plenty of adventure of a sort to be had. You can even make it pay, with a little care; for it is easy to attract public attention to any exploit which is at once highly improbable and absolutely useless. You can lay the foundations of a brief but glorious career on the Music Halls by being the 'First Girl Mother to swim twice round the Isle of Man'; and anyone who successfully undertakes to drive a well-known make of car along the Great Wall of China in reverse will hardly fail of his reward. And then there are always records to be broken. Here you can make some show of keeping within the best traditions, and set out to take the illustrious Dead down a peg by repeating their exploits with a difference. Rivers which they ascended in small boats you can ascend in smaller; if they took five months to cross a desert, go and see if you can do it in four. Where they went in litters, you can ride; where they went on mules, you can go on foot: and where they went on foot, you can go (for all I care) on roller-skates. It is a silly business this statistical eye-wiping. These spurious and calculated feats bear about as much relation to adventure as a giant gooseberry does to agriculture.

The old men who grumble that modern youth is not adventurous make two cardinal mistakes. They fail to appreciate the facts and they have got their values all wrong.

PETER FLEMING *Brazilian Adventure*

Section Three

Essays

Essay-writing is a valuable exercise in self-expression. An essay should be the creation of the writer: his thought and imagination, his taste and intelligence, are all brought into play and have to be expressed fluently and accurately with attention to style, idiom and logical arrangement of ideas.

To become fluent and competent in writing Spanish, considerable and regular practice is required, for it is only by continual practice that real progress can be made in the assimilation of vocabulary, idiom and constructions of the language.

'*Problem*' *subjects* (e.g. what would you do in such a situation or emergency?) stimulate inventiveness and imagination. When writing the resultant narrative, including perhaps some dialogue, it is essential to use the appropriate tenses.

Descriptive essays enlarge and consolidate vocabulary, especially adjectives, and encourage the occasional use of metaphors and similes as well as inspiring the inner eye. Before writing an essay of this type it is rewarding to study one or more descriptive passages composed by a Spanish author (e.g. nos. 4, 11, 18, 35, 50, 60).

Character sketches of imaginary or real people require creative ability. It is fascinating to invent and develop a person, an animal or even an inanimate 'gimmick'. Before attempting such an exercise it is helpful to inspect the portrait of a character invented and portrayed by a Spanish novelist (e.g. nos. 12, 26, 34, 35, 37, 45, 68).

If a *refrán* subject is given, it is obviously insufficient at 'A' Level to write a little story and use the proverb as a conclusion or moral. The origin, meaning and consequences of its influence on behaviour, have to be expounded and a judgement given as to its validity in the modern world.

Philosophical topics and those asking for an evaluation can be dealt with in many ways. One simple way is to state the problem in the intro- duction, put the arguments for and against and sum up at the end giving your own final opinion or, perhaps, an indication of future developments.

To learn how to assemble ideas and plan an essay, analyse a few good articles written in English or in Spanish. Examine carefully the first paragraph and the last. Notice how a brilliant beginning usually leads one's thoughts into the subject of the essay and how a satisfying concluding paragraph rounds off the work. The end of each paragraph should also provide a link with the next and ideas should follow each other logically to the end.

In the examination room the choice of subject is all important: don't make up your mind till you have studied all the titles. Select one on which you have interesting ideas or opinions – it is asking for trouble to try to write about a technical subject in detail, for example 'a trip to the moon', if you do not possess the necessary technical vocabulary. However, if you feel confident you can treat the subject in a general, pleasing manner, go ahead.

In any case first assemble your ideas, put them in a logical order and think of a suitable introduction and conclusion before attempting to write the essay. If sufficient time is available write a rough draft of the introduction and conclusion and polish them up before your final version is written, because these, when they are attractive, create a good impression on the reader.

Before handing your work in you must revise what you have written, and correct all the obvious, avoidable errors. Bear in mind that a well-composed, well-organized and well-revised effort of about 300 words is worth more in an 'A' Level Spanish examination than a long, hastily written one marred by elementary and careless errors, even if the ideas expressed may be interesting and original. And don't forget that legible handwriting helps to convey your ideas quickly: anything illegible is a brake on this transmission.

To sum up then, you have to convince the examiner that you have ideas and that you can express them clearly in good Spanish. Bad writing, careless mistakes and lack of logical arrangement are the usual barriers to a successful result. Remember that a sparkling, original introduction, a well constructed body and an easy natural conclusion will make your essay more readable, attractive and convincing.

A Problemas

1

Imagínese que es usted el capitán de una banda de delincuentes (en cualquier país o período que prefiera). Le han capturado y ocupa un calabozo en un castillo que se eleva sobre rocas escarpadas. Algunos miembros de la banda todavía están en libertad y ponen en ejecución un plan para rescatarle. ¿En qué consiste el plan y qué éxito tienen?

2

Haciendo el "auto-stop" en España, el conductor del vehículo que le ha invitado a subir cae enfermo en una carretera solitaria, sin poder detener el vehículo. ¿Qué hace usted?

3

Después de varias horas en una cueva practicando la espeleología advierte usted un resplandor en la lejanía, al salir de la cueva. Pronto se da cuenta por la forma de hongo de la explosión de que se trata de una bomba atómica. ¿Cómo actúa usted en tal situación?

4

Llega usted al aeropuerto para tomar un avión a Palma de Mallorca y descubre que le falta el pasaporte. Relate el incidente y explique cómo resuelve el problema de llegar a Mallorca.

5

Si estando de vacaciones en el extranjero perdiese usted su cartera con todo el dinero y el pasaporte, ¿qué haría?

6

Conduciendo un automóvil en España por una carretera solitaria se le acaba la gasolina. Describa lo que hace para solucionar el problema y reanudar el viaje.

7

Está usted viajando en tren por España. Se baja del tren en una estación para ir a la cantina y para comprar un periódico. El tren se pone en marcha inesperadamente. ¿Qué hace usted?

8

Un día ve usted que unos ladrones salen corriendo de un banco. Explique cómo reacciona usted y cómo captura la policía a los ladrones.

9

Está usted en el piso más alto de un hotel (o una casa de vecindad). Se produce un incendio a medianoche. Huele a algo que quema. ¿Qué hace?

10

Va usted de piloto en un avión que se ve forzado a aterrizar en un claro del bosque. Refiera usted el incidente y explique cómo hace para volver a casa sano y salvo.

B Inventos

1

Invente un personaje masculino y colóquelo en una situación: (a) cómica; (b) triste; o (c) trágica.

2

Invente un truco publicitario, explique sus usos y calcule sus probabilidades de éxito.

3

¿Seguirá habiendo mecanógrafas en el siglo XXI? Si no, ¿cómo se comunicarán unas oficinas con otras?

4

Invente y describa un nuevo juego que se practique dentro o fuera de casa.

5

En su opinión, ¿cuál será el próximo descubrimiento que se consiga en el desarrollo de la televisión en color?

6

¿Cómo resolvería usted el problema actual de la circulación en las ciudades grandes?

7

Invente y describa un nuevo tipo de vehículo que ayude a resolver el problema de la circulación tanto en el campo como en la ciudad.

8

Invente un método o métodos de conservar los suministros de agua en Gran Bretaña o en España.

9

Invente un nuevo método de enseñar idiomas.

10

¿Cómo mejoraría usted los servicios postales y telefónicos de Gran Bretaña o de España?

C Descripciones

1

Describa la capital o pueblo donde nació.

2

Describa la vista más hermosa que recuerde haber visto en Inglaterra o en otro país.

3

Describa el hogar o la escuela ideales.

4

Describa una fiesta en España.

5

Describa su automóvil o motocicleta favoritos.

6

Describa una catedral hermosa que haya visitado usted en Gran Bretaña o en España.

7

Describa la ciudad más fea que conozca.

8

Describa la tormenta más impresionante de que tenga memoria.

9

Describa el programa de televisión o la película cinematográfica más interesante que haya visto.

10

Describa su animal preferido: perro, gato, jaquita o caballo.

D Retratos

1

¿Cuáles son las cualidades esenciales del hombre que triunfa?

2

Relate los acontecimientos principales de la vida de Sir Winston Churchill.

3

Describa brevemente el carácter del amigo que, en su opinión, es más probable tenga éxito en la vida.

4

¿Cuál es su actor (actriz) o cantante preferido? Describa sus cualidades profesionales y físicas más destacables.

5

Haga una descripción del carácter de su pariente más viejo.

6

Relate brevemente la vida y la obra del General Franco.

7

Narre la vida y la obra de Harold Wilson, Edward Heath o de cualquier otro Primer Ministro del Reino Unido.

8

Relate la vida y la obra de su autor favorito.

9

¿Cuál es el deportista que más le gusta? Describa su carrera, sus facultades y sus éxitos.

10

Describa la vida de un piloto de prueba o de un astronauta.

E Profecías

1

Los métodos de transporte en el año 2.000.

2

La vida en Inglaterra en el año 2.050.

3

El futuro de Hispanoamérica.

4

¿Qué ocupación piensa usted ejercer dentro de cinco años? Explique por qué quiere entrar en esa profesión o cargo.

5

¿Que forma de transporte será más popular dentro de diez años: el helicóptero o el avión particular, el automóvil o el auto deslizante (*hovercraft*)? ¿Por qué?

6

La futura universidad (o escuela) del aire, ¿cómo cree que funcionará y competirá con la universidad (o escuela) tradicional?

7

"El gobierno inglés será comunista antes de que termine el siglo." Razone esta profecía.

8

El futuro de África.

9

Se dice que en el futuro será casi inevitable el hambre en el mundo entero. ¿Cómo haría usted para solucionar este grave problema?

10

¿Habrá otra guerra mundial? Si cree que sí, diga qué forma tomará; si cree que no, diga cómo se evitará.

F Opiniones

1

¿Qué sistema de calefacción elegiría usted para su casa: ¿petróleo, carbón, gas o electricidad? Explique las ventajas del sistema que elija.

2

¿Cree que sea útil para la humanidad invertir dinero en la exploración del espacio? Explique las razones de su afirmación o negativa.

3

¿Qué defecto físico le parece peor: la ceguera o la sordera? Enumere las razones de su opinión.

4

"Cada persona un voto": ¿es ésta la base auténtica de la democracia? ¿Es aceptable universalmente y funciona igual de bien en todas partes?

5

"Igual paga por tarea igual": ¿cree que esto sea justo en todas las circunstancias?

6

¿Cree que la democracia y el patriotismo están pasados de moda? Dé las razones en que basa su respuesta.

7

¿Cuáles cree que son las ventajas y desventajas de estudiar idiomas modernos?

8

¿Es el clima de Gran Bretaña una ventaja o una desventaja en lo que concierne al carácter, la economía y el turismo británicos?

9

La época del ferrocarril ha terminado ya. Razone esta tesis.

10

¿Por qué necesita España ejército, marina y aviación?

G Refranes

1

El que a hierro mata, a hierro muere.

2

El hombre en la plaza y la mujer en casa.

3

No por mucho madrugar amanece más temprano.

4

Hombre prevenido vale por dos.

5

Amigo de muchos, amigo de ninguno.

6

Nunca la pereza hizo cosa bien hecha.

7

Con viento limpian el trigo y los vicios con castigo.

8

Por las obras, no por el vestido, es el hipócrita conocido.

9

Poderoso caballero es don Dinero.

10

El que pone al juego sus dineros no ha de hacer cuenta de ellos.

H Literatura

1

Influencia de la novela picaresca española en la novela inglesa del siglo XVIII.

2

Influencia de Inglaterra en el romanticismo español.

3

Don Quijote.

4

Federico García Lorca.

5

Haga la crítica de cualquier obra de teatro o novela española modernas.

6

¿Qué clase de poesía prefiere usted?

7

¿Qué características nuevas han aparecido en la novela española a partir de 1939.

8

¿Fue una obra en vano la de la "generación del 98" (1898)?

9

Poesía española contemporánea.

10

¿Considera usted que estudiar literatura sea perder el tiempo?

Section Four

Exercises and Tests on Grammar

(*The numbers in brackets refer to paragraphs in the Grammar section.*)

1 Adjectives (*3*)

Make any necessary changes to the adjectives in brackets.

1 Quiero un (bueno) bistec con patatas (frito).
2 Tengo una (excelente) miniatura de mi (viejo) abuela.
3 El agua del acueducto es (fresco).
4 Hemos comprado en el almacén unos calcetines de algodón (rosa), un chal de seda (japonés) y unos guantes (castaño).
5 Los soldados (belga) son muy (valiente).
6 (Este) mapa pertenece al autor del (tercero) libro del curso.
7 (Tal) personas no pueden aprender la lengua (castellano).
8 Mi (mejor) alumna (joven) visitó (ese) catedral (antiguo).
9 (Alguna) día visitaremos una ciudad (semejante).
10 Hay (demasiado) gente (holgazán) en las (tranquilo) calles.
11 En (cada) uno de los (ciento) libros hay más de (doscientos) páginas.
12 El padre nos ha hablado de (Santo) Pedro, (Santo) Domingo y (Santo) Ana.
13 Nos acercamos a las tierras (fértil) y (plano) de los viñedos.
14 Se me quedó mirando con sorpresa y azoramiento (infinito).
15 Nos despertó el ruido (ensordecedora) de un trueno.

2 Prepositions (*9*) and (*11(b)*)

Fill in the gaps, if necessary, with an appropriate preposition and translate:

1 Eres el primero — llegar — casa.
2 Hiciste bien — venir — ver — tu tío.
3 El secretario se apresuró — explicar lo sucedido.
4 — todos modos saldremos — Méjico, mañana.
5 Pasé — aquí — camino — casa.
6 Le agradezco — su interés.
7 El secreto consiste — no vacilar — el juez.

8 ¿Quién le enseñó — dibujar y — tocar el piano?

9 Carlos se esfuerza — leer el periódico.

10 Yo no me atrevo — decirle que miente.

11 — informaciones, pregunte — la dirección.

12 Hay que fijarse — los detalles antes — ir — vacaciones.

13 No se ha dado cuenta — nada, ni — nadie.

14 Todos queremos — asociarnos — la protesta.

15 ¿Por qué se empeña usted — hacerlo si es difícil?

16 ¿Por qué se mete usted — mis asuntos?

17 Lentamente, — la puerta derecha entra Daniel — ropa de dormir.

18 Lleva una pistola — la mano derecha.

19 — este momento, Pedro, — su abstracción, hace un leve movimiento — la mano izquierda, como — expulsar una visión inoportuna.

20 Cierra los ojos un segundo y vuelve — abrirlos.

21 Hablaba mecánicamente, casi — voz baja mientras se acercaba — nosotros.

22 El profesor regresa acompañado — un chico — catorce años.

23 — mi parecer, no vendrán nunca — vernos.

24 La madre se había visto obligada — trabajar.

25 Unos ladrones intentaron — introducirse — la planta baja pasando — la terraza.

26 La fiesta varió — carácter, porque no tardó — aparecer el vino.

27 Corrían — su auxilio.

28 Trabajaban hora — hora, día — día.

29 Vive — mi protección, porque carece — pan.

30 Me niego — darle al doctor el trabajo que me pide.

31 El terreno despedía un olor penetrante — tierra húmeda.

32 Trabajé desde las ocho — la una.

33 Había un gatito — la mesa.

34 No puedo contar — mi hermano.

35 Depende — lo que vaya — hacer.

36 Acabo — ayudar — un ciego — cruzar la calle.

37 Los pobres se asomaron — las ventanas, pero no se atrevieron — saltar — tierra.

38 ¿ — qué se quejan? No les obligo — quedarse.

39 Nos ha prometido — pronunciar un discurso.

40 Estaba sentada — la puerta y pretendía — enterarse — lo que ocurría en la calle.

3 *Para* and *Por* (*10*)

Insert **para** *or* **por**, *whichever is appropriate, in the gaps and translate.*

1. Salieron — Madrid.
2. Nadie sabía — quien llorábamos.
3. Luchan — la victoria.
4. Construyó la casa — su hijo.
5. No tienen bastante dinero — comprar un coche.
6. Se marchó — muchas razones.
7. Ha venido — la Navidad.
8. Su compañía fue un gran alivio — mí, pues me hacía reír.
9. No puede acompañarnos — estar enfermo.
10. — ser pobre no vino al concierto.

11. Dame 50 céntimos — el autobús.
12. Estos libros son — usted.
13. Me dieron mil pesetas — el tocadiscos.
14. Costaba cincuenta pesos — mes.
15. — eso no quería volver a casa.
16. — ser francés habla muy bien el inglés.
17. Fueron — el vino.
18. La vi — casualidad en la calle.
19. Vendió la casa — mucho dinero.
20. Hay que trabajar — ganarse la vida.

21. Quiero vivir en este pueblo — siempre.
22. — término medio, van a verle dos veces al año.
23. Lo haré — el jueves próximo.
24. Lo hace todo — ellas.
25. Hemos estudiado mucho — el examen.
26. Ha comprado un traje de noche — el baile.
27. Irán a Buenos Aires — cinco años.
28. Estamos ahorrando — las vacaciones.
29. Preguntaba — usted.
30. Entraron — la puerta.

31. Es una región famosa — sus vinos.
32. Hay dos cartas — mí.
33. Hicieron el viaje — avión.
34. Esta iglesia nos sorprende — su belleza.
35. Compramos el regalo — los niños.

36 No le gusta ir — agua.
37 — difícil que sea, lo haré.
38 Está muy amable — conmigo.
39 — beber agua envenenada murieron cien personas.
40 No van a tomarla — tonta.

41 Entremos en esta tienda — que yo pueda comprar una maleta.
42 Mi amigo me prestó una peseta — el billete.
43 Discúlpeme usted — haberme dejado llevar — la impaciencia.
44 Te lo aconsejo — tu bien.
45 Me necesitas más de lo que piensas: — hacerme daño, — lo menos.
46 Sentiré piedad — ti cuando haya logrado olvidar tu maldad.
47 Pondría mi mano en el fuego jurando — él.
48 No tengo tiempo — tonterías.
49 Tengo miedo que se haya matado — eso.
50 Quiero un hogar lujoso — mi hijo.

4 Exercise on Order of Words (12)

Rewrite in a better Spanish order.

1 — Tengo mucha hambre — el esposo dijo.
2 La voz del criado que decía: — Puede usted pasar a almorzar — le despertó.
3 Aquí ustedes tienen la casa de mis padres.
4 El hombre con los cangrejos y el pescado y el vino volvió al poco rato.
5 Esta palabra no despertaba ni amor, ni odio, ni vergüenza en su corazón.
6 Así el padre lo hizo porque así las leyes lo querían.
7 Escuchen las cosas tan curiosas por favor que este señor cuenta.
8 No tomaba nadie tan serias cosas en broma.
9 Allí ese titiriteo de alegría es natural.
10 Hay castañuelas colgadas en los escaparates de objetos de música con optimista profusión.

11 Allá el intérprete y su jefe fueron.
12 El edificio Empire State ha estado mirando a todos los demás rascacielos neoyorquinos por encima del hombro durante un período de cuarenta años.
13 Un grito se oyó en la galería a esta sazón.
14 La administración y el despacho de Eugenia, todo cerrado y a oscuras también, estaban en un recodo de la galería más allá de la biblioteca.

15 Desde que su esposa murió a quien amaba con ternura don Augusto vivía consagrado a su misión en absoluto.

5 Subjunctive (*18*)

(*a*) *Change* if necessary, *the infinitive in brackets into the appropriate form of the verb and explain why the subjunctive, indicative or infinitive is needed. Then translate into English.*

1 Ya la conocerá usted cuando (venir) para la Navidad.
2 Les pido que (permanecer) tranquilos.
3 He de ir a esa casa aunque tú (oponerse).
4 Antes de que (llegar) las nieves, regresé a la ciudad.
5 No debe beber agua mientras (no saber *nosotros*) si (estar) envenenada.
6 Llevo medio año en esta casa y no he visto (pasar) por ella ninguna mujer que (valer) un piropo.
7 Tal vez si me ven me (matar *ellos*).
8 Siento (haber) olvidado el apellido de esos señores.
9 Mi trabajo se limitaba a evitar que los hijos (matarse).
10 Póngalo donde (querer).

11 No quiero (comprar) un coche que no (tener) radio.
12 Nunca puedo hacer nada sin que (enterarse *ella*).
13 Con tal que (volver él) pronto, no me importa que tú (salir).
14 Si (haber) llovido habría sido un desastre.
15 Mis padres habían prohibido a mi hermano que (fumar). Sin embargo, lo hacía sin que ellos lo (saber).
16 Le exigimos que (mostrar *él*) su pasaporte.
17 El garaje me llamará cuando (estar) arreglado el coche.
18 Espero que no me (descubrir *tú*).
19 Nunca dije nada que (poder) revelar el secreto.
20 Hay cosas que por inocentes que (ser) suenan mal al decirlas.

21 Tengo que cerrar los ojos para que no me (doler).
22 El sacerdote les había ordenado (acudir) en peregrinación.
23 Nos indigna que algo (ocurrir) pudiendo ser evitado.
24 Niegan que Pablo (haber) encontrado el reloj.
25 Prefiero (comer) aquí, en casa.
26 Llámeme cuando (venir) mis padres.
27 ¿Qué quieres que nosotros te (decir)?

28 Por fuerte que (ser) Pedro no podrá hacerlo.
29 Es lástima que (estar) enfermos.
30 Es verdad que Manuel (ser) muy inteligente.

31 Si vienen, yo les (hablar).
32 Si (venir) yo les hablaría.
33 Parece que ellos (partir) hace dos horas.
34 ¿Cree usted que ellas (haber) encontrado el tesoro?
35 No es verdad que Carlos (haber) mentido.
36 ¡Ojalá ella le (haber) visto más tarde!
37 Se alegra de que sus hijos (haber) dormido bien.
38 Es vergonzoso que usted (beber) tanto vino.
39 Joaquín también salía a recorrer oficinas ministeriales con la
esperanza de que le (dar) una pensión.
40 Deje a José que (responder).

41 No vamos a rechazar lo que tú (escoger).
42 ¿Tiene usted unas tijeras que (servir)?
43 Como no (sentirse) tranquilos, no pueden dormir.
44 Tan pronto como (llegar *ellos*) avíseme.
45 Puesto que (valer) tanto, no lo vamos a vender.
46 Compraron una casa que (tener) siete habitaciones.
47 Me dijo que (buscar) otro empleado (*two ways*).
48 Sugerí que nos (quedar) en casa.
49 Es ridículo que (suceder) una cosa tan grave.
50 Sentimos que le (doler) tanto la cabeza.

51 Como el barrio (ser) sucio y miserable no transcurrían muchos días
sin que alguien (morir).
52 ¿Te parece lógico y sencillo que dos individuos (arriesgarse) para
robar un libro ordinario?
53 Si Pepe (haber) querido robar algo, hubiera cogido un objeto de
más valor.
54 ¿Cómo puede ser que ella no (estar) en casa?
55 Era preciso que el avión (despegar) en seguida.
56 Espero que (seguir *ellos*) mis consejos.
57 El que ellos (haber) protestado, molestó mucho a las autoridades.
58 Me molesta que ustedes (hablar) tan mal de sus padres.
59 Da vergüenza que ella (comportarse) así.
60 Importa que usted lo (hacer).

61 El alcalde no permite que se (celebrar) el desfile.
62 Es verdad que (llegar *nosotros*) tarde.
63 Doña Teresa había rogado al maestro que (seguir) dando clases a su nieto con objeto de que (poder) presentarse a un examen de bachillerato sin necesidad de (ir) a un colegio de la capital.
64 Aunque le (decir) que (venir), no vendrá.
65 Salió sin que nadie la (ver).
66 Pueden pensar que el chico (haber) huído.
67 Los padres le habían dicho cuánto deseaban que Juanita (poder) adquirir una buena cultura.
68 ¿Quién te dice que (haber *ellos*) robado la casa?
69 Era natural que el perro (ser) el único cariño de la niña.
70 El abuelo mandó a Marta que (ir) a cuidarle y le (llevar) cuanto (necesitar).

71 A ti Marta te encarga que (usar) el tesoro como mejor te (placer).
72 Le había aconsejado varias veces que no lo (hacer).
73 Es posible que yo sola (haber) fracasado.
74 No creo que me (ir) de aquí.
75 Necesito un tocadiscos que (ser) portátil.
76 Ojalá (saber) escribir.
77 Me di cuenta de ello sin que me lo (decir).
78 Yo no iba a menos que él me (acompañar).
79 Voy temprano para que (poner *nosotros*) unos discos.
80 Espero que (estar *ella*) allí.

81 Quiero (encontrar) un banco donde (cambiar) un cheque.
82 Mis padres propusieron que yo (seguir) otra carrera.
83 Es fantástico que él (escapar) de nuevo.
84 El viejo se sentó dejando que el niño (jugar) allí cerca.
85 Si ustedes (desear) descansar, llamaré al botones para que les (acompañar) a la mejor habitación de nuestra casa.
86 Ruego a usted (excusar) mi retraso en contestarle.
87 Todo ha salido como yo (suponer).
88 Lo que les interesa es (tener) una prueba pública de que Pedro ha cometido una falta que le (impedir) recibir la herencia.
89 Hasta que no (tener) la prueba puede interesarles que Pedro (vivir), acaso para obligarle a que (escribir) al alcalde confesando su robo.
90 Ellos deben ignorar que alguien (sopechar) de ellos.

91 Desean regresar a América tan pronto (recibir) el dinero.
92 Suplicarás al dueño del hotel que me (tomar) a su servicio.
93 Cuando ya (estar *yo*) instalado en el hotel, tú regresarás al pueblo.
94 Yo te contaré lo que (pasar).
95 Estoy seguro de que usted no (arrepentirse).
96 No le pido le (pagar); me contento con que le (dar) de comer.
97 ¡Que Dios se lo (pagar)!
98 Es evidente que el maestro no (desear) perjudicar a su protegido.
99 ¿Qué quieres que (hacer) ese niño?
100 Dile al dueño del hotel que (subir) un momento.

101 Necesitamos alguien que nos (ayudar) a llevar las provisiones.
102 Bueno, venga lo que Dios (querer); quizá (ser) una oportunidad para mí.
103 El sacerdote les había ordenado (acudir) en peregrinación.
104 No sé por qué se oponía a que (aceptarse) la oferta.
105 Los padres preferían que ella no (salir) sin permiso.
106 No hay nadie que (saber) tantos idiomas.
107 Esto hacía que (estar) dispuestos a marcharse.
108 Sus provocaciones determinaron que la policía le (conducir) a la cárcel.
109 Estaban satisfechos de su disfraz que les (permitir) ir despacio.
110 Deben inventar una ventana que (cerrarse) y (abrirse) con facilidad.

111 Tampoco pueden impedir que (despedir *nosotros*) a nuestros familiares.
112 Tan pronto como ella (llegar), dictó una carta.
113 ¿No te he pedido cien veces que no (fumar) en casa?
114 Se hace insufrible la angustia de suponer que el hombre (ser) un mal chófer.
115 Cuando (enterarse) su antiguo compañero le prestaría dinero.
116 Aurelio podría tener una cama donde (pasar) la noche.
117 Importa que ellos (irse).
118 No te (hacer) el tonto; es inútil que (negarlo).
119 Si (pedir *tú*) nadie te oye.
120 Era necesario que (salir) de cualquier manera de la prisión.

121 Espero que la luna (aparecer) entre dos árboles.
122 Le prometeré la libertad si escribe cuanto yo le (dictar).
123 Una vez que (tener *yo*) la carta escrita de su puño y letra, podemos acabar con él.

124 No podíamos dejarle con la duda de que (poder) denunciarnos.

125 Sea como (ser), después de cenar iremos a ver a la policía.

126 Los dos hombres se odiaban porque cada uno pensaba en lo que le correspondería si no (existir) el otro.

127 ¡Que (cenar) abundantemente, que (beber) mucho hasta emborracharse y (dormir) toda la noche!

128 Escribirá cuanto le (dictar).

129 Diles que te (cuidar), para que (poder *tú*) obedecerles mejor.

130 No es posible que el chico (haber) subido solo.

131 Les oyó llamar repetidas veces hasta que (hacer) caer con rabia la piedra que cerraba el subterráneo.

132 Así se habrían quedado a menos que (llegar) otra vez los criminales con una escalera.

133 Era inútil (pensar) en todo esto.

134 Dicen que es una mujer terrible, capitana de un grupo de bandoleros encargados de asesinar a cuantos (intentar) oponerse a sus designios.

135 Cuando usted (querer), patrón, podemos continuar el viaje.

136 Ahí todo está tal como lo dejó el difunto, que en paz (descansar).

137 — ¿Y usted quién es? – inquirió Luzardo como si no (sospechar) quién (poder) ser.

138 Quería conocer al hombre y por fin logré que me lo (mostrar *ellos*).

139 El que lo (hacer) mis hijos me avergüenza.

140 Como la actitud de los perros hacia nosotros no (parecer) tranquilizadora, permanecimos en el interior del coche, aunque los pastores les (agarrar) por la oreja para contenerlos.

141 Sentía que ellas (estar) enfermas.

142 Le mandaré a usted un regalo dondequiera que (estar).

143 La patrona sugirió que usted (dormir) en el parque mientras no pague el alquiler.

144 Ella saldrá de paseo con quien (venir) a buscarla más tarde.

145 Mi madre le aconseja a mi hermanita que (dormir) un poco todas las tardes.

146 Encuentro muy feo que me (insultar) así, sin tener ninguna certeza.

147 Merezco que (ser *tú*) sincera conmigo.

148 ¿Cómo puedes creer que (ser *yo*) capaz de hacer eso?

149 ¿Crees que (estar) ciego?

150 Al general no le ha gustado que tú te (haber) dirigido a mí y no a él. De modo que yo te (aconsejar) que no te (ir) allá.

(*b*) *Translate into Spanish.*

1 I am sorry you are ill.
2 I was sorry you were ill last year.
3 I always tell her to go to bed early.
4 I always told her to go to bed early.
5 They asked us to wait for them.
6 I'll come and see them when they arrive.
7 I went to see them when they had arrived.
8 He realizes that it is better for him to confess.
9 It is certain they have left for Madrid.
10 I am not certain they have left for Madrid.

11 Perhaps they are still at the airport.
12 They cannot prevent us from going to see our friends off.
13 He promised to come and see us as soon as he returned to London.
14 If he had returned I am sure he would have come to see us.
15 What do you want us to do now?
16 We shall need someone to help us buy a car.
17 The fact that you have enough money is very important.
18 We shall not say that he is rich until we know.
19 Wherever you are we will send you a Christmas card.
20 Although he was satisfied he did not say so.

21 The artist asked me to go with him so that he could show me his studio.
22 However foolish you may be, don't go out before I arrive.
23 We fear there has been a bad car accident in the street.
24 The people were talking as if nothing had happened.
25 It is important for you to advise your son not to smoke.

6 *Ser* and *Estar* (*19*)

(*a*) *Translate the following sentences and determine why* **ser** *or* **estar** *was used in each case.*

1 El canto era grave.
2 Llegamos aquella tarde al hotel. Fuimos recibidos por el gerente.
3 Estábamos muertos de hambre.
4 Somos ingleses.
5 Cuando estamos juntos el ruido del cuarto es infernal.
6 Es seguro que están en la ciudad.
7 Estoy seguro de que ellos no llegarán hoy.

8 El incendio no era grande.
9 Estamos contentos que ya estén todos en casa.
10 La madre no estaba desanimada.

(*b*) *Insert the correct form of* **ser** *or* **estar** *in the gaps in the following sentences.*

1 El reloj, que — en la mesa, — de oro.
2 Mi hermano y yo — contentos de — en casa.
3 El café — malo: no — caliente.
4 Los alumnos — de pie y — listos para salir.
5 (*Al teléfono*): – ¿Oiga? ¿El doctor Sánchez? ¿ — tú, Fabián? . . . — yo: Jaime. ¡ — un caso gravísimo!
6 El pobre — en un apuro y vino a pedirme ayuda. Eso —. — que — urgente ¿sabes?. Una cuestión de vida o muerte.
7 El desayuno — bueno. El café — hecho sin achicoria, y el panecillo — bien cocido. Mi patrona — radiante. Se conoce que el matrimonio — feliz.
8 El camino — húmedo y el cielo — gris.
9 Ella — seria y muda aquel día.
10 Yo — a punto de salir.

11 Esta cosa sí que — rara.
12 Ya — todo en orden, señor doctor.
13 La luna inspira a los poetas y a los que no lo —.
14 — todo ya muy gris en la penumbra de los árboles.
15 ¡La música — de todos!
16 Mujer, — los tres juntos.
17 Vallecas — un poquito a la izquierda, allá abajo.
18 Mira, mejor — que veamos lo que — haciendo los niños.
19 Yo — a punto de gritar cuando llegó mi amigo.
20 No le — posible fomentar el descontento, porque el pueblo — más contento que unas pascuas.

21 ¿Cuál — la capital de España?
22 En una plaza redonda y antigua — el palacio real.
23 El castigo no — demasiado grave.
24 El príncipe — un militar muy belicoso, pero su ejército — chiquitín.
25 La frontera — a media hora de galope.
26 Julia podía — orgullosa de su novio.
27 (*Al teléfono*): – ¿Quién —? . . . ¿Madrid? ¿—tú, mamá? . . . ¿Cómo —, mamá?

28 Ya sabe usted lo sociable que — yo.

29 Yo — feliz; — educando a mis hijos.

30 Allí — los dos en este momento: el bote y Pablo. Me dijo que — listo esta mañana. ¡Y — verdad, mira!. Lo — empujando ahora hacia el agua . . . ¡Ya — a flote! Pablo — subido en la popa.

7 Deber (20(b))

(a) *Study and translate these sentences.*

1 Sabemos lo que debemos hacer.

2 Debo reconocer la fuerza de la ley.

3 Antonio yacía en la acera. Debió morir instantáneamente.

4 No debí haberle dejado salir.

5 Sus ideas deben haberse modificado.

6 Los camiones de la policía deberían conducirles a la cárcel.

7 Era algo que debería ocurrir fatalmente.

8 Debían sufrir a un tirano.

9 Debió tomar parte en la lucha.

10 Usted debe convenir conmigo en que tengo razón.

11 Debo salvarlos a todos.

12 Después, ¡qué malas horas debió pasar cuando tuvo que esperar el diagnóstico del médico!

13 Supongo que usted debe de ser el amo.

14 El viajero de tren correo, puesto que viaja lo mismo que un paquete, debería certificarse en la estación de salida para poder reclamar por daños en la de llegada.

15 A las cinco debía haber salido usted con el pelotón de ejecución.

(b) *Rewrite the above sentences omitting **deber**.*

1 Sabemos lo que hacemos, etc.

(c) *Translate into Spanish using **deber** where possible.*

1 There must be plenty of money in the box.

2 I had to listen to him because he did not stop talking.

3 You ought to have bought another suitcase.

4 He said we must get up early.

5 We ought to go to Madrid every year.

6 If they had had to speak no one would have believed them.

7 If you had gone to Spain you would have had to speak Spanish.
8 I said that she must learn to drive.
9 I had to leave at noon to catch the plane.
10 They asked whether we would have to pay for the book ourselves.

8 Poder *(20(m))*

(a) Study the tenses in the following sentences and translate into English.

1 Podría escribirse un libro en aquella ventana.
2 De lo demás podía carecerse.
3 No me moví de mi asiento. De todos modos no podía ir entonces a casa.
4 Los músculos de mi cuerpo no podían dar más de sí.
5 Me dijo que podía darme habitación, porque varios huéspedes se habían marchado de pronto.
6 No podía haber duda. Era un coche que se acercaba.
7 Pablo, no te he olvidado nunca. No podía olvidarte.

(b) Translate the following sentences into Spanish.

1 You may always come to my house and play the piano.
2 He told me I could always go to his house and play the piano.
3 Can you swim? Yes I can, but I can't swim today because the water is too cold.
4 I asked her if she could swim. She said she could, but added that she couldn't swim then because the water was too cold.
5 I shall see him when he can come to London.
6 If I could see the manager I could explain what I have already done.
7 He could have read many more books if they could have given him more time.
8 Can you tell me the time, please?
9 We could have done this before, couldn't we?
10 Yes, they might have come last night while we were at the theatre.

9 Misleading similarities *(25)*
Find in column B, the meaning of each word in column A.

A		B	
a	el cobrador	1	*to remain*
b	la lectura	2	*to ignore s.t.*
c	abrasar	3	*the account (bill)*

d	el cuento	4	*to introduce (socially)*
e	los padres	5	*the subject (of a king, etc.)*
f	el engaño	6	*the conductor (bus)*
g	tener éxito	7	*the parents*
h	restar	8	*to be successful*
i	introducir	9	*to happen*
j	por último	10	*lately*
k	ignorar algo	11	*the date (fruit)*
l	el súbdito	12	*to be ignorant of (not to know) s.t.*
m	la cita	13	*the deception*
n	abrazar	14	*the relatives*
o	el conductor	15	*the driver*
p	últimamente	16	*to burn*
q	la decepción	17	*the reading*
r	suceder	18	*at last*
s	el dátil	19	*to embrace*
t	presentar	20	*to subtract*
u	el sujeto	21	*the subject (topic)*
v	no hacer caso	22	*the story*
w	la cuenta	23	*the reader*
x	quedar	24	*the disappointment*
y	los parientes	25	*to insert*
z	el lector	26	*the date (appointment)*

10 Spelling (*26*)

Give the Spanish equivalent of the following words. (Beware of the spelling!)

1	the admiral	13	loyal
2	the attack	14	the mustard
3	the adventure	15	to occur
4	the character	16	the prejudice
5	the comprehension	17	the chemistry
6	the conscience	18	to rejoice
7	the enthusiasm	19	respectable
8	the giant	20	the richness
9	the hymn	21	sacred
10	the interim	22	to surprise
11	invincible	23	suspicious
12	the judge	24	the treasure

11 Countries, cities, etc. (27(d))

(a) *Replace the words in brackets by the appropriate adjective:*

1 la costa (de Portugal)
2 las calles (de Madrid)
3 los países (de Europa)
4 las montañas (de Chile)
5 los ríos (de Brasil)
6 las ciudades (de Andalucía)
7 los molinos (de la Mancha)
8 la catedral (de Barcelona)
9 la lengua (de Cataluña)
10 los estudiantes (de Dinamarca)

(b) *Translate:*

1 un país hispanoamericano
2 cigarros cubanos
3 flores holandesas
4 un príncipe austríaco
5 los héroes griegos
6 jugadores antillanos
7 una sueca rubia
8 el acento rioplatense
9 la lengua vascuence
10 un banquero costarricense

12 Test sentences in Spanish (11(b)) and (24), etc.

Study and translate.

1 Las calles estrechas estaban muy concurridas, aunque llovía a cántaros.
2 Hacía mucho tiempo que mi amigo estaba acostado sobre cubierta, boca arriba.
3 El actor joven ha representado bien el papel.
4 Me han gastado una broma. Excusado es decir que me encogí de hombros al salir de la sala.
5 El autobús se paró al final de la calle y tuve que volver a casa bajo la lluvia.

6 Los soldados pegaron fuego a la casa de al lado.

7 Ella me miró de reojo y después rió a carcajadas.

8 Entonces me di cuenta de que me habían tomado el pelo.

9 Tarde o temprano se armará la de San Quintín.

10 Aquí hay gato encerrado – dijo el guardia civil al descubrir la carta escondida.

11 En la cocina se estaba bien, porque don Julio nos había enviado como regalo de Navidad un saco de carbón.

12 Aunque daba pena echar a la lumbre aquellos trozos de un negro tan reluciente, que valían un dineral, no hubo más remedio que sacrificar un par de kilos de carbón.

13 Una motocicleta pasó haciendo un gran ruido por la estrecha callecita a la que daba la habitación.

14 Recordaba, siendo él aún joven, haber visto a don Pedro y a otros muchos parientes.

15 Por las noches no se alejaba de los lugares concurridos y se le hacía sospechoso cualquiera que por azar le mirase con alguna fijeza.

16 Es ahora el periódico *The Times* el que pasa revista a la situación de Gibraltar.

17 Un reloj da las dos. Nosotros pensamos en esas noches en que un aire glacial barre la calle, en cuya soledad un hombre soporta, impávido, el frío y la lluvia, la nieve y el hielo.

18 De cara al necesario y armónico desarrollo económico ha surgido un plan para reorganizar la enseñanza universitaria.

19 En la pensión cabían cómodamente siete u ocho huéspedes.

20 Salí en pos de la muchacha, que se me perdió como una idea a medio comprender. Deambulé a la deriva por los pasillos, cada vez más despacito.

21 Estábamos sentados, la abuela y yo, en sendas sillas, muy calladitos.

22 Ni siquiera se atrevían a gritarme; me veían al borde de un barranco y temían despeñarme con sus voces.

23 Todo pasó como una ráfaga de aire, en mucho menos tiempo del que me lleva contarlo.

24 Apenas si le oí decir "ya" y retirarse pensativo. Me contrarió aquello inexplicablemente. Hubiese ido detrás de él para decirle que se metiese en lo que le importaba.

25 Pero venía Juanita, al cabo; porque era ella la que venía, silenciosa y mohina.

26 Bajé a brincos, salí como un loco del caserón, vi al perro corriendo como alma que llevase el diablo por el camino de la estación y corrí detrás.

27 Lo he visto así gracias a no sé qué oscuro olfatear de recuerdos que me ha llevado a releer un pasaje sin cuya ayuda me habría quedado quizá para siempre con mi desazón.

28 Otra posibilidad sería que sea colocado un satélite artificial en órbita venusiana para que estudie y envíe datos sobre la atmósfera, fotografíe el planeta y quizás pueda retornar luego a la tierra.

29 – Es la Emperatriz – dijo el doctor cuando la noble dama salió –. El huracán de la guerra hizo pedazos su poderoso imperio, le arrebató su marido, su corona, su patrimonio familiar y la trajo a España con sus hijos, uno de los cuales tengo aquí para intentar una operación de vida o muerte.

30 Devoré mis recuerdos: no dejé que ellos me devorasen a mí. Extenuado, había dejado de cavilar y aceptado de cara mi fracaso, tragándome a solas mi orgullo.

31 Por extraño que parezca, quien me tranquilizaba con su actitud era María.

32 María se conducía con tal aplomo que llegaba a hacerme pensar no sólo que ni su padre ni nadie se lo figuraba sino que, aun cuando todo se descubriese, carecería de importancia.

33 Ésta fue la gota que hizo rebasar la copa.

34 La suerte de Consuelo fue la que siempre suele caber al que media en riñas de casados.

35 El rígido orgullo de casta de su padre prefirió verla enterrarse en el convento antes que consentir en su enlace con un guerrero de fama equívoca y de bajo linaje.

36 Ahí tienen ustedes el porqué de lo que voy a referir.

37 No se le ocurra enviar semejante carta.

38 Esta mañana se sortearon los seis toros entre los tres matadores. Al nuevo matador le toca torear el tercer toro y el sexto.

39 – Bueno, Laurita, no te alteres, que yo te daré los veinte duros en cuanto cobre.

40 – Bueno. Resulta que van a tener que jubilar a los catedráticos de las facultades y aumentar las plantillas de los laboratorios.

41 Ahora bien, si Cortés se alejaba no era traidor al rey, pues un traidor hubiera procurado quedarse, hacerse cada vez más indispensable, allegar mayores recursos y perfeccionar los preparativos de la rebelión.

42 – Pues lo mismo me da – respondió el centinela –, pero tengan ustedes cuidado de que no me mate el enemigo.

43 Empecé a andar sin rumbo fijo, seguido del nutrido grupo cuyos componentes habían entablado animada conversación.

44 – Pase, pase – me invitó el director a entrar en el manicomio – está usted en su casa.

– El que está en su casa es usted – gruñí por si era una indirecta –. Yo vengo de paso nada más —. Y entré sin quitarme la gorra.

45 Entonces me despierto mojadito. Sí, mojadito de sudor. Luego viene papá a besarme, porque se va a la oficina, y a mí me da rabia porque el bigote le huele a tabaco.

13 Test sentences in English *(11(b)), (13), (18), (20), (21), (24)*, etc.

1 They entered the dining room without washing their hands, but the soup was already cold.

2 I was sitting at the table and was about to begin my meal, when the waiter came running in carrying a telegram on a tray.

3 It was my turn to be disappointed! He passed me by and handed the telegram to an officer's wife who was seated at a table in the corner of the room.

4 Mrs Martin used to be a teacher before Colonel Martin fell in love with her and married her.

5 She now calls the tune and the Colonel has to do everything she tells him to do.

6 'What do you think of this novel?' 'Well, I don't really know what the author wishes to say. Is he making fun of his readers?'

7 At what time will the sun set tonight? Last night it set at seven thirty-five.

8 Being hungry and tired we ought to go to bed but we don't want to be asleep when our friend telephones.

9 I miss all my friends, especially the young lady whom I met last Sunday. I hope she will remember me from time to time.

10 She likes to play the piano and can also play the violin very well. Her younger brother plays tennis in the summer and football in the winter.

11 Whatever happens, I must see her again as soon as she comes back to Madrid.

12 It is a pity that I have to earn my living in the capital of Spain.

13 On the way to Barcelona we decided to go and visit our eldest sister in the Hospital of the Holy Cross.

14 Because she was seriously ill and did not want us to leave her, we had to spend several hours at her bedside.

15 How is she now? I am told she is much better and, although she has been treated with great kindness by the nurses, she is longing to return home.

16 However, the doctor says that she will have to stay there for another week at least.

17 I have no money and I need some immediately. Will you lend me some, please?

18 I have already had to spend all the money which I borrowed from my cousin six months ago.

19 You realize now how I depend on my friends and relatives for financial aid but even they refuse to lend me money sometimes.

20 I often dream of the day when I shall be a millionaire and can give back everything I owe them.

21 Fortunately, it was the retired detective who recognized the disguised men in the street.

22 When he saw them enter the bank he ran and telephoned the police and the bank manager, telling them that the uniformed men were not policemen but well-known criminals.

23 The police arrived and arrested the men. Needless to say they did not fail to thank the ex-detective for his valuable help.

24 'They are experiments of great importance that the Russians are carrying out at present', said Sir Bernard Lovell, the director of the famous observatory.

25 There were about fifty people there when we arrived, most of whom we had never met before and few of them over the age of twenty-five.

26 Then the manager rang and asked for the letters to be brought to him at once.

27 The secretary who brought them to him remained standing at the window with her back to him.

28 Her hair was already beginning to turn grey and it seemed strange to him that she had grown so much older.

29 As there was no time to lose he told her to go to the station and get on the first train for London without waiting for him to arrive.

30 If he had been allowed to buy a ticket he could have caught the bus easily.

31 At last Mrs Martin was able to telephone the police to whom she had to give her name and address before explaining to them what had happened.

32 Needless to say, none of the stolen articles was found in their possession and the burglars denied having entered the house.

33 They promised to let me know as soon as she was ready to leave the hotel.

34 Although it is not yet twelve o'clock, I can already see the young children running happily out of school.

35 We have been in bed for more than half an hour. You should have telephoned us to say that you could not arrive before midnight.

36 It was pouring with rain, we were cold and hungry and were a hundred kilometres from our destination when the accident happened.

37 'I am certain,' she said, 'that you will do everything possible to help my mother whatever happens in the future.'

38 While his friend went shopping in the biggest shop in the town, George went to have his hair cut.

39 Please tell the family not to do anything until the police have examined everything, the house, the garden, and the garage.

40 It's a good job you did not catch that train. It arrived three hours late.

41 Whose umbrella have I got? Is it yours? I don't think it belongs to my family.

42 Let's see. Aren't you going to the cinema one day next week to see the new English film?

43 It seems to me that you could have done that better than anyone if you had tried to do it.

44 You had better come with us: I am not at all sure that your car will hold so many people.

45 Smoking and taking photographs are not allowed in this theatre, gentlemen.

46 Our parents must have missed us while we were going round the world.

47 They did not realize that the eggs they had sat upon and broken belonged to a poor woman who was bringing them to sell in the market.

48 Whoever he is, he will have to wait until we come back. Tell him we are very sorry about it.

49 My apple trees have more fruit than we thought a month ago. Would you like us to send you some?

50 Good-bye. Don't forget to come to see us whenever you are in England. We shall be delighted to see you.

Section Five

Grammar

This is not a complete grammar: it deals particularly with those parts which seem to give most trouble to English-speaking students. If used sensibly, this section should suffice for 'A' Level candidates who are assumed to know the elementary stages of Spanish grammar and syntax.

The footnotes to the passages, on pages 3 — 90, refer to specific points in this Grammar Section – the Spanish passages to provide examples, the English to remind the student of what he has to think about as he translates into Spanish.

The exercises (pages 101 to 120) should give the student adequate practice, if he needs it, on especially difficult points of grammar and vocabulary.

NOTE: The abbreviation *s.o.* stands for someone and *s.t.* for something.

1 Nouns

(a) GENDER OF NOUNS

i. The following nouns are **masculine** despite ending in

- **-a:** el día, *day*; el mapa, *map*; el profeta, *prophet*; el sofá, *sofa*; el tranvía, *tramway*

- **-ma:** el aroma, *scent*; el clima, *climate*; el dilema, *dilemma*; el drama, *drama*; el idioma, *language*; el panorama, *panorama*; el síntoma, *symptom*; el sistema, *system*; el telegrama, *telegram*

- **-ista:** (when referring to men): el artista, *artist*; el comunista, *communist*; el futbolista, *footballer*; el oculista, *optician*; el bañista, *bather*, etc.

ii. Infinitives also are **masculine** when used as nouns (see *11*).

iii. Nouns ending in **-ión** are usually **feminine** but the following are exceptions to the rule:

el avión, *aeroplane*; el camión, *lorry*; el gorrión, *sparrow*

iv. Nouns ending in **-d** or in **-z** are usually **feminine** except

el arroz, *rice*; el ataúd, *coffin*; el césped, *turf*; el lápiz, *pencil*; el matiz, *tint*; el tapiz, *tapestry*

v. All letters of the alphabet are **feminine**:
la erre, *r*; la equis, *x*; etc.

vi. Some nouns may have either **gender,** depending on the meaning. Here are a few examples:

el capital, *capital (money)*
la capital, *capital (city)*

el cólera, *cholera (disease)*
la cólera, *anger*

el corriente, *ordinary (wine), current (month)*
la corriente, *stream (water), current (electrical), trend*

el corte, *cut*
la corte, *Court* (hacer la corte, *to court*)

el frente, *front (war)*
la frente, *forehead*

el guardia, *policeman*; *guardsman*
la guardia, *guard*

el guía, *guide* (*man*)
la guía, *guide* (*directory, book*)

el orden, *order* (*arrangement*)
la orden, *order* (*command*); *order of knighthood*

el papa, *pope*
el papá, *father*
la papa, *potato* (*in Latin America*)

el pez, *fish*
la pez, *pitch* (*tar*)

el radio, *radius*; *radium*
la radio, *radio* (*wireless*)

(b) PLURAL OF NOUNS

i. To form the plural of nouns ending in **-z**, change **z** into **c** and add **-es**:

la actriz: las actrices, *actresses*
la cicatriz: las cicatrices, *scars*
el lápiz: los lápices, *pencils*
el tapiz: los tapices, *tapestries*

ii. Remember that a stressed final **-í** is followed by **-es** in the plural:

el rubí: los rubíes, *rubies*
el colibrí: los colibríes, *humming birds*

iii. Family names are usually invariable:

los Roca, *the Rocas* (*Roca family*)
los Pascual, *the Pascuals* (*Pascual family*)

BUT

los Goyas del Museo del Prado
the Goyas (*pictures*) *in the Prado Museum*

iv. **Padres**, usually refers to both parents:

los padres de Emilio, *Emilio's parents*

Otherwise it refers to priests:

los padres dominicanos, *the Dominican fathers*

2 Articles

(a) OMISSION

In many instances calling for the article in English, no article is required in Spanish, as follows:

i. Before nouns in apposition:

> Aquel hombre era Carlos, hijo de Gregorio.
> *That man was Charles, the son of Gregory.*

ii. Usually before nouns and pronouns depending on **ser**, **hacerse**, **convertirse en**:

> Es profesor.
> *He is a teacher.*
>
> Son nuestros.
> *They are ours.*
>
> Los tres éramos poetas.
> *The three of us were poets.*
>
> Me hice capitán.
> *I became a captain.*
>
> Se convirtió en persona de provecho.
> *He became a useful person.*

iii. Before **cierto**, **otro**, **tal** and, often, **medio**:

> Cierto día nos reunimos para cenar.
> *We gathered for supper on a certain day.*
> Uno habló y otro añadió unas palabras.
> *One spoke and another added a few words.*
> Nunca se ha visto tal cosa.
> *Such a thing has never been seen.*
> Le telefoneé media hora después.
> *I telephoned him half an hour later.*

iv. In many prepositional phrases (see 9):

> en manos de la policía, *in the hands of the police*
> en brazos de su madre, *in his mother's arms*
> en forma de interrogación, *in the form of a question*
> a mitad del camino, *in the middle of the way*

v. Idiomatically, before such nouns as **casa, palacio, voz**:

> Ella y yo íbamos a casa.
> *She and I were going home.*

> Se dirigió a palacio.
> *He went towards the palace.*

> Mi amigo me habló en voz baja.
> *My friend spoke to me in a low voice.*

vi. In some idiomatic expressions:

> camino de Madrid, *on the way to Madrid*
> rumbo a Buenos Aires, *on course for Buenos Aires*

NOTE: Words classified as prepositions in English do not necessarily coincide with those so described in Spanish, which are: *a, ante, bajo, cabe* (nigh), *con, contra, de, desde, en, entre, hacia, hasta, para, por, según, sin, so, sobre* and *tras*. The word 'preposition' is therefore used here and elsewhere in this book in its English definition, unless specifically stated otherwise.

(b) THE ARTICLE 'LA' BECOMES 'EL'

before a stressed **a** or **ha** syllable:

> el agua fría, *cold water*
> el águila negra, *the black eagle*
> el ala derecha, *the right wing*
> el hacha de acero, *steel hatchet*
> el hambre espantosa, *awful hunger*

but remains **la** before an unstressed **a** or **ha**:

> la Alhambra, *Alhambra*
> la aventura, *adventure*
> la harina, *flour*
> La Habana, *Havana*

(c) USE OF THE ARTICLE WITH PARTS OF THE BODY AND WITH PERSONAL CLOTHING

i. When referring to parts of the body or personal clothing, the definite article is used, unless these are the subject of the sentence or clause:

> Luciano volvió la cabeza.
> *Luciano turned his head.*

> Sus ojos me contemplaron.
> *His eyes watched me.*

Sentí que mis labios temblaban.
I felt that my lips were trembling.

La señora se puso los guantes.
The lady put on her gloves.

Sus guantes eran blancos.
Her gloves were white.

ii. If necessary, the owner is indicated by an indirect pronoun:

Ella me colgó del cuello el collar de perlas.
She hung the pearl necklace around my neck.

La fatiga y el alcohol le cerraron los párpados.
Weariness and alcohol closed his eyes.

BUT

Ella tenía los brazos y los hombros cubiertos.
She had her arms and shoulders covered.

iii. In Spanish, the logical singular is used where in English the plural form would apply:

Ellos salieron con la cabeza vendada.
They came out with their heads bandaged.

Dándole la espalda, los hombres se marcharon.
Turning their backs on him, the men walked away.

(d) TITLES AND RANK

i. These are preceded by the definite article and begin with a small letter:

el señor Roca, *Mr Roca*
la señora de López, *Mrs López*
el duque de Alba, *the Duke of Alba*
el rey de Bélgica, *the King of Belgium*
la reina de Inglaterra, *the Queen of England*

NOTE: *Presidente*, the Spanish equivalent of 'chairman', follows the rule and is written also with a small letter. When referring to the president of a country, however, a capital P is normally used:
el presidente del casino, *the club's chairman.*

BUT

el Presidente Nixon, *President Nixon*

ii. **The article is omitted when talking to the person who is mentioned:**

– Sí, señor Roca, *'Yes, Mr Roca'*

1. When the person addressed holds a professional title, this is normally mentioned either by itself (without the article) or preceded by *señor*, though the former is to be preferred:

– Sí, doctor, el enfermo ha mejorado.
'Yes, doctor, the patient has improved.'

– No, señor doctor, no han telefoneado del hospital.
'No, doctor, the hospital has not telephoned.'

2. In the Armed Forces when talking to the holder of a higher rank, instead of 'Sir', Spaniards quote the rank, preceded by the possessive *mi*:

– ¿Qué desea, mi capitán?
'What do you wish, Sir?'

iii. a **El señor don, la señora doña** are terms of respect used in speech only when both the Christian and family names are quoted. In less formal but nevertheless respectful forms of address, **don** and **doña** alone are used preceding the Christian name:

El señor don Luis Miró va a pronunciar un discurso.
Mr Luis Miró is going to make a speech.

– ¿Podría hablar un momento con usted, doña María?
'Could I speak to you for a moment, Mrs X?'

b In correspondence, the full name of the addressee is preceded by *señor don*, *señora doña* or *señorita*, normally abbreviated to **Sr. D.**, **Sra. Da.** or **Srta.** (notice the capital letters):

Sr. D. José Rodríguez, *Mr José Rodríguez*
Sra. Da. Luisa Calvo de Rodríguez, *Mrs Rodríguez*

c The plurals are abbreviated to **Sres.**, **Sras.** and **Srtas.** *Sres.* is also the equivalent of 'Messrs' and of 'Mr and Mrs':

Sres. Alcocer y Cía., *Messrs. Alcocer & Co.*
Sres. de Ortega, *Mr and Mrs Ortega*

1. Married women retain their family name and add to it their husband's preceded by *de*:
Sra. Luisa Calvo de Rodríguez.

2. In Latin America, correspondence is also addressed to *señor* (*Sr.*), *señora* (*Sra.*) or *señorita* (*Srta.*) but the words *don* (*D.*) and *doña* (*Da.*) are rarely written.

3 Adjectives

(a) ADJECTIVES OF NATIONALITY

If they end in a consonant, **-a** is added to show the feminine form:

> alemán: alemana, *German*
> español: española, *Spanish*
> inglés: inglesa, *English*

(b) OTHER ADJECTIVES ENDING IN '-ÁN', '-ÓN', '-OR'

These also add **-a** in the feminine form:

> burlón: burlona, *mocking*
> charlatán: charlatana, *prattling*
> hablador: habladora, *talkative*

NOTE: Irregular comparatives ending in *-or*, such as: *anterior*, *posterior*, *exterior*, *interior*, *inferior*, *superior*, *mayor*, *menor*, *mejor*, *peor* follow the basic rule, i.e. they do not add an *-a* in the feminine singular:

> la habitación interior, *inside room*
> la hija mayor, *eldest daughter*

(c) SUPERLATIVE OF ADJECTIVES

To form the superlative of an adjective add **-ísimo (-a, -os, -as)** and apply the necessary spelling changes:

> fácil, *easy*; facilísimo, *very easy*
> blanco, *white*; blanquísimo, *very white*

The prefix **re-** is sometimes used to indicate intensity:

> las paredes recalentadas, *very hot walls*
> los campos requemados por el sol, *fields burnt up by the sun*

There are a few purely colloquial expressions of this type, such as:

> un problema redifícil, *an extremely difficult problem*

(d) ADJECTIVES OF COLOUR

Nouns used as adjectives of colour may not agree grammatically with the nouns to which they are attached. This is accounted for by the words **de color** being mentally inserted between the noun and the noun-adjective:

> los cabellos castaño claro, *light brown hair*

Sometimes, in fact, **de color** is inserted:

> la blusa de color rosa, *the pink-coloured blouse*

(e) POSITION OF ADJECTIVES

i. The position of adjectives is on the whole a matter of style and feeling which may be acquired by much reading of, and listening to, Spanish (see *12*).

There are many exceptions to the general rule that adjectives of colour, shape and nationality come after the noun:

> a figuratively, as in:
> la negra melancolía, *deep melancholy*

> b to express a quality already inherent in the noun, in order to enhance it:
>
> la blanca nieve, *the white snow*
> la olorosa flor, *the scented flower*

> c for stylistic reasons:
> una leve brisa, *a light breeze*

ii. In some instances, the meaning of an adjective changes according to its position:

> una ciudad grande, *a large city*
> una gran ciudad, *a great city*
>
> un hombre pobre, *a poor (not wealthy) man*
> un pobre hombre, *a man to be pitied*
>
> una nueva casa, *another (e.g. recently-occupied) house*
> una casa nueva, *a newly-built house*
>
> varios ejercicios, *several exercises*
> ejercicios varios, *various exercises (of different type)*
>
> una iglesia antigua, *an ancient church*
> una antigua iglesia, *a building that used to be a church*

(f) APOCOPATION OF ADJECTIVES

i. The following adjectives drop the final **-o** when preceding a masculine singular noun:

uno, *one*; alguno, *some*; ninguno, *no(ne)*; bueno, *good*; malo, *bad*; primero, *first*; tercero, *third*; postrero, *last*.

alguno and *ninguno* require an accent in their shortened form:

> algún día, *some day*
> ningún hombre, *no man*

ii. Remember that:

    a *grande* becomes *gran* before any noun;

    b with the exception of Santo Domingo, Santo Tomás and Santo Toribio, *santo* becomes *san* when followed by a name: *San José*, Saint Joseph;

    c certain numbers drop the ending when followed by another word (see Appendix A):

        veintiún libros, *twenty-one books*
        cien soldados, *one hundred soldiers*

(g) SOME DIFFICULT ADJECTIVES

i. **Demasiado**, *too much*, precedes the noun and agrees with it in the usual way:

    Tenemos demasiadas clases.
    We have too many lessons.

    Hay demasiada agua.
    There is too much water.

When used as an adverb, *demasiado* is invariable.

ii. **Demás**, *remaining*, *other*, is always invariable and requires the definite article in front:

    los demás libros, *the remaining books*
    las demás casas, *the rest of the houses*

As a noun, *los demás* means 'the others', 'the rest of them', and *lo demás* 'the remainder'.

iii. **Sendos, (-as)**, *one apiece*, *each*:

    Las mujeres llevaban sendas cestas.
    The women were carrying one basket apiece.

    Llegaron con sendos cubos de agua.
    They came each carrying a bucket of water.

NOTE: The infinitive can sometimes be used as an adjective:
un cigarrillo a medio fumar, *a half-smoked cigarette*

4 Pronouns

(a) ESSENTIAL POINTS

i. The appropriate pronoun is often inserted when the object is placed before the verb:

Esto también lo sabían.
This they also knew.

La niebla se la llevaba el viento.
Fog was being carried away by the wind.

The above rule helps us to determine that *el viento* is the subject of the sentence.

ii. ¿De quién?, *Whose?*:

Whose? is not translated by **cuyo** nowadays but by ¿**de quién**?:
¿De quién es el libro que lee usted?
Whose book are you reading?

iii. ¿Cuál? is used in preference to ¿que? when the questioner requires specific information about one of several choices: (see p. 174)

¿Cuál es el cuarto de Juan?
Which is John's room? (which one)

¿Qué? usually precedes a more general, often abstract, question:

¿Qué es la verdad?
What is the truth? (definition requested)

iv. Conmigo, contigo, and consigo are invariable:

– Venga conmigo – dijo ella.
'*Come with me,' she said.*

– Venga conmigo – dijo él.
'*Come with me*', he said.

Llevaban un perro blanco consigo.
They had a white dog with them.

La decisión trajo consigo preocupaciones.
The decision brought with it some worries.

v. **El que, la que, lo que, los que, las que** are needed for emphasis when **ser** is added to a noun or pronoun plus a relative clause:

> ¿Fuiste tú el que telefoneó?
> *Was it you who telephoned?*

> Es ella la que dice esto.
> *It is she who says this.*

> Son mis padres los que me mandan hacerlo.
> *It is my parents who order me to do it.*

> Quiero que sean mis hermanas las que ocupen la nueva casa.
> *I should like it to be my sisters who would occupy the new house*

> Son ustedes los que juegan a la pelota.
> *It is you who play pelota.*

(b) SE

i. **Se** is used as an ordinary reflexive pronoun (third person):

> Se afeita todas las mañanas.
> *He shaves every morning.*

ii. **Se** is also used to indicate the owner of clothing, parts of the body, etc. (see 2(c)):

> Se puso el sombrero.
> *He put his hat on.*

> Se lavó la cara.
> *He washed his face.*

iii. **Se** replaces **le, la, les** when two third-person object pronouns are used. As it can have six meanings, the appropriate prepositional pronoun is often added to avoid ambiguity:

> Se lo dieron a él, a ella, a ellos, a ellas, a usted, a ustedes.
> *They gave it to him, to her, to them, to you.*

iv. **Se** is used idiomatically to form impersonal expressions:

> Se dice que . . .
> *It is said that . . .*

> Se trata de un empleo.
> *It is a matter of a job.*

Se está bien aquí.
It is comfortable here.

A ella se le ocurrió decir . . .
It occurred to her to say . . .

5 Lo

(a) In addition to its use as an ordinary object pronoun, **lo** combined with an adjective forms an abstract noun:

Ante lo inevitable me resigno.
I give up in the face of the inevitable.

No quería convencerse de lo evidente.
He did not wish to be convinced of what was obvious.

A nosotros nos sucede lo contrario.
The opposite happens to us.

(b) **Lo** followed by an adjective and by **que** has the meaning of 'how' (note the agreement of adjective and noun):

Tú sabes lo curiosos que son los niños.
You know how inquisitive children are.

Advirtieron lo dura que era la vida.
They realized how hard life was.

(c) **Lo** followed by **de** means 'the business (matter, affair, question) of':

Lo de ayer fue muy peligroso.
That affair of yesterday was very dangerous.

NOTE: In Argentina *lo de* means 'at' in the sense of somebody's place or home:
Fuimos a lo de Jorge.
We went to George's place.

(d) **Lo** is needed with verbs such as **ser**, **parecer**, **poder**, to complete the predicate when the idea expressed by a previous noun or adjective or phrase is present:

¿Es usted profesor? Sí, lo soy.
Are you a teacher? Yes, I am (it).

Está enferma, pero no lo parece.
She is ill but does not seem so.

Lo puedo.
I can (do it).

(e) **Lo** completes the sentence in Spanish with such verbs as **decir, pedir, jurar, preguntar**:

Dígamelo.
Tell me (it).

Se lo pedí a él.
I asked him (for it).

Te lo juro.
I swear (it) to you.

No me lo pregunte.
Don't ask me (it).

(f) **Lo** is used with **más** to form the superlative of adverbs:

Habló lo más claramente posible.
He spoke as clearly as possible.

Por favor, conduce lo más cuidadosamente posible.
Please drive as carefully as possible.

(g) SOME USEFUL PHRASES WITH **Lo**:

a lo lejos, *in the distance*
de lo negro a lo blanco, *from black to white*
en lo alto, *on the top*
lo de menos, *the least of it*
lo malo es que, *the worst of it is*
lo mío, *mine*
lo mismo que, *just like*
por lo demás, *besides*
por lo menos, *at least*
todo lo ocurrido, *everything that happened*
todo lo que, *all that which*
ya lo creo, *I think so*
a lo sumo, *at most*

6 Adverbs and *como*

(a) When two or more adverbs ending in **-mente** are separated only by commas or by the conjunction **y**, the **-mente** is removed from all but the last:

Los vecinos vigilaban la calle ansiosa y nerviosamente.
The neighbours watched the street anxiously and nervously.

Hablaba rápida, clara y correctamente.
He spoke rapidly, clearly and correctly.

(b) Adverbs are sometimes replaced by adjectives, especially after verbs of motion:

Van y vienen silenciosos.
They come and go silently.

Todos iban alegres por el parque.
They were all going cheerfully through the park.

Vivíamos felices.
We used to live happily.

(c) Adverbs usually follow the verb (see also *12*) but adverbs of time like **hoy, ayer, ya**, tend to go at the beginning of the sentence:

Hoy hace mucho calor.
It is very hot today.

Ayer fuimos a Londres.
We went to London yesterday.

Ya me lo contaron.
I have already been told.

Ahora voy.
I am coming now.

(d) Many of the English adverbs ending in '-ly', especially the long ones, are frequently expressed in Spanish by **con** followed by the appropriate noun, (see *9(b)*):

con estridencia, *stridently*
con alegría, *joyfully*

Sometimes **en** is used instead of **con**:

en secreto, *secretly*
en confianza, *confidently*

(e) COMO

The following are some of the points to remember in the use of **como**:
i. **¿Cómo?**, **¡Cómo!** when interrogative or exclamatory have an accent:

¿Cómo está usted?
How are you?

¡Cómo llueve, buen Dios, cómo llueve!
How it rains, good heavens, how it rains!

ii. **Como**, *how, in what way*:

> Le diré como tiene que hacerlo.
> *I will tell him how he must do it.*

iii. **Como**, *as, how, in what way*:

> Como usted quiera.
> *As you like.*

iv. **Como**, *as, since* (cf. **pues**):

> Como no tenemos dinero, no podremos ir a Madrid.
> *As we have no money, we shall not be able to go to Madrid.*

v. **Como un(a)**, *like a*

> Nadaba como un pez.
> *He was swimming like a fish.*

> Permaneció inmóvil como una estatua.
> *He remained motionless like a statue.*

> Vive como un rey.
> *He lives like a king.*

vi. **Como** plus personal noun, *as a*:

> Trabajó seis años como profesor.
> *He worked six years as a teacher.*

> Colón navegó como corsario.
> *Columbus sailed as a pirate (implying he was one).*

vii. **Como**, *as if*:

> Quedó como muerto.
> *He remained as if dead.*

> Corrían como si volaran.
> *They ran as if they were flying.*

viii. **Como si** plus subjunctive, *as if* (see *18(k)*):

ix. **Como** plus subjunctive, *if* (see *18(k)*):

x. **Tan (to) ... como**, *as ... as* (see *8*).

NOTE: *Como* can never mean 'while' or 'when'. These words are rendered by *cuando, según* or *mientras*.

7 Comparisons with clauses

(a) COMPARISON OF NOUNS WITH A CLAUSE

Del que, de la que, de los que, de las que, are used according to the gender and number of the noun 'understood' in the clause:

> Volvió con más dinero que yo.
> *He came back with more money than I.*
> (noun – pronoun but no clause)

> Volvió con más dinero del que habíamos calculado.
> *He came back with more money than we had estimated.*
> (masculine singular noun, therefore *del que* before the clause)

> Han encontrado más agua de la que necesitaban.
> *They have found more water than they needed.*
> (feminine singular noun, therefore *de la que* before clause)

> Compraron más diarios de los que podrían leer.
> *They bought more newspapers than they could read.*
> (masculine plural noun, therefore *de los que* before the clause)

> La casa tiene más ventanas de las que ven ustedes.
> *The house has more windows than you can see.*
> (feminine plural noun, therefore *de las que* before the clause)

(b) COMPARISON OF ADJECTIVES AND ADVERBS WITH A CLAUSE

De lo que is used instead of **que** when the adjective or adverb is compared with a clause:

> Es más inteligente de lo que parece.
> *He is cleverer than he appears.*
> (adjective plus clause, therefore *de lo que*)

> El asunto ha resultado mejor de lo que esperábamos.
> *The matter has turned out better than we hoped.*
> (adverb plus clause, therefore *de lo que*).

8 Correlatives and *sino*

(a) Correlatives not only join two clauses or phrases but also add fluency and variety to the language.

i. **O . . . o,** *either . . . or:*

El árbitro o no oyó los gritos o se hizo el sordo.
The referee either did not hear the shouts or turned a deaf ear.

(*Ni . . . ni,* neither . . . nor (see Negation, *16*))

NOTE: *o* becomes *u* when the following word begins with *o* or *ho:*

o siete u ocho, *either seven or eight*
o mujer u hombre, *either man or woman*

ii. **Ora . . . ora,** *now . . . now*
Ya . . . ya, *sometimes . . . sometimes*

Ora baila, ora canta.
Now he dances, now he sings.

Viajan ya de noche, ya de día.
They travel sometimes by night, sometimes by day.

iii. **Tanto . . . como,** *as much . . . as; both . . . and:*

Sabe tanta literatura inglesa como española.
He knows as much English literature as Spanish.

Tanto María como Juana decidieron marcharse.
Both Mary and Joan decided to leave.

iv. **Tan** (plus adjective or adverb) **. . . como,** *as . . . as;* and, of course,
no tan . . . como, *not so . . . as:*

Tan difícil es leer como escribir.
It is as difficult to read as to write.

Aquí no hablan tan bien el castellano como en Burgos.
Here they do not speak Castilian so well as they do in Burgos.

v. **Cuanto más (menos) . . . tanto más (menos),** *the more (less) . . .
the more (less):*

Cuanto más (menos) estudiamos, tanto más (menos) aprendemos.
The more (less) we study, the more (less) we learn.

Similarly with other comparatives:

Cuanto mejor (peor) escribe, mejor (peor) se le entiende.
The better (worse) he writes, the better (worse) he is understood.

vi. **Quien(es) ... quien(es)**, *one (some) ... another (others)*:

Quienes dormían de bruces, quienes tendidos boca arriba.
Some were sleeping face downward, others stretched out on their backs.

vii. **No bien (apenas) ... cuando** (the latter word may be omitted in Spanish) *no sooner (hardly) ... when (than)*:

No bien (apenas) hubimos llegado, (cuando) salieron.
No sooner had we arrived when they left.

Apenas (no bien) hubo abierto la carta, (cuando) llamaron a la puerta.
Hardly had he (she) opened the letter when someone knocked at the door.

viii. **De ... a; desde ... hasta**, *from ... till*:

De marzo a junio es primavera.
From March to June is springtime.

Duermen desde las once hasta las cuatro.
They sleep from eleven till four (o'clock).

(b) SINO

i. **Sino** (not *pero*) is used to introduce a positive clause contradicting a previous negative statement. The original verb is implied in the positive clause:

No es rico sino (es) pobre.
He is not rich but (is) poor.

No quieren estudiar sino (quieren) jugar.
They do not want to study but (want) to play.

ii. **No** plus verb plus **sino** (or **más que**), meaning 'only':

No busca sino su provecho.
He only looks for his own advantage.

No piensan más que en él.
They only think of him.

iii. **Sino que** is required if a clause follows the negative statement:

Él no quiere que tú vayas al cine, sino (quiere) que le acompañes al teatro.
He does not want you to go to the cinema but (wants you) to accompany him to the theatre.

iv. **No sólo ... sino también**, *not only ... but also*:

No sólo tiene una mujer muy agradable, sino también tres hijas guapas.
He has not only a very pleasant wife but also three pretty daughters.

9 Prepositions[1]

[1] For list of Spanish prepositions see note to *2(a) iv.*

(a) THE PREPOSITION 'A' is used:

i. To indicate motion:

Vamos a España (a Madrid).
We are going to Spain (to Madrid).

Van a pescar al río.
They are going to fish in the river

Salimos a la huerta.
We went into the orchard.

El chico cayó al agua.
The boy fell into the water.

Nos acercamos a la frontera.
We approach the frontier.

Van a pasar el fin de semana al campo.
They are going to spend the week-end in the country.

ii. To indicate place. Study the following phrases:

a doce kilómetros del pueblo, *at twelve km. from the village*
a la derecha, *to (on) the right*
a la izquierda, *to (on) the left*
a la luz, *in the light*
a la mesa, *at the table*
a la puerta, *at the door*
a la sombra, *in the shade*
al final de la calle, *at the end of the street*
a lo lejos, *in the distance*
al pie del árbol, *at the foot of the tree*
al sol, *in the sun*
a su alcance, *within his reach*

iii. To relate the action to a personal object. The personal **a is** essential sometimes to indicate the object of the verb, as otherwise the meaning may be ambiguous:

    a Juan conocía a Francisco mejor que nadie.
       John knew Francis better than anyone did.

    b Juan conocía a Francisco mejor que *a* nadie.
       John knew Francis better than anyone else.

iv. To form some adverbial expressions:

    a caballo, *on horseback*
    a cántaros, *raining heavily*
    a carcajadas, *laughing heartily*
    a ciegas, *blindly*
    a cuestas, *on one's back*
    a escondidas, *under cover*
    a fondo, *deeply*
    a galope, *at a gallop*
    a gatas, *on all fours*
    a hurtadillas, *by stealth*
    a la francesa, *in the French way*
    a mano, *by (at) hand*
    a medias, *by halves*
    a mujeriegas, *side-saddle (riding)*
    a nado, *swimming*
    a oscuras, *in the dark*
    a pie, *on foot*
    a propósito, *on purpose*; *by the way*
    a rastras, *dragging*
    a raudales, *in abundance*
    a sabiendas, *knowingly*
    a solas, *alone*; *lonely*
    a tientas, *gropingly*
    a toda prisa, *at full speed*
    a zancadas, *with strides, striding*

v. In many adverbial expressions related to time:

    a deshora, *inopportunely*, *late*
    a eso de las diez, *at about ten o'clock*
    a fines de octubre, *at the end of October*
    a las dos, *at two o'clock*

a la vez, *at the same time*
a los pocos días, *a few days later*
a mediados del año, *in the middle of the year*
a menudo, *often*
a principios del siglo, *at the beginning of the century*
a tiempo, *in time*
a veces, *occasionally*

vi. In some widely used prepositional phrases beginning with **a** and ending with **de**:

a base de, *based on*
a cambio de, *in exchange for*
a causa de, *because of*
a costa de, *at the cost of*
a diferencia de, *unlike*
a excepción de, *except*
a falta de, *for lack of*
a fuerza de, *by dint of*
a impulso de, *driven by*
al servicio de, *in the service of*
a manos de, *at the hands of*
a partir de hoy, *from today onwards*
a pesar de, *in spite of*
a punto de, *on the point of*
a través de, *through*

vii. To indicate separation:

Robaron el dinero al abuelo.
They stole the money from the grandfather.

Compré la casa a mi amigo.
I bought the house from my friend.

viii. In certain idiomatic expressions where a different preposition (usually 'of') would be needed in English including expressions with the verbs **oler** (to smell) and **saber** (to taste):

el amor al trabajo, *love of work*
el olor a flores, *scent of flowers*
el sabor a fruta, *taste of fruit*
el temor a la muerte, *fear of death*

ix. After verbs of beginning, encouraging, learning, persuading, preparing and teaching, as well as following reflexive verbs of deciding and refusing, before an Infinitive (see 11(a) and (b)).

Empezó a explicar la lección.
He began to explain the lesson.

Le animé a venir.
I encouraged him to come.

Aprendimos a nadar.
We learned how to swim.

Le indujo a escribir.
He induced him to write.

Se disponían a salir.
They were getting ready to go out.

Mi amigo se decidió a comprar el diccionario.
My friend decided to buy the dictionary.

(b) CON is used:

i. With nouns to form many adverbial expressions:

con mucho gusto, *very willingly*
con prisa, *in haste*
con retraso, *with delay*
con temor, *in fear*

ii. In idioms, combined with certain verbs (see 11(b)):

Mis colegas cuentan conmigo.
My colleagues rely on me.

Ella va a casarse con un español.
She is going to marry a Spaniard.

Sueño con mis vacaciones.
I am dreaming of my holidays.

Tropezó con su amigo en la calle.
He bumped into his friend in the street.

Se encontró con ella en la plaza.
He (she) met her in the square.

(c) DE is used:

   i. To precede descriptive adjectival phrases:

      la casa de más allá, *the house further away*
      la escalera de caracol, *the winding staircase*
      la hoja de afeitar, *the razor-blade*
      el reloj de oro, *the gold watch*
      el sello de cinco pesetas, *the five-peseta stamp*
      el sofá de dos asientos, *the sofa for two people*
      el tren de Valencia, *the Valencia train*

   ii. After the hour of the day or following a superlative when the preposition 'in' would be required in English:

      Fuimos a misa a las seis de la mañana.
      We went to mass at six o'clock in the morning.

      Me esperaba a las dos y media de la tarde.
      He waited for me at half past two in the afternoon.

      Aquélla era la iglesia más grande de la ciudad.
      That one was the largest church in the city.

      Fuimos al Canadá en al avión más moderno del mundo.
      We went to Canada in the most modern aeroplane in the world.

   iii. Also in other sentences where 'in' could be replaced by 'of':

      La criada ocupa una habitación de la casa.
      The maid occupies a room in the house.

      La oficina está en una calle de Madrid.
      The office is in a street in Madrid.

      El momento culminante del programa vino después.
      The high spot in the programme came later.

   iv. In some adverbial phrases:

      como de costumbre, *as usual*
      de bruces, *face downwards*
      de buena (mala) gana, *willingly (unwillingly)*
      de cara, *opposite*
      de improviso, *unexpectedly*
      de la misma manera, *in the same way*
      de memoria, *from (by) memory*

de nuevo, *again*
de pie, *standing*
de prisa, *quickly*
de pronto, *suddenly*
de puntillas, *on tiptoe*
de remate, *utterly*
de repente, *suddenly*
de tarde en tarde, *occasionally*
de todos modos, *in any case*
de una vez, *in one go*
de un modo elemental, *in an elementary way*
de veras, *truly*
de vez en cuando, *from time to time*
ir de compras (de vacaciones), *to go shopping (on holiday)*
mirar de hito en hito, *to look closely*
mirar de reojo, *to look askance*
viajar de día y de noche, *to travel by day and night*

v. After verbs of ending, emotion and others, as well as after nouns introducing an infinitive (see *11(a)*, *(b)*):

Las mujeres terminaron de discutir.
The women finished arguing.

Me alegro de ver cuanto se divierten.
I am glad to see how much they enjoy themselves.

Nos cansamos de jugar al ajedrez.
We got tired of playing chess.

Tenga usted la bondad de hablar más despacio.
Please speak more slowly.

vi. Immediately after some verbs that are followed by a noun or pronoun (see *11(a)* and *(b)*):

burlarse de alguien, *to make fun of someone*
cambiar de tren, *to change trains*
carecer de dinero, *to lack money*
disfrazarse de payaso, *to disguise as a clown*

vii. After certain past participles (see *13(b)*):

cubierto de polvo, *covered with dust*
seguido de los niños, *followed by the children*

viii. In exclamations and some idiomatic expressions

> ¡ay de mí!, *woe is me!*
> ¡pobre de mí!, *poor me!*
> camino de Londres, *on the way to London*
> de aquí en adelante, *henceforth*
> de nada, *don't mention it; (you are welcome)*
> de ninguna manera, *by no means; not at all*
> de sol a sol, *from sunrise to sunset*

NOTE: Followed by an infinitive, *de* may be translated by 'if' (see *II* (*a*)):
de saberlo, *if I had known.*

(d) EN is used:

i. In many everyday idioms:

> en alta mar, *on the high seas*
> en cambio, *on the other hand*
> en casa, *at home*
> en cuclillas, *squatting*
> en cueros vivos, *stark naked*
> en el fondo, *at heart*
> en esto, *whereupon*
> en forma, *in form; in shape*
> en la actualidad, *at the present time*
> en mi vida, *(never) in my life*
> en otros términos, *in other words*
> en pelota, *naked*
> en plena lucha, *in the midst of the struggle*
> en pleno día, *in broad daylight*
> en primer lugar, *in the first place*
> en punto, *on the dot (punctual)*
> en seguida, *at once*
> en todo caso, *in any case*
> en un abrir y cerrar de ojos, *in the twinkling of an eye*
> en vigor, *in force*
> en voz baja (alta), *in a low (loud) voice*

ii. Following certain verbs (see *II*(*a*) and (*b*)):

> consistir en algo, *to consist of s.t.*
> convenir en algo, *to agree on s.t.*
> convertirse en algo (alguien), *to become s.t. (s.o.)*
> fijarse en algo (alguien), *to stare at s.t. (s.o.)*

147

pensar en algo, *to think of s.t.*
volver en sí, *to regain consciousness*

iii. In certain idioms, followed by an infinitive (see also *II* (*a*) and (*b*)):

Mi hijo fue el primero en llegar.
My son was the first to arrive.

Luisa se ocupaba en cocinar.
Louise was busy cooking.

La niña no tardó mucho en dormirse.
The little girl soon went to sleep.

Los prisioneros se esforzaron en salir de la cárcel.
The prisoners struggled to get out of the prison.

No perdió tiempo en buscar la llave.
He did not waste time looking for the key.

El acusado insiste en hablar.
The accused man insists on speaking.

Me obstiné en conducir el coche.
I persisted in driving the car.

iv. To form many prepositional phrases:

en busca de oro, *in search of gold*
en contra de mi voluntad, *against my will*
en cuanto a España, *as for Spain*
en dirección al teatro, *in the direction of the theatre*
en forma de protesta, *as a protest*
en medio del almuerzo, *in the middle of lunch*
en pos de los otros, *after the others*
en señal de peligro, *as a danger signal*
en vez de su amigo, *instead of his friend*

v. To indicate the time taken to do something:

Aprenderé el español en tres años.
I shall learn Spanish in three years.

Saldrá para Madrid dentro de dos meses.
He will leave for Madrid in two months time.

NOTE: *Dentro de* is used when 'in' implies 'within a certain time'.

(e) ANTE, ANTES DE, ANTES QUE, DELANTE DE

i. **Ante** is used in a figurative sense meaning 'in the presence of', 'in the face of':

> ante el público, *before (in the presence of) the public*
> ante el peligro, *in the face of danger*

ii. **Antes de** refers to time and frequently precedes an infinitive:

> Nos reunimos antes de comer.
> *We gathered before eating.*

iii. **Antes que** also refers to time but usually precedes nouns or pronouns:

> Mi hermano llegó antes que nosotros.
> *My brother arrived before us.*

NOTES:
1. The adverb *antes* means 'beforehand':

> La habíamos visto antes.
> *We had seen her beforehand.*

2. The conjunction *antes que* governs the subjunctive mood (see *18*).

(f) SIN

i. Followed by a noun, **sin** does not require the indefinite article as its English equivalent does. In many instances, however, the definite article is used between *sin* and the noun:

> Generalmente sale sin sombrero.
> *Generally, he goes out without a hat.*

But if referring to a specific item:

> – No salgas a la calle sin *la* bufanda.
> *'Don't go out into the street without your scarf.'*

ii. Followed by an infinitive **no** is not required as **sin** implies a negative:

> La muchacha se fue sin decir nada.
> *The girl went away without saying anything.*

NOTE: Observe the adjectival use of **sin** + infinitive: (see *11* (*a*) *vii*):
una camisa sin lavar, *an unwashed shirt*

iii. **Sin que** is a conjunction which governs the subjunctive (see *18(f)*).

(g) TRAS, DETRÁS DE, DESPUÉS DE

i. **Tras** means 'after' or 'behind' and may be used in phrases of time or place:

Esperamos hora tras hora.
We waited hour after hour.

Veraneaba en el mismo sitio año tras año.
He spent his holidays in the same place, year after year.

Fumaba cigarrillo tras cigarrillo.
He smoked cigarette after cigarette.

El perro corría tras él.
The dog ran behind him.

Tras la puerta colgaba la llave.
The key was hanging behind the door.

ii. **Detrás de** refers to place only, meaning 'behind':

El jardín está detrás de la casa.
The garden is behind the house.

NOTE: *Por detrás* is an adverbial expression also meaning 'behind':
Por detrás no hay nada.
There is nothing behind.

iii. **Después de** refers to time only and means 'after':

Después del partido volvimos a casa.
After the game we returned home.

Te telefonearé después de comer.
I'll ring you up after eating.

NOTE: *Después* is an adverb and means 'afterwards', 'then', 'next':
Ella abrió el cajón y después volvió a cerrarlo.
She opened the drawer and afterwards (then, next) closed it again.

(h) HASTA may mean:

i. As far as:

Iremos hasta la catedral.
We shall go as far as the cathedral.

Te acompañaré hasta el puente.
I shall accompany you as far as the bridge.

ii. Until, till:

No volveremos hasta el miércoles.
We shall not return until Wednesday.

hasta luego, *so long*
hasta la vista, *be seeing you*

iii. Even, up to:

Hasta los ricos tienen hambre.
Even the wealthy are hungry.

No ha llegado nadie hasta ahora.
No one has arrived up to now.

(i) BAJO, DEBAJO DE, SO

Debajo, being an adverb of place, gives **debajo de** a more precise physical connotation than **bajo,** as will be seen from the following examples:

i. **Bajo,** *under*:

Los niños están bajo mi protección.
The children are under my protection.

Lo prometí bajo juramento.
I promised it under oath.

ii. **Debajo de,** *under*:

Estamos debajo del árbol.
We are under the tree.

NOTE: *Debajo* and *abajo* are both adverbs:

Los vecinos del piso de debajo no nos hablan nunca.
The neighbours in the flat below never talk to us.

¿Están arriba o abajo?
Are they upstairs or downstairs?

iii. **So** is only found nowadays in a few expressions, mostly legal ones:

so capa de, *under the cloak of*
so pena de muerte, *under penalty of death*
so pretexto de, *under the pretext of*

151

10 *Para* and *Por*

(a) PARA, *for*, is used implying:

i. Purpose:

> ¿Para qué van a España?
> *For what purpose do they go to Spain?*

> Para aprender el idioma.
> *To learn the language.*

> Déme dinero para (comprar) el billete.
> *Give me money for the ticket.*

ii. Destination (place, people or time):

  a Place:

> ¿A qué hora sale el avión para Palma?
> *At what time does the aeroplane leave for Palma?*

> Antonio salió para casa.
> *Antonio left for home.*

  b People:

> Es un libro (escrito) para niños.
> *It is a book meant for children.*

> Mi madre preparaba un postre para mí.
> *My mother was preparing a dessert for me.*

  c Time:

> ¿Qué lecciones han estudiado para hoy?
> *What lessons have they studied for today?*

> Le veré cuando venga para la Navidad.
> *I shall see him when he comes for Christmas.*

iii. Suitability or unsuitability:

> Es un juego difícil para chicos de diez años.
> *It is a difficult game for ten-year old boys.*

> Este modo de vivir no es bueno para la salud.
> *This way of life is not good for health.*

iv. **Para con**, denotes mental attitude towards someone; emotion rather than motion:

> Usted es muy amable para con ellas.
> *You are very kind towards them.*

v. The following are some common expressions with *para*:

> para su sorpresa, *to his (her, their, etc.) surprise*
> para asombro de todos, *to everybody's astonishment*
> para siempre, *for ever*

(b) POR, *for*, is used implying:

i. Exchange:

> Demandaron ojo por ojo, diente por diente.
> *They demanded an eye for an eye, a tooth for a tooth.*

> Dieron cien pesetas por el libro.
> *They gave one hundred pesetas for the book.*

ii. Reason (because of, on account of):

> Ella se desmayó por la falta de aire.
> *She fainted because of the lack of air.*

> No iré a España por culpa del calor.
> *I won't go to Spain on account of the heat.*

iii. On behalf of, in favour of, for the sake of:

> Este señor viaja por su compañía.
> *This gentleman travels on behalf of his firm.*

> Murió por la patria.
> *He died for his country.*

> El arte por el arte.
> *Art for art's sake.*

iv. An introduction to the object of a feeling:

> Enrique siente cierta atracción por ella.
> *Henry feels a certain attraction for her.*

> Nadie sabía por quién lloraban.
> *No one knew for whom they were weeping.*

v. Length of time intended to be spent:

> Iremos a Barcelona por dos semanas.
> *We shall go to Barcelona for two weeks.*

> Pidió hospitalidad por una noche.
> *He requested hospitality for one night.*

NOTE: When expressions of length of time actually spent are used in past tenses, *durante* is required rather than *por*:

> Trabajó mucho durante un mes.
> *He worked hard for one month.*

vi. After certain verbs, such as: **ir por, mandar por, preguntar por**:

> Fuimos por agua.
> *We went for water.*

> Le mandamos por fruta.
> *We sent him for fruit.*

> Preguntó por el director.
> *He asked for the manager.*

11 Verbs

(a) INFINITIVE

It should be remembered that when a verb is governed by a preposition, the verb must be in the infinitive.

> Voy a telefonear tan pronto como pueda.
> *I am going to telephone as soon as I can.*

> Por ser pobre viajaba en tercera clase.
> *Through being poor he travelled third class.*

> Mi amigo me esperaba a pesar de llegar tarde yo.
> *My friend was waiting in spite of my arriving late.*

i. When an infinitive is a logical subject, no preceding preposition is needed:

> Es fácil decir eso.
> *It is easy to say that.*

> Vale la pena trabajar bien.
> *It is worth the trouble to work well.*

> Es posible no hacer nada.
> *It is possible not to do anything.*

ii. The infinitive is often preceded by **el** when used as a noun:

No estaba en su mano el remediarlo.
To remedy it was not in his own hands.

No puedo evitar el tener pensamientos tristes.
I cannot avoid having sad thoughts.

iii. An infinitive is often used to express the action perceived by the senses (verbs of seeing, hearing, feeling, etc.):

Vi relampaguear sus ojos en la oscuridad.
I saw his eyes flashing in the darkness.

Me oyó tocar el piano.
He heard me playing the piano.

iv. Remember the use of **que** followed by the infinitive when a noun object precedes:

No había tiempo que perder.
There was no time to lose.

Tenemos mucho trabajo que hacer.
We have much work to do.

NOTE: Before *beber* and *comer*, **de** is often used instead of **que**:

¿Hay algo de comer?
Is there anything to eat?

No hay nada de beber.
There is nothing to drink.

v. **Al** followed by an infinitive is interchangeable with **cuando** and the pertaining verbal form:

Al llegar (cuando llegamos) a casa nos lavamos.
On arriving home we washed.

Vi a mi tío al salir (cuando salí) a la calle.
I saw my uncle on going out into the street.

El profesor se levantó al terminar (cuando terminó) la lección.
The teacher stood up when the lesson ended.

vi. **Por** followed by an infinitive (see *10*) implies reason and often replaces **porque**:

Por ser (porque es) mi cumpleaños.
Because it is my birthday.

Por confiar (porque confié) en él.
Because I trusted him.

vii. Accompanied by certain prepositions and adverbs, (**sin, a medio**, etc.), the infinitive has some idiomatic adjectival uses:

Era una mesa de madera sin pintar.
It was a table of unpainted wood.

Me dio un cuaderno con hojas a medio arrancar.
He gave me an exercise book with leaves half-torn out.

viii. In some expressions, **de** preceding the infinitive must be translated by 'if':

De no haber llovido estaría seco al jardín.
If it had not rained the garden would be dry.

Habría telefoneado, de saber que estabas en casa.
I would have telephoned, if I had known that you were at home.

ix. The meaning of some verbs varies slightly when used as reflexives:

caer, *to fall; to drop*	caerse, *to fall over*
comer, *to eat*	comerse, *to eat up*
despedir, *to dismiss; to see s.o. off*	despedirse, *to take leave*
dirigir, *to direct; to manage*	dirigirse a, *to make for*
divertir, *to divert; to amuse*	divertirse, *to amuse oneself*
dormir, *to sleep*	dormirse, *to fall asleep*
encontrar, *to find*	encontrarse, *to be; to find oneself*
estar sentado, *to be seated*	sentarse, *to sit down*
hacer, *to do; to make*	hacerse (*followed by a noun or an adjective*), *to become*
hallar, *to find*	hallarse, *to find oneself; to be*
ir, *to go*	irse, *to go away*
levantar, *to raise*	levantarse, *to get up*
llamar, *to call*	llamarse, *to be named*
llevar, *to wear; to take away*	llevarse algo, *to carry away s.t.*
	llevarse bien (mal), *to get on well (badly) with*
poner, *to put; to place*	ponerse (*plus adjective*), *to become; (followed by a garment) to put on s.t.*
sentar, *to suit*	sentarse, *to sit down*
sentir, *to feel; to be sorry*	sentirse, *to feel (within oneself)*
vestir, *to wear; to dress*	vestirse, *to dress oneself*

(b) GOVERNMENT OF VERBS

The following is a list of verbs which, together with their construction, should be learnt by use and by frequent revision.

a

abrirse paso, *to make way*
acabar de hacer algo, (i) *to finish doing s.t.*
                   (ii) *to have just done s.t.*
acabar por hacer algo, *to end by doing s.t.*
acercarse a algo (a alguien), *to approach s.t. (s.o.)*
acertar en algo, *to find the right solution to s.t.*
acordarse de algo (de alguien), *to remember s.t. (s.o.)*
acostumbrarse a hacer algo, *to be used to doing s.t.*
afanarse por algo, *to strive for s.t.; to toil*
agradecer algo a alguien, *to be grateful to s.o. for s.t.*
alabarse de algo, *to boast about s.t.*
alegrarse de haber hecho algo, *to be glad to have done s.t.*
alejarse de algo, *to go away from s.t.*
apoderarse de algo, *to take possession of s.t.*
apretar el paso, *to quicken one's step*
apropiarse de algo, *to take possession of s.t.*
aprovecharse de algo, *to take advantage of s.t.*
aproximarse a algo, *to approach s.t.*
asomarse a, *to look outside (or inside), to lean out of*
atreverse a hacer algo, *to dare to do s.t.*
ayudar a alguien a hacer algo, *to help s.o. to do s.t.*

b

bajar (se) del tren, *to get out of the train*
bajar la escalera, *to come down the stairs*
burlarse de alguien, *to make fun of s.o.*
buscar algo (a alguien), *to look for s.t. (s.o.)*

c

caber (see 20)
caer en la cuenta, *to see the point*
cambiarse de ropa, *to change clothing*
cambiar de tren, *to change trains*
carecer de algo, *to lack s.t.*
casarse con alguien, *to marry s.o.*

cerrar con llave, *to lock up*
cesar de hacer algo, *to stop doing s.t.*
conseguir algo, *to obtain s.t.*
conseguir hacer algo, *to succeed in doing s.t.*
constar de algo, *to consist of s.t.*
contar con alguien, *to count on s.o.*
contestar (a) una pregunta, *to answer a question*
costar trabajo a alguien, *to give trouble to s.o.*
cuidar de algo, *to look after s.t.*
cumplir (con) una promesa, *to keep a promise*

d

dar (see *20*)
deber (see *20*)
dedicarse a algo, *to devote oneself to s.t.*
dejar (see *20*)
depender de algo, *to depend on s.t.*
derramar lágrimas, *to shed tears*
deshacerse de algo, *to get rid of s.t.*
despedir a alguien, *to dismiss s.o.; to see s.o. off*
despedirse de alguien, *to take leave of s.o.*
dirigirse a alguien, a algo, *to go towards s.o., to go to s.t., to make for s.t.*
dirigir una pregunta a alguien, *to ask s.o. a question*
disfrutar (de) algo, *to enjoy s.t.*
disimular hacer algo, *to pretend to do s.t.*
doler (see *20*)
dormir la siesta, *to take an afternoon nap*
dudar en hacer algo, *to hesitate to do s.t.*

e

echar (see *20*)
empeñarse en hacer algo, *to insist on doing s.t.*
enamorarse de alguien, *to fall in love with s.o.*
encogerse de hombros, *to shrug one's shoulders*
encontrar a alguien, *to find s.o.*
encontrarse con alguien, *to meet (run into) s.o.*
entablar una conversación, *to start a conversation*
entrar al servicio de alguien, *to enter the service of s.o.*
entrar en un cuarto, *to enter a room*
esforzarse en (por) hacer algo, *to try to do s.t.*
estar (see *19*)
estrechar la mano, *to shake hands*

f

faltar (see *20*)
fiarse de alguien, *to trust s.o.*
figurarse algo, *to imagine s.t.*
fijarse en algo, *to gaze at s.t.*
fruncir las cejas, *to frown*

g

gozar de algo, *to enjoy s.t.*
guardarse de alguien, *to guard against s.o.*
guardar silencio, *to keep silent*
gustar (see *20*)

h

haber (see *20*)
hacer (see *20*)

i

informar a alguien de algo, *to inform s.o. of s.t.*
invitar a alguien a hacer algo, *to invite s.o. to do s.t.*

j

jugar al fútbol, *to play football* (see *to play*, *21*)

l

lanzarse a (sobre) algo o alguien, *to rush upon s.t. or s.o.*
lavarse las manos, *to wash one's hands*
librarse de algo, *to escape from s.t.*
limitarse a (hacer) algo, *to confine oneself to (doing) s.t.*
lograr hacer algo, *to succeed* (see *21*) *in doing s.t.*

ll

llamar la atención, *to draw attention*
llegar a, *to arrive at*
llegar a ser, *to become* (see *21*)
llevar a cabo algo, *to carry out s.t.*
llevarse algo, *to carry (take) away s.t.* (see *21*)
llevar un año (aquí), *to have been (here) one year*

m

mandar hacer algo, *to order s.t. to be done*
meter algo en algo, *to put* (see 21) *s.t. into s.t.*
meterse en algo, *to meddle in s.t.*
mirar a alguien, *to look at s.o.*
mirar algo, *to look at s.t.*
mudarse de casa, *to move house*

n

necesitar algo, a alguien, *to need s.t., s.o.*
negarse a hacer algo, *to refuse to do s.t.*
negar hacer algo, *to deny doing s.t.*

o

obligar a alguien a hacer algo, *to force s.o. to do s.t.*
obstinarse en hacer algo, *to persist in doing s.t.*
ocuparse en (hacer) algo, *to be busy with s.t.*
ofrecerse para hacer algo, *to volunteer to do s.t.*
oír algo, *to hear s.t.*
oír decir algo, *to hear (say) s.t.*
oír hablar de algo, *to hear (talk) of s.t.*
oler a algo, *to smell of s.t.*
oler algo, *to smell s.t.*
olvidar(se), *to forget* (see 20)

p

pagar algo (por alguien), *to pay for s.t., (for s.o. else)*
parecerle a alguien, *to seem to s.o.*
parecerse a alguien, *to resemble s.o.*
parecer hacer algo, *to seem to do s.t.*
pasar (see 20)
pasear(se), *to stroll*
pensar en algo, *to think* (see 21) *of s.t.*
poner (see 20 and 21)
perder de vista algo (a alguien), *to lose sight of s.t. (s.o.)*
prender fuego a algo, *to set fire to s.t.*
prestar atención, *to pay attention*
procurar hacer algo, *to try to do s.t.*
prometer hacer algo, *to promise to do s.t.*
pronunciar un discurso, *to deliver a speech*
proveerse de algo, *to provide oneself with s.t.*

q

quedar(se), *to remain; to stay behind*

quedarse con algo, *to keep s.t.; to take (purchase) s.t.*

quejarse de algo (de alguien), *to complain about s.t. (s.o.)*

querer (see 20) a alguien, *to love s.o.*

querer hacer algo, *to wish (want) to do s.t.*

quitar algo, *to remove s.t.*

quitarse algo, *to take (see 21) s.t. off*

r

recordar algo, *to remember s.t.*

recorrer una distancia, *to travel (cover) a distance*

rehusar hacer algo, *to refuse to do s.t.*

reírse de algo (de alguien), *to laugh at s.t. (at s.o.)*

reparar en algo, *to notice s.t.*

reprochar algo a alguien, *to reproach s.o. for s.t.*

resistir algo, a alguien, *to resist s.t., s.o.*

resultar ser, *to turn out to be*

s

saber a algo, *to taste of (like) s.t.*

saber algo, *to know s.t.*

salir a la calle, *to go out into the street*

salir bien (mal) *to do well (badly)*

sentir algo, *to be sorry for s.t.*

servir, (see 20)

sobrar, *to be in excess*

sobrar(le) algo a alguien, *to have s.t. left over*

soler (see 20)

subir al coche (tren), *to get into the car (train)*

subir la escalera, *to go up the stairs*

t

tardar (poco or mucho) en hacer algo, *to take (little or much) time in doing s.t.*

temblar de emoción, *to tremble with emotion*

tocarle a alguien hacer algo, *to be one's turn to do s.t.*

tomar, *to take (see 21)*

trabar conversación, *to strike up a conversation*

traducir del (al) inglés, *to translate from (into) English*

tratar a alguien, *to treat s.o.*
tratar algo, *to treat s.t.*
tratar con alguien, *to have dealings with s.o.*
tratar de algo, *to deal with s.t.*
tratarse de algo, *to be a question of (about) s.t.*
tratar de hacer algo, *to try to do s.t.*

v

vacilar en hacer algo, *to hesitate to do s.t.*
valerse de algo, *to use s.t.*
vengarse de alguien, *to take revenge on s.o.*
venir a las manos, *to come to blows*
vestir, *to clothe*
vestirse, *to dress oneself*
volver a hacer algo, *to do s.t. again*
volver en sí, *to regain consciousness*
volverse, *to turn round*

(c) TENSES

General remarks
Students are strongly recommended to form the habit of inspecting
closely a complete paragraph of Spanish in order to discover the pattern
of tenses used by an author. Several passages in Section One are ideal for
this purpose, and occasionally in other excerpts, too, the notes draw
attention to the tense or tenses being used.

i. *The use and sequence of tenses in the indicative mood:*

  a **The Present Tense:**

  1. **Estar** added to the **gerundio** (*14*) is used more or less as the
     continuous present in English:

     Están jugando al tenis.
     They are playing tennis.

  2. Unlike English usage, the present tense is often used
     in Spanish in sentences indicating how long a particular
     action or state has been going on:

     Hace tres años que vivimos aquí.
     We have been living here for three years
     (implying that we are still living here).

Llevan dos meses en Londres.
They have been in London for two months
(implying that they are still there).

3. As in English the present tense is used in a stylistic and narrative sense to make past events more vivid and dramatic:

Colón desembarca, pisa tierra americana y, arrodillándose, da gracias a Dios.
Columbus disembarks, sets foot on American soil and, kneeling down, thanks God.

b The Compound Past or Perfect Tense:

The best rule to follow here is to use this tense for actions or events which have taken place in a period of time not yet fully lapsed:

Mis amigos han salido para Toledo.
My friends have left for Toledo.

En este siglo han muerto en vano muchos soldados.
Many soldiers have died in vain in this century.

NOTE: If the action has taken place at a definite time which has fully lapsed, the *pretérito* should be used:

Dos minutos después llegaron mis amigos.
My friends arrived two minutes later.

Esta mañana vino el médico.
The doctor came this morning.

c The Pretérito Tense:

1. This past tense usually recounts events or actions that began, happened, followed successively or ended at some definite past time (see Passage *17*):

Ayer hubo un accidente en la calle.
Yesterday there was an accident in the street.

Anoche cenamos a las nueve.
We dined at 9 o'clock last night.

2. The *pretérito* is also used to recount events or actions which lasted for a specified length of time:

El emperador reinó muchos años.
The emperor reigned for many years.

163

Hablé con él un rato.
I spoke to him for a while.

Estuvieron enfermos algún tiempo.
They were ill for some time.

¿Dónde estuvo usted el lunes?
Where were you on Monday?

3. From (1) and (2) it will be seen that the *pretérito* is used to denote an event or action that cuts across something that was already going on (expressed by the imperfect):

Me paseaba por el parque cuando vi a un amigo mío.
I was walking in the park when I saw a friend of mine.

Mi pobre marido (se) murió cuando el niño tenía dos años.
My poor husband died when the child was two years old.

Mientras jugábamos al tenis, empezó a llover.
While we were playing tennis it began to rain.

NOTE: Study carefully the use of the *pretérito* in the following and similar situations when *ser* is used to single out one part of a sentence for the sake of emphasis:

Quien más me ayudó fue el profesor.
It was the teacher who helped me most.

But if the imperfect is used in the main clause, the subordinate clause must also be in the imperfect:

Quien más me ayudaba era el profesor.
It was the teacher who used to help me most.

d The Imperfect Tense:

1. The imperfect tense is used to express habitual action or state of affairs, i.e. what used to happen or to exist:

Iban a misa todos los domingos.
They went (used to go) to mass every Sunday.

El árbol estaba al final del jardín.
The tree stood (existed) at the bottom of the garden.

2. The imperfect is also the tense used in descriptions (see Passage *18*) of scenery, people, background, etc.:

Daba un poco de luna en lo alto de los árboles.
The moon was shining a little on the tops of the trees.

Alicita y su tía estaban radiantes de alegría.
Alice and her aunt were radiant with joy.

El cuarto era pequeño.
The room was small.

3. The imperfect expresses what was already going on when something else happened that interrupted the action or state (see **c** 3):

Estábamos comiendo cuando llegó mi madre.
We were eating when my mother arrived.

4. The imperfect is used as a logical consequence of **a** 2 above in sentences expressing how long a particular action or state had been going on within the past:

Hacía tres años que no respiraban el aire de la montaña.
They had not breathed the mountain air for three years.

Llevaba ya veinte años de estudiante.
He had already been a student for twenty years.

5. The imperfect is often used in the description, explanation or development of a main event or statement (see Passage *16*):

Cuando llegó con el pato, fue recibido con ruidosa hilaridad: la gente *reía* a carcajadas, alguien *disculpaba* el error del cazador, pero las mujeres *se apretaban* la nariz.
When he arrived with the duck he was received with noisy hilarity: the people burst out *laughing, someone* forgave *the hunter his mistake but the women* held *their noses.*

NOTE: Although the last three actions took place after the arrival and reception of the duck, the imperfect is used to bring the reader closer to the scene; the pretérito would fail to do this, as it would underline the action being a past one, concluded in a distant time.

6. The imperfect tense is also used, of course, in the appropriate indirect statements and questions:

Le dije que mis padres salían para París.
I told him that my parents were leaving for Paris.

Me preguntó si yo quería acompañarle al colegio.
He asked me if I wanted to go with him to the school.

e **The Future Tense:**

This tense is used for the most part as in English. Sometimes, however, it implies conjecture or supposition:

¿De quién será ese paraguas?
Whose umbrella can that be?

Será el de mi hermana.
I suppose it is my sister's.

NOTE: The use of 'will' in English requests is translated into Spanish by *querer*:
¿Quiere usted cerrar la ventana?
Will you close the window?

f The Conditional Tense:

1. This tense has sometimes been called the **future in the past**. In addition to its basic use in introducing clauses that contain a conditional or potential element, it often implies conjecture or supposition, but referring to past, not current actions as the future tense does (see **e**):

Y estas personas, ¿quiénes serían?
And who could these people be?

Serían amigos suyos.
They could (might) be his friends.

Tendría unos veinte años.
He could be twenty years old.

Serían las seis de la mañana cuando llegó.
It could have been (it was about) six a.m. when he came.

2. The conditional tense is also used in indirect statements or questions, to represent the future of a direct statement:

Dijo que iría a verla al día siguiente.
He said he would go and see her on the following day.

El ministro afirmó que dimitiría dentro de un mes.
The minister affirmed that he would resign within one month.

3. For the general use of the conditional see *18 k*

4. The word 'would' in English requests should be translated into Spanish by *querer* (see note to **e**):

– ¿Querría abrir la puerta?
'Would you open the door?'

No quiso abrirla.
He wouldn't (refused to) open it.

ii. *The use and sequence of tenses in the Subjunctive Mood* (see *18*):

a The Present Subjunctive:

When the main verb is in the present or future tense, the present subjunctive is used in the dependent clause:

Queremos que venga pronto.
We want him to come soon.

Cuando lleguen saldremos en seguida.
When they arrive we shall leave at once.

b The Past Subjunctive (ending in -se or -ra):

When the main verb is in a past tense or in the conditional, the past subjunctive is used in the dependent clause:

Queríamos que viniesen (vinieran) pronto.
We wanted them to come soon.

Dijo que cuando llegasen (llegaran) saldríamos en seguida.
He said that when they arrived, we should leave at once.

c The Compound Tenses follow the scheme in a and b with the auxiliary verb taking the subjunctive:

Cuando hayan comido irán al teatro.
When they have eaten, they will go to the theatre.

Si hubiesen (hubieran) llegado antes, habrían visto a mis padres.
If they had arrived earlier, they would have seen my parents.

(d) AVOIDANCE OF THE PASSIVE VOICE

The passive voice is not used in Spanish as frequently as it is in English. To convert the English passive into the Spanish active, use one of the following methods:

i. Use the agent as the subject:

We were fascinated by the mystery.
Nos fascinaba el misterio.

He was accused of the theft by his secretary.
Le acusó del robo su secretario.

ii. If no agent is mentioned, use the verb in the indefinite third person plural:

The prisoners were set free (they set the prisoners free).
Libertaron a los prisioneros.

The house was knocked down (they knocked the house down).
Derribaron la casa.

iii. When the subject is non-personal and no agent is mentioned, use the reflexive pronoun:

Apples are sold here.
Aquí se venden manzanas.

The books are kept in the library.
Los libros se guardan en la biblioteca.

None of the articles was found.
No se encontró ninguno de los artículos.

iv. Frequently, when the subject is a person, the impersonal reflexive **se** is used:

It is said that he has a girl friend.
Se dice que tiene novia.

I am asked to keep the secret.
Se me pide que guarde el secreto.

The villagers were promised a new bridge.
A los aldeanos se les prometió un nuevo puente.

We were consulted about the programme.
Se nos consultó acerca del programa.

12 Order of words in a sentence

Obviously the order of words in a sentence is, to a large extent, a matter of style and emphasis. Style is the result and expression of an individual's characteristics, experience and personal taste, whereas emphasis is governed by the tone and effect intended by the author (or speaker).

However, a few general rules may be helpful in showing the normal Spanish order of words when this differs from the English.

(a) The subject may follow the verb:

  i. When the subject is long or modified by a clause:

    Se presentó uno de los chicos que acababan de jugar al fútbol.
    There appeared one of the boys who had just been playing football.
    Lit.: *One of the boys, who had just been playing football, appeared.*

    Llegaron los hombres que buscaba.
    The men he was looking for arrived.

  ii. When an adverb of place or time is placed at the beginning of the sentence:

    Desde entonces han pasado por aquí muchas personas.
    Since then many people have passed through here.

    A ambos lados de la carretera se extendían praderas verdes.
    Green fields stretched away on both sides of the road.

  iii. When the verb of statement is placed after one or more words of direct speech:

    – Está loco – repitió el maestro.
    'He is mad', repeated the teacher.

    – ¡Mentira! – exclamaron ambos.
    'Lies!' both exclaimed.

  iv. In adjectival and adverbial clauses, especially at the end of a compound sentence:

    Hemos visto el coche en que viajaban los bandidos.
    We have seen the car in which the bandits were travelling.

    Fuimos al café donde se reunía toda la gente.
    We went to the café where everybody used to meet.

  v. When the author wishes to emphasize the idea in the verb:

    Salieron primero las mujeres y luego los hombres.
    The women left first and then the men.

    Murieron muchos soldados en la batalla.
    Many soldiers died in the battle.

(b) The indirect object or adverbial phrase may precede the direct object when the latter is more lengthy than the former:

Vieron en la calle coches, bicicletas y autobuses.
They saw cars, bicycles and buses in the street.

Las comadres compraron en el mercado lechugas, fruta y legumbres.
The women bought lettuce, fruit and vegetables in the market.

Les daba a mis hijos todo lo que querían.
I used to give my children everything they wanted.

(c) See (3(*e*) and 4(*a*)).

13 Participles

(a) PRESENT PARTICIPLES

The present participle when used like an adjective agrees with the noun it qualifies:

La habitación tiene agua corriente.
The room has running water.

Mi primo empleó los argumentos más convincentes.
My cousin employed the most convincing arguments.

La mujer tenía una mirada penetrante.
The woman had a penetrating look.

(b) PAST PARTICIPLES

i. In addition to the following well-known irregular past participles:

abrir	abierto, *open(ed)*
cubrir	cubierto, *covered*
decir	dicho, *said*
escribir	escrito, *written*
freír	frito, *fried*
hacer	hecho, *done*
imprimir	impreso, *printed*
morir	muerto, *dead*
poner	puesto, *put*
romper	roto, *broken*
ver	visto, *seen*
volver	vuelto, *returned.*

Note the following derivatives and other past participles:

absorber	absorto, *absorbed*
bendecir	bendito, *blessed*
componer	compuesto, *composed*
describir	descrito, *described*
descubrir	descubierto, *discovered*
devolver	devuelto, *given back*
disolver	disuelto, *dissolved*
disponer	dispuesto, *disposed*
entrever	entrevisto, *half-seen*
maldecir	maldito, *cursed*
proponer	propuesto, *proposed*
proveer	provisto, *provided*
resolver	resuelto, *resolved*
satisfacer	satisfecho, *satisfied.*

ii. Past participles agree, like adjectives, with the noun to which they refer, but there is no agreement when conjugated with *haber*:

Nuestras obras serán leídas en España.
Our works will be read in Spain.
Casi todos los españoles han leído los libros.
Nearly all Spaniards have read the books.

iii. In many instances, the Spanish past participle is best rendered into English not by the past but by the present participle:

aburrido, *boring*
acostado, *lying down*
apoyado, *leaning*
asomado, *looking out of*
atrevido, *daring*
caído, *falling*
cargado, *carrying*
colgado, *hanging*
divertido, *amusing*
dormido, *sleeping*
encendido, *burning*
osado, *daring*
reclinado, *reclining*
ruborizado, *blushing*
sentado, *sitting.*

iv. The past participle is sometimes used for economy, to condense an otherwise long introductory clause:

Concluida la cena, Carlos se puso a tocar el piano.
When supper was over, Charles began to play the piano.

Dispuesto el viaje, escribió una larga carta.
When the journey was organized, he wrote a long letter.

Picada por la curiosidad, se acercó a la ventana.
When curiosity overcame her, she approached the window.

v. After a past participle, the agent is usually introduced by the preposition **por**:

El libro fue escrito por mi amigo.
The book was written by my friend.

Las casas han sido compradas por un hombre rico.
The houses have been bought by a wealthy man.

Sometimes **de** is used, instead:

Entró precedido de su mujer.
He came in preceded by his wife.

NOTE: The widespread use of *por* after the participle is relatively contemporary. A number of expressions where *de* is used instead, have been preserved from classical Spanish which in turn evolved them from Latin.

14 Gerundio

(a) Formation exceptions:

i. **I** becomes **y** between two vowels:

creyendo, *believing*
leyendo, *reading*
oyendo, *hearing*

ii. Radical-changing verbs ending in **-ir** change the stem vowel **e** into **i** and **o** into **u**:

dormir	du**r**miendo,	*sleeping*
morir	m**u**riendo,	*dying*
pedir	p**i**diendo,	*asking for*
preferir	pref**i**riendo,	*preferring*
reír	r**i**endo,	*laughing*
sentir	s**i**ntiendo,	*feeling*

iii. Irregular formations:

pudiendo, *being able*
viniendo, *coming*
yendo, *going*

(b) The *gerundio* has the force of an ordinary finite verb:

Dejando (dejó) la luz encendida, salió a la calle.
Leaving the light burning, he went out into the street.

Se sentó y, abriendo (abrió) el libro, comenzó a leer.
He sat down and opening the book began reading.

(c) The *gerundio* is used in Spanish with **estar, ir** and **seguir** to form continuous tenses:

Todo el mundo está yéndose.
Everybody is going away.

El padre siguió leyendo.
The father went on reading.

(d) The *gerundio* often fulfils in Spanish the functions of the English 'by', 'while' and 'through' plus the -ing form of a verb:

Viajando por avión, llegaré esta noche.
By taking a plane, I shall arrive to-night.

– No importa – exclamó, sonriendo vagamente.
'It does not matter' he exclaimed, while smiling vaguely.

No gastes dinero comprando tales trastos.
Do not waste money through buying such rubbish.

(e) The *gerundio* is sometimes needed to help in the translation of certain English idiomatic verbal constructions:

He swam to the shore.
Llegó nadando a la playa.

She ran out of the flat.
Salió corriendo del piso.

15 Interrogatives

Remember that accents (see 26) are required on the interrogative word:

(a) **¿Qué?** may be used as a pronoun or adjective:

¿Qué pasa?
What's the matter?

¿De qué hablamos?
What are we talking about?

¿Qué llavín han perdido?
Which key have they lost?

(b) **¿Qué?** followed by *ser* is used when a definition is asked for:

¿Qué es esto?
What's this?

¿Qué es la vida?
What is life?

(c) **¿Cuál?** followed by *ser* is used to obtain information:

¿Cuál es la capital de la Argentina?
What's the capital of the Argentine?

¿Cuál es su nombre?
What's his name?

¿Cuál? is also used to elicit an answer that may clarify which out of several choices is the right one:

¿Cuál de los jugadores marcó el gol?
Which one of the players scored the goal?

¿Cuál de los tres vino?
Which one of the three came?

(d) i. **¿Quién?** *who?*:

¿Quién?, es?
Who is it?

ii. **¿A quién?**, *whom? to whom?*

¿A quien ha visto hoy?
Whom have you seen today?

iii. **¿De quién?**, *whose? from whom?*:

> ¿De quién es el libro?
> *Whose book is it?*

NOTE: Except in poetry and in classic writers, **cuyo** is only used as a relative pronoun.

(e) **¿Cuánto?**, *how much?*, is used as a pronoun or adjective:

> ¿Cuánto es?
> *How much is it?*

> ¿Cuántos libros compró usted?
> *How many books did you buy?*

(f) **¿Por qué?**, *why?* (*for what reason?*):

> ¿Por qué está triste?
> *Why is he sad?*

The expected answer is preceded by **porque**:

> Porque su madre está enferma.
> *Because his mother is ill.*

(g) **¿Para qué?**, *why?* (*for what purpose?*):

> ¿Para qué hace usted todos estos preparativos?
> *Why (for what purpose) are you making all these preparations?*

The expected answer is preceded by **para** or **para que** followed by the subjunctive:

> Para ir a los Estados Unidos.
> *To go to the United States.*

16 Negation

(a) When a negative word or phrase precedes the verb, **no** is not used in Spanish:

> Nunca leo libros.
> *I never read any books.*

> Nadie llegó.
> *No one arrived.*

> Tampoco vamos nosotros.
> *We are not going, either.*

> Ningún hombre civilizado hará eso.
> *No civilized man will do that.*

Nada estaba en orden.
There was nothing in order.

En la vida los he visto.
I have not seen them in my life.

Sin que habitante alguno lo supiera.
Without a single inhabitant knowing it.

Ni una gota tienen de nuestra sangre.
They do not have a single drop of our blood.

(b) When the verb is negative, **ni** is used instead of **o**; in that case most indefinite pronouns and adverbs become negative, too:

No vi marcharse ni a don Manuel ni a las señoras.
I did not see either don Manuel or the ladies leaving.

Era un perro feo que nadie había visto ni en la aldea ni en los alrededores.
It was an ugly dog which no one had seen before, either in the village or in the neighbourhood.

Ni Juan ni Carlos podrán venir nunca.
Neither John nor Charles will ever be able to come.

(c) **Ni** sometimes stands for **ni siquiera,** *not even*:

No viene ni Pedro.
Not even Peter is coming.

No quiere que salgamos ni por un momento.
He does not want us to go out even for a moment.

(d) **Nada** sometimes means 'not at all':

El juez tenía un rostro nada simpático.
The judge's face was not at all friendly.

No es nada bonita.
She is not pretty at all.

No me importa nada lo que piensas.
What you think does not matter to me at all.

(e) Sometimes **alguno(-a, -os, -as)** is preferred to **ninguno** for emphasis, in which case it follows the noun and has the force of a negative:

No tengo libro alguno.
I have not a single book.

No me gusta en forma alguna.
I do not like it in any shape (form).

(f) **No . . . más**, *no longer; no more*:

No beberá más vino.
He will not drink any more wine.

(g) After comparisons, **nadie** is used for 'anyone else':

Ganaba más que nadie.
He earned more than anyone else.

Ella toca el piano mejor que nadie.
She plays the piano better than anyone else.

(h) Some common expressions using negative forms:

de nada, *do not mention it*
más vale tarde que nunca, *better late than never*
nada más, *nothing else*
creo que no, *I think not*
no lo creo, *I do not think so*

17 Imperatives see also *18(a)*

The following points should be remembered:

(a) The subjunctive form of the verb is used in every imperative sentence, except the positive familiar commands (*tú* and *vosotros*):

First person plural, positive command: hablemos
First person plural, negative command: no hablemos

Polite positive command: hable usted, hablen ustedes
Polite negative command: no hable usted, no hablen ustedes

Familiar positive command: habla tú, hablad vosotros
Familiar negative command: no hables, no habléis

(b) The positive plural familiar command is formed by simply changing the **-r** of the infinitive ending into a **-d**:

hablar: hablad
hacer: haced
ir: id

This **-d** is omitted in the reflexive form:

levantad: levantaos
poned: poneos
introducid: introducíos

(Exception: id: idos)

(c) All object pronouns are enclitic in the positive imperatives.
Accents are needed to indicate the stress:

Démelo.
Give it to me.

Probémoslo.
Let us prove it.

Fíngete enfermo.
Pretend to be ill.

Díganoslo.
Tell it to us.

(d) In negative commands, object pronouns occupy their normal
position before the verb, and the verb is used in the subjunctive form:

No te finjas enfermo.
Don't pretend to be ill.

No nos lo digan.
Don't tell it to us.

No os vayáis nunca.
Never go away.

18 Subjunctive mood

(a) The subjunctive form of the verb is used in main clauses:

i. For all commands except in the positive familiar form (see
imperatives, *17*):

Que traigan al prisionero.
Bring the prisoner in.

ii. To express wishes, prayers, hopes:

Ojalá (from Arabic *wa-sǎ' Allah!*) que vengan pronto.
Let us hope they come soon.

¡Viva la República!
Long live the Republic!

– ¡Que tengas suerte en los exámenes!
'*I wish you good luck in your exams!*'

iii. To introduce polite requests:

Quisiera pedirle un favor.
I would like to ask you a favour.

iv. Frequently (though not always) after **acaso**, **quizá(s)**, **tal vez**, *perhaps*:

Acaso sea mejor que venga usted mañana.
Perhaps it would be better if you would come tomorrow.

But when referring to actions that have actually taken place, the indicative is often used:

Tal vez guardó la llave en el bolsillo.
Perhaps he kept the key in his pocket.

(b) The subjunctive mood is used in subordinate noun clauses depending on verbs expressing **wishes**, **requests**, **orders**, **advice**, **permission**, **prevention** and **opposition**, etc., except when both clauses have the same subject, in which case an infinitive is employed:

i. **Wishing**, *desear, necesitar, preferir, querer*:

Desean que alguien les escriba.
They want someone to write to them.

Mi primo necesitaba que (yo) fuese a verle.
My cousin wanted me to go and see him.

No quiero hablar más.
I do not want to speak any more.

ii. **Requesting**, *pedir, rogar, suplicar*:

Les pedí que vinieran.
I asked them to come.

Le rogaron que fuese a Madrid.
They requested him to go to Madrid.

iii. **Ordering** and **getting things done**, *decir, exigir, hacer, insistir en, mandar, ordenar*:

Dígales que salgan a la pizarra.
Tell them to come to the blackboard.

Haga que salgan todos.
Make them all go out.

iv. **Advising**, *aconsejar*, *proponer*, *recomendar*:

El empleado aconsejó a los niños que esperaran.
The clerk advised the children to wait.

El escritor propone que se traduzcan sus obras al inglés.
The writer suggests that his work should be translated into English.

v. **Permitting** and **approving**, *permitir*, *aprobar*, *consentir*, *dejar*:

Por favor, permitan ustedes que Pedro entre.
Please allow Peter to come in.

Consiento que lo hagas tú.
I consent to your doing it.

vi. **Preventing** and **opposing**, *impedir*, *evitar*, *oponerse*, *prohibir*:

Mi padre se oponía a que me marchara al extranjero.
My father was opposed to my going abroad.

El maestro ha prohibido que los chicos fumen.
The teacher has forbidden the boys to smoke.

(c) The subjunctive mood is used in subordinate clauses depending on verbs and phrases expressing **emotion**: anger, fear, joy, hope, pity, shame, sorrow, surprise, mistrust, etc., when the subject of the principal and the subordinate clause are not the same:

i. **Anger**, *indignar*, *irritar*, *molestar*:

Me indigno de que suceda algo que pudo evitarse.
I am annoyed that anything should happen which could have been avoided.

Lo que más le irrita es que hagan ruido.
What irritates him most is that they make a noise.

ii. **Fear**, *temer*, *tener miedo*:

Temían que la niña se cayera al pozo.
They feared that the little girl might fall into the well.

Los niños tienen miedo de que el perro les muerda.
The children are afraid the dog will bite them.

iii. **Joy**, *alegrar(se), gustar, estar alegre, estar contento*:

> Me alegro de que Juanito haya podido venir.
> *I am glad that Johnny was able to come.*

> Me gusta que estudien ustedes.
> *I am pleased you are studying.*

iv. **Hope**, *confiar, esperar*:

> Confiamos en que nos des buenas noticias.
> *We trust you will give us good news.*

> Esperan que sigamos sus consejos.
> *They hope we shall follow their advice.*

NOTE: For *esperar* meaning 'to wait', see *18(i)*.

v. **Pity** and **shame**, *sentir, sentir lástima, tener pena, dar vergüenza, avergonzarse*:

> Siento lástima que se encuentre usted tan débil.
> *It's a pity you feel so weak.*

> Le dio vergüenza de que su familia se portase mal.
> *He felt ashamed of his family's bad behaviour.*

vi. **Sorrow**, *doler, estar triste, lamentar, sentir*:

> Nos duele que se haya ido nuestro hermano.
> *We are sorry our brother has gone.*

> Lamentamos que esté usted enfermo.
> *We are sorry you are ill.*

vii. **Surprise**, *asombrar(se), extrañar(se), sorprender(se)*:

> No te sorprendas de que quieran vernos.
> *Don't be surprised that they want to see us.*

> Ella se extrañó de que nos riéramos.
> *She was astonished that we laughed.*

viii. **Suspicion**, *desconfiar, recelar, sospechar*:

> No creo que sea un hombre honrado.
> *I do not believe him to be an honest man.*

> Luis sospechaba que fuese yo el culpable.
> *Louis suspected that I was the culprit.*

(d) The subjunctive mood is used in subordinate clauses depending on verbs expressing **doubt** or **denial**, as well as verbs of **thinking**, used negatively or interrogatively, when the subjects of the clauses are different from each other:

i. **Doubt**, *dudar*:

Dudamos (de) que ellos tomen un taxi.
We doubt that they will take a taxi.

Dudo (de) que Pedro llegue mañana.
I doubt whether Peter will arrive tomorrow.

ii. **Denial**, *negar*:

Negué que ella lo supiera.
I denied that she knew it.

But in the negative the indicative is used as there is no longer doubt:

No negamos que es perezoso.
We do not deny he is lazy.

iii. **Thought**, *no creer, no estar seguro, no pensar, no suponer*:

No creo que puedas escribir un ensayo.
I do not believe you are able to write an essay.

¿Estamos seguros de que lo sepan?
Are we sure that they know it?

(e) The subjunctive mood is used in **temporal clauses** depending on conjunctions such as *antes* (*de*) *que, así que, cuando, después que, en cuanto* (*que*), *hasta que, luego que, mientras* (*que*), *tan pronto como*, when no definite fact is implied or when future possibility is referred to. *Antes de que* always governs the subjunctive:

Salió antes (de) que llegasen sus amigos.
He left before his friends arrived.

Iré a España cuando tenga bastante dinero.
I shall go to Spain when I have enough money.

NOTES:

i. The infinitive, governed by the corresponding preposition, is often used in the dependent clause when the subject of both verbs is the same:

Se lavaron las manos antes de comer.
They washed their hands before eating.

ii. *Al* followed by an infinitive may replace a clause beginning with *cuando*:

Al entrar se quitará la corbata.
When he comes in he will take off his tie.

(f) The subjunctive mood is used in adverbial clauses depending on the
following **conjunctions**:

  i. Those implying condition or supposition, except **si**, *if*, (see *18(k)*):

> a condición de que, *provided that*
> a menos que; a no ser que, *unless*
> como, *when it means 'if'*
> con tal que; siempre que, *provided that*
> dado que, *given (granted) that*
> en caso (de) que, *in case*
> supuesto que, *supposing that*

> Le invitaré, a condición de que se quede dos días.
> *I shall invite him, provided that he will stay two days.*

> Iré al pueblo, a no ser que llueva a cántaros.
> *I shall go to the village, unless it pours with rain.*

  ii. **Sin que**, *without*:

> Lo demás sucedió sin que ella se diese cuenta.
> *The rest happened without her realizing it.*

But when the subject is the same in both clauses, *sin* followed by
the infinitive is used:

> Ella había salido sin ser vista.
> *She had left without being seen.*

  iii. **A pesar de que**, *despite*; **aun cuando**, *even if*; **aunque**, *although*,
when no actual fact is stated:

> A pesar de que no sea inteligente, obtendrá el puesto.
> *Despite not being clever, he (she) will obtain the position.*

> Aunque griten nadie les oirá.
> *Although they may shout, no one will hear them.*

BUT

> A pesar de no ser inteligente (*fact*), ha obtenido el puesto.
> *Despite not being clever, he obtained the position.*

> Aunque gritaban (*fact*), nadie les oía.
> *Although they were shouting, no one heard them.*

  iv. **Conjunctions** such as *a fin de que, de manera que, de modo que, con
(el) objeto de (que), para que*, meaning 'in order that', 'so that', with

183

the sense not of result but of purpose, are followed by the verb in the subjunctive mood:

Le escribiré a fin de que nos veamos.
I shall write to him so that we may meet.

Colocó el cuadro de manera que se viese desde el estudio.
He placed the picture so that it could be seen from the study.

(g) The subjunctive mood is used in subordinate clauses depending on an **indefinite** or a **negative antecedent**.

i. Indefinite antecedents occur frequently in Spanish. Here are some examples in which a vague future possibility is implied:

Vamos a buscar un lugar que sea más tranquilo que éste.
We are going to look for a place (unknown) which may be more peaceful than this one.

Estudie usted lo que más le guste.
Study what you (may) like best.

Ella bailará con los que la inviten.
She will dance with those who (may) invite her.

The two following examples illustrate how a change from unknown or imprecise to known and precise takes place when substituting the indicative for the subjunctive:

Necesitamos una joven que *sepa* escribir bien a máquina.
We need a girl (unknown, any) who can type well.

Haré lo que me *digan*.
I shall do what(ever) (unspecified) they tell me.

BUT

Conocemos a una joven que *sabe* escribir bien a máquina.
We know a (specific) girl (notice the personal a) who can type well.

Haré lo que me han dicho.
I shall do what they have told me to do (specifically).

ii. Negative antecedents:

Aquí no hay nadie que se llame Jorge.
There is no one here called George.

No hay quien me lo explique.
There is no one who can explain it to me.

(h) In clauses depending on several **indefinite expressions**, when the main verb does not refer to what happened in the past. This resembles (g) above, but is a little more complicated, and studying some of the following models may be useful:

Por ricos que sean, no pueden comprar esto.
However rich they may be, they cannot buy this.

Quienquiera que lo haya hecho será castigado.
Whoever may have done it will be punished.

Les daremos cualquier cosa que pidan.
We shall give them whatever they ask for.

Dondequiera que se hayan escondido les encontraré.
Wherever they may have hidden, I shall find them.

BUT in the past tense:

Por más empeño que ponía, me era imposible descifrarlos.
However much trouble I took, it was impossible for me to decipher them.

(i) The subjunctive mood is used in noun clauses depending on **impersonal verbs** which do not indicate certainty:

Importa que escribas a tu mujer.
It is important for you to write to your wife.

Basta que vengan tres testigos.
It is sufficient that three witnesses come.

Resultaría mejor que ella estudiara bien su papel.
It would be better for her to study her part well.

Puede (ser) que lleguen mañana.
They may come tomorrow.

Hay duda de que puedan comprar una casa.
It is doubtful whether they can buy a house.

Es probable que hayan leído la noticia.
It is probable they have read the news.

Es hora de que salga el tren.
It is time the train left.

Será mejor que vengan todos mañana.
It will be better for all to come tomorrow.

When a definite fact is stated, however, the indicative mood is used in Spanish:

> Es cierto que trabajas.
> *It is certain that you are working.*

> Es seguro que vendrán pronto.
> *It is certain they will come soon.*

NOTES:
1. When these impersonal locutions are negative or interrogative, doubt is implied and consequently the subjunctive mood is required:

> No es verdad que pronuncien mal.
> *It is not true that they pronounce badly.*

> ¿Es cierto que hayan llegado?
> *Is it certain they have arrived?*

2. The same principle applies to sentences using such expressions as *es dudoso* (*hay duda*) which calls for the subjunctive and *no es dudoso* (*no hay duda*) which requires the indicative.

> Hay duda de que haga buen tiempo esta tarde.
> *There is doubt that it will be fine (weather) this afternoon.*

> No hay duda que hará buen tiempo esta tarde.
> *There is no doubt that it will be fine (weather) this afternoon.*

(j) The subjunctive mood is found in noun clauses used as the subject of a sentence when they are introduced by, **el (hecho de) que, eso que**, *etc.*, meaning 'the fact that', 'this fact, etc.':

> El hacerlo me gusta; el (hecho de) que ellos lo hagan me gusta más aún.
> *I like doing it; the fact that they do it pleases me even more.*

> El oírlo les satisface; el (hecho de) que yo lo oiga les satisface más.
> *They get satisfaction from hearing it; the fact that I hear it gives them more satisfaction.*

(k) The subjunctive mood is also used:

i. In conditional clauses using **si**, *if*, **como si**, *as if* and **como** (meaning 'if'), in the past tense, when the fulfilment of the condition is impossible or improbable or when there are, at any rate, doubts as to whether the action will be fulfilled:

> Si tuviese mucho dinero, compraría otro coche.
> *If I had plenty of money (but I have not), I would buy another car.*

> Gasta dinero como si tuviese millones.
> *He spends money as if he had millions (but he has not).*

ii. When the fulfilment is a distinct possibility, the indicative is required:

Dijeron que si trabajaban era sólo para gastar el dinero en vino.
They said that if they worked it was only to be able to spend the money on wine.

Si ha escrito la carta la ha echado al correo.
If he has written the letter he has posted it.

iii. In **si** clauses where the verb is in the present tense, only the indicative is used:

Si va a Madrid verá a mis amigos.
If he goes to Madrid he will see my friends.

Llévame si vas a Madrid.
Take me if you go to Madrid.

iv. **Si ... o no**, *whether ... or not* is usually followed by the future or the conditional and not by the subjunctive:

No sé si iré a los Estados Unidos o no.
I do not know whether I shall go to the United States or not.

No sabía si ellas irían de compras o no.
I did not know whether they would go shopping or not.

19 *Ser* and *estar*

(a) SER, *to be*, is used:

i. With predicate nouns:

¿Qué es esto?
What is this?

Es un sombrero.
It is a hat.

Soy profesor.
I am a teacher.

Somos estudiantes.
We are students.

ii. With adjectives and adjectival phrases to express permanent or inherent qualities, character, origin, possession, etc.:

El libro es interesante.
The book is interesting.

Las casas son sólidas.
The houses are solid.

La mesa era de madera.
The table was made of wood.

Este hombre es de Colombia.
This man comes from Colombia.

El clima es bueno.
The climate is good.

Las ropas son de Juan; no son mías.
The clothes are John's; they are not mine.

iii. With past participles to form the passive voice:

Ha sido declarado el estado de sitio.
A state of siege has been declared.

La puerta fue cerrada por el viento.
The door was closed by the wind.

iv. In impersonal sentences introducing a clause:

Es necesario trabajar.
It is necessary to work.

Era cierto que llegarían tarde.
It was certain they would arrive late.

v. In many everyday expressions:

¿Qué hora es? *What is the time?*
¿No es verdad? *Is it not so?*
Era tarde. *It was late*
ser aficionado a, *to be keen on*
ser desgraciado, *to be unhappy* (*by nature*)
ser feliz, *to be happy* (*by nature*)
ser joven, *to be young*
ser médico, *to be a doctor*
ser rico (pobre), *to be wealthy* (*poor*)
ser viejo, *to be old*

(b) ESTAR, *to be*, is used:

i. To express position:

> ¿Dónde están los periódicos?
> *Where are the newspapers?*

> Estoy en casa.
> *I am at home.*

> El museo está en Sevilla.
> *The museum is in Seville.*

ii. With adjectives, to express transitory qualities, moods, state of health, etc.:

> La mesa está limpia.
> *The table is clean.*

> El café está frío.
> *The coffee is cold.*

> Mis hijos estaban enfermos.
> *My children were unwell.*

> Estoy triste, pero ellos están contentos.
> *I feel sad but they are happy.*

> La casa estaba vacía.
> *The house was empty.*

iii. With past participles to express a state resulting from a previous action:

> Estábamos muy cansados.
> *We were very tired.*

> La puerta está abierta.
> *The door is open.*

iv. With the *gerundio* to form continuous tenses:

> Estábamos cantando el himno nacional.
> *We were singing the national anthem.*

> Están leyendo y escribiendo.
> *They are reading and writing.*

v. In many everyday expressions, such as:

¿A cuántos estamos?
What is today's date?

Estamos a quince de enero.
It is the fifteenth of January.

¿Está el señor Rodríguez?
Is Mr. Rodríguez at home?

estar contento, *to be satisfied*
estar de buen (mal) humor, *to be in a good (bad) mood*
estar de compras, *to be shopping*
estar de maestro (de médico), *to be working as a teacher (doctor)*
estar de servicio, *to be on duty*
estar de vacaciones, *to be on holiday*
estar de vuelta, *to be back*
estar listo para salir, *to be ready to go out*
estar loco de furia, *to be mad with rage*
estar para (a punto de) comer, *to be about to eat (on the point of eating)*
estar sano y salvo, *to be safe and sound*
estar seguro, *to be sure*
estar triste, *to be sad (temporarily)*

20 Some idiomatic Spanish verbs

(a) CABER

This very irregular verb means literally 'to be able to be contained in' and translates the English verbs 'to hold' and 'to fit in'. Its use can best be learned from examples:

En la famosa plaza de toros de Madrid caben 23.000 personas.
The famous Madrid bullring holds 23,000 people.
(*Lit.: 23,000 people can be contained in the Madrid bullring.*)

Nunca hubieran pensado que en una maleta tan pequeña cupieran tantas cosas.
They would never have thought that such a small suitcase could hold so many things.

No cabían en sí de alegría.
They could not control themselves for joy.

No cabe duda que vendrán mañana.
There is no doubt that they will come tomorrow.
(*Lit.: There is no room for doubt that they will come tomorrow.*)

(b) DAR

In addition to its first meaning of 'to give', **dar** is used in many expressions where a different verb would be required in English:

dar a conocer algo, *to make s.t. known*
dar a entender algo, *to suggest s.t.*
dar de comer a alguien, *to feed (give food to) s.o.*
dar la espalda a alguien, *to turn one's back on s.o.*
dar las doce, *to strike twelve o'clock*
dar gusto a alguien, *to please s.o.*
dar las gracias, *to thank s.o.*
dar la vuelta, *to turn back*
dar la vuelta al mundo, *to go round the world*
dar los buenos días (noches, etc.), *to say good morning (night, etc.)*
dar oídos a algo (alguien), *to pay attention to s.t. (s.o.)*
dar palmadas, *to clap*
dar pena a alguien de algo, *to feel sorry for s.t.*
dar puntapiés (golpes, patadas, etc.), *to kick*
dar que pensar, *to give food for thought*
dar saltos, *to jump*
darse cuenta de algo, *to realize s.t.*
darse con alguien, *to run into s.o.*
darse por vencido, *to consider oneself defeated*
darse prisa, *to hurry*
dar un paseo, *to take a walk*

La casa da al parque.
The house looks out onto the park.

Le dio un golpe en la cabeza.
He struck him on the head.

Lo misma me da.
It is all the same to me.

Se le da mucho (bien) la música.
He is very good at music.

No me da la gana.
I don't fancy doing it.

(c) DEBER

Like most verbs of mood, **deber** presents English students with the problem of choosing the correct tense. One way to tackle this is to use the auxiliary *deber* in the tense one would have used with the main verb:

> *I must work (I work =* trabajo), debo trabajar.
> *He said I must work (he said I was working).*
> Dijo que yo debía trabajar (dijo que trabajaba).
>
> *There must be 2,000 pesetas in the wallet (there are).*
> Debe haber 2.000 pesetas en la cartera (hay).
>
> *They had to sing at 6 p.m. (they sang at 6 p.m.).*
> Debieron cantar a las 6 (cantaron a las 6).
>
> *They had to sing every day (they used to sing every day).*
> Debían cantar todos los días (cantaban todos los días).
>
> *They must have arrived (they have arrived).*
> { Han debido llegar (han llegado).
> { Deben haber llegado.
>
> *He ought to sing (he would sing).*
> { Debería cantar (cantaría).
> { Debiera cantar.
>
> *He ought to have sung (he would have sung).*
> { Debería haber cantado (habría cantado).
> { Habría debido cantar.

NOTE: *Deber de* implies supposition:
Debió de trabajar ayer.
He must have worked yesterday.

(d) DEJAR

i. **dejar la casa, la ciudad,** etc., *to leave the house, city, etc.*:

> Dejó la oficina a las dos.
> *He left the office at two o'clock.*

ii. **dejar olvidado algo,** *to leave s.t. behind; to forget s.t.*:

> Dejamos olvidado el llavín.
> *We left the key behind.*

iii. **dejar atrás a alguien,** *to overtake s.o.*:

> El muchacho dejó atrás al viejo.
> *The boy overtook the old man.*

iv. **dejar hacer algo a alguien,** *to let s.o. do s.t.*:

El profesor nos dejó tocar el piano.
The teacher let us play the piano.

v. **dejar caer algo,** *to let fall (drop) s.t.*:

Dejé caer el lápiz.
I dropped the pencil.

vi. **dejar de hacer algo,** *to stop doing s.t.*:

La niña dejó de llorar.
The girl stopped crying.

vii. **dejar (or no dejar) de hacer algo,** *to fail (or not to fail) to do s.t.*:

No dejaán de llegar pronto.
They are bound to arrive soon.

(e) DOLER

i. **Doler,** *to ache, to feel pain, to grieve*:

Me duelen los dientes.
I have toothache.

Me duele mucho la conducta de ellos.
Their conduct grieves me.

ii. **Dolerse,** *to repent, to complain, to sympathize*:

Se duele de sus pecados.
He repents of his sins.

iii. **El dolor,** *pain, grief, sorrow, repentance*:

Tiene un fuerte dolor de cabeza.
He has a bad headache.

Les causó dolor separarse de sus padres.
They were grieved to leave their parents.

(f) ECHAR

i. **Echar a** (with certain verbs of motion only), *to begin to*:

Echar a andar.
To start walking.

ii. **Echar al buzón (correo) una carta,** *to post a letter*:

> Voy a echar esta carta al correo.
> *I am going to post this letter.*

iii. **Echar de menos algo (a alguien),** *to miss s.t. (s.o.)*:

> Echan de menos a sus amigos.
> *They miss their friends.*

iv. **Echar de ver algo,** *to catch sight of s.t.*:

> Al salir echó de ver la llave en la puerta.
> *When leaving he caught sight of the key in the door.*

(g) FALTAR

i. **Faltar** means 'to be missing', 'to be absent', 'to lack', 'to fail':

> Al niño le faltaban varios dientes.
> *The boy had several teeth missing.*

> Veo que falta el portero.
> *I see that the goalkeeper is missing.*

> Me faltan las fuerzas.
> *I lack the strength.*

NOTE: *No faltaba más sino que . . .* is the equivalent of 'the last straw'. In answer to a request, however, ¡*No faltaba más!* is the Spanish for 'but of course!'

ii. **Faltar poco para que** (plus subjunctive), *to be a close thing*:

> Faltaba poco para que Cortés se pusiera en camino.
> *Cortés was almost ready to set out.*

iii. **Hacer falta,** *to need; to be missing to s.o.; to be necessary*:

> Justina me hace falta aquí.
> *I need (miss) Justina here.*
> (Lit.: *Justina is missing here to me.*)

iv. **Hace falta que** (followed by subjunctive), *it is necessary that*:

> Hace falta que usted salga en seguida.
> *It is necessary for you to leave at once.*

v. **Una falta,** *an error; fault; absence; lack*:

> Ha hecho muchas faltas.
> *He has made many errors.*

vi. Idiomatic (a) **sin falta,** *without fail*; (b) **a falta de,** *for lack of.*

(h) GUSTAR

i. When **gustar** means **dar gusto,** lit: *to give pleasure*

    a it is used frequently in the third person;
    b it rarely has a personal subject;
    c the subject is usually a singular or plural thing or idea;
    d the subject often follows the verb:

Le gustan las manzanas.
He likes apples.
(Lit.: *apples give pleasure to him.*)

Les gusta conducir.
They like driving.
(Lit.: *driving gives them pleasure.*)

Me gustaba que ella fuese a Londres.
I liked her to go to London.

ii. **Gustar de hacer algo,** *to enjoy doing s.t.*:

Gustamos de leer.
We enjoy reading.

iii. **Gustar algo,** *to taste s.t.*:

Gustamos el vino que nos ofrecieron.
We tasted the wine which was offered to us.

iv. The noun **gusto** is used in certain idiomatic expressions:

tener gusto en, *to have pleasure in*
tener buen (mal) gusto, *to have good (bad) taste*
tanto (mucho) gusto, *delighted (in introductions)*

(i) HABER

i. When used with a past participle to form compound tenses, the past participle does not agree and should not be separated from **haber** by any other word:

¿Han llegado los hombres?
Have the men arrived?

ii. **Haber** is the infinitive of **hay,** there is (are); **había,** there was (were), etc.:

Ha habido muchos accidentes en esta calle.
There have been many accidents in this street.

Después hubo una explosión.
Then there was an explosion.

Habrá mucha gente en el teatro.
There will be many people in the theatre.

iii. **Hay que** followed by the infinitive is an impersonal verb indicating necessity:

Hay que salir pronto.
It is necessary to leave soon.

Habría que telefonear.
It would be necessary to telephone.

iv. **Haber de** followed by the infinitive has less force than *deber* or *tener que*:

Ha de comer con amigos.
He is to dine with friends.

Habremos de volver a casa.
We shall have to return home.

(j) HACER

The uses of **hacer** are inexhaustible. Here are a few important examples:

i. ¿Qué tiempo hace?
What is the weather like?

Hacía calor (frío).
It was hot (cold).

ii. ¿Cuánto tiempo hace que está usted aquí?
How long have you been here?

Hacía dos horas que estaban en casa.
They had been at home for two hours.

NOTE: Only the present *hace*, used for something still going on, and the imperfect, *hacía* used for something that was going on, can be employed in this situation.

iii. Salieron para Lima hace un año.
They left for Lima a year ago.

iv. Hágame el favor de cerrar la puerta.
Please close the door.

v. hacer una pregunta a alguien, *to ask* (see *21*) *s.o. a question.*

vi. hacer caso a alguien, *to pay heed to s.o.*

vii. hacer un regalo a alguien, *to give a present to s.o.*

viii. hacer fuego contra alguien, *to fire against s.o.*

ix. hacer daño a alguien, *to hurt (to damage) s.o.*

x. hacer señas a alguien, *to signal, (make signs) to s.o.*

xi. hacer cola, *to queue, stand in line.*

xii. hacer alto, *to halt (stop).*

xiii. hacer las maletas, *to pack the suitcases.*

xiv. hacer lo posible, *to do one's best.*

xv. hacerse, *to become* (see *21*).

xvi. hacer un papel, *to play a part (in a play, etc.).*

xvii. hacer el muerto, *to float*; hacerse el muerto, *to pretend to be dead.*

xviii. hacerse atrás (a un lado), *to stand back (aside).*

xvix. hacer frente a alguien, *to face s.o.*

xx. hacer las paces, *to end a quarrel, to make it up.*

xxi. hacer hacer algo, *to get s.t. done*; *to cause s.t. to be done*:

> Pedro se lo hizo repetir dos veces.
> *Peter had it repeated twice to himself.*

xxii. No hacer más que (sino) followed by the infinitive is equivalent to 'only' plus verb:

> No hacía más que (sino) cazar tigres, leones y otras fieras.
> *He only hunted tigers, lions and other wild animals*
> *(He did nothing except hunt)*

(k) OLVIDAR

Notice the various constructions of this verb:

i. Like many Spanish verbs it is used transitively or reflexively with practically no difference in meaning:

a Olvidar algo, olvidar hacer algo:

> Olvidó el incidente, la fecha.
> *He forgot the incident, the date.*
>
> Olvidaron abrir las ventanas.
> *They forgot to open the windows.*

b **Olvidarse de algo, olvidarse de hacer algo:**

Se olvidó de la carta.
He forgot the letter.

Se olvidaron de cerrar las ventanas.
They forgot to close the windows.

ii. **Olvidársele algo a alguien**

Here it is used in a fully reflexive form, the subject being the thing or things (or persons) which are forgotten:

Se me olvidaron (*plural verb*) los guantes (*plural subject*).
I forgot my gloves.

Se les olvidó la fecha.
They forgot the date.

iii. **Dejar olvidado algo,** *to leave s.t. behind*:

Dejó olvidada la maleta.
He left his suitcase behind.
(*He forgot to take his suitcase.*)

(l) PASAR

Pasar has many meanings, some obvious, others idiomatic. Here are several examples:

i. To hand s.t. to s.o.:

Haga el favor de pasarme el pan.
Please pass me the bread.

ii. To cross:

Tiene que pasar el puente (el río).
He has to pass over the bridge (the river).

iii. To overtake:

El automóvil quiere pasar a la bicicleta.
The motor-car wants to pass the bicycle.

iv. To spend time:

Pasó el tiempo leyendo.
He passed the time reading.

v. To happen:

> ¿Qué pasó anoche?
> *What happened last night?*

vi. To transfer:

> Pasaron el enfermo a otro hospital.
> *They passed the patient on to another hospital.*

vii. To call (the roll):

> Pasaban (la) lista a las ocho.
> *They used to call the roll at eight o'clock.*

viii. To pass by (without stopping or without taking notice):

> Nos pasarán de largo.
> *They will pass us by.*

ix. To have an enjoyable (a bad) time:

> Pasamos bien (mal) la tarde.
> *We had a good (bad) time in the afternoon.*

x. To be bad:

> El pescado estaba pasado.
> *The fish was bad.*

xi. To overlook, to pass over s.t.:

> Lo pasó por alto.
> *He passed it over.*

xii. To do without:

> No podemos pasar(nos) sin ella.
> *We cannot do without her.*

xiii. Some common idiomatic phrases:

> Pase usted, *come in (go in)*
> ¿Qué pasa?, *what's the matter?*
> Pase lo que pase, *come what may (whatever happens).*

(m) PODER

Poder, like *deber*, is a verb of mood and it is not always easy for English-speaking students to select the correct equivalent tense. The method suggested for *deber* (see *20(c)*) may also be applied here. Another way of tackling the problem is to convert 'can' and 'could', 'may' and 'might' into the verb 'to be able' before translation:

Present

The house (can) is able to be seen from here.

Se puede ver (se ve) la casa desde aquí.

Imperfect

He said they (could) were able to hear the noise of the sea as they moved forward.

Dijo que podían oír (oían) el ruido del mar mientras avanzaban.

Pretérito

The robber escaped and was able to cross (crossed) the river.

El ladrón (se) escapó y pudo cruzar (cruzó) el río.

Conditional

If we had enough money, we (could) would be able to buy a plane.

Si tuviéramos bastante dinero podríamos comprar (compraríamos) un avión.

Future

We (can) shall be able to swim tomorrow in the swimming pool.

Podremos nadar (nadaremos) mañana en la piscina.

Indirect statement

I said we (could) would be able to swim tomorrow in the swimming pool.

Dije que podríamos nadar (nadaríamos) mañana en la piscina.

NOTES:
1. With verbs of perception, *poder* is not needed in Spanish:

    se podía ver = se veía
    se podía oír = se oía

2. *Puede ser*, maybe, perhaps

3. ¿Se puede entrar?
   May I come in?

(n) PONER (see *to put, 21(g)*)

    poner en libertad, *to set free*
    poner huevos, *to lay eggs*
    poner la mesa, *to lay the table*
    ponerse a jugar, *to begin to play*
    ponerse de acuerdo, *to come to an agreement*
    ponerse en camino, *to begin a journey; to set off on the road*
    ponerse en marcha, *to set off; to start*
    ponerse en pie, *to stand up*
    ponerse los zapatos, *(el sombrero, etc.), to put on one's shoes (hat, etc.)*
    ponerse pálido, *to turn pale*
    el sol se pone (sale), *the sun sets (rises)*
    la puesta (salida) del sol, *sunset (sunrise)*

(o) QUERER

i. **Querer** is often used as a verb of mood. Refer to **deber** and the following examples for help on tense selection:

Present
I want to sell the car (I sell the car).
Quiero vender (vendo) el coche.

Past
I said I wanted to sell (I was selling) the car.
Dije que quería vender (vendía) el coche.

Future
I shall want to sell (I shall sell) the car.
Querré vender (venderé) el coche.

Conditional
I said I would like to sell (I would sell) the car.
Dije que querría vender (vendería) el coche.

ii. **Querer a alguien,** *to love s.o.*:

No me quiere.
He (she) does not love me.

iii. **Querer,** *to want* (see *18(b)*):

¿Qué quiere usted?
What do you want?

iv. **Desear(le) algo a alguien,** *to wish s.o. s.t.*:

Le deseamos buenas vacaciones.
We wish you good holidays.

v. **Querer decir,** *to mean*:

¿Qué quiere decir la palabra "castizo"?
What does the word castizo *mean?*

(p) SERVIR

Servir is a very common verb with many idiomatic constructions:

i. **Servir,** *to serve (food, etc.), to be in service*:

Sirva café, por favor. *Serve coffee, please.*
Sirvió a la patria. *He served his country.*

ii. **Servir de,** *to serve as*:

> Sirvió de embajador.
> *He served as ambassador.*

iii. **Servir para algo,** *to be useful for some purpose*:

> ¿Para qué sirve este cuchillo?
> *What is this knife used for?*
>
> Esto no sirve para nada.
> *This is no use at all.*

iv. **Servirse de algo (de alguien)** *to make use of s.t. (s.o.)*:

> Se sirven del disco para aprender español.
> *They use the record to learn Spanish.*

v. Some useful phrases:

> Sírvase sentarse.
> *Please sit down.*
>
> Sírvase usted.
> *Help yourself.*
>
> para servir a usted, *at your service*
> estar de servicio, *to be on duty*

(q) SOLER

Soler means 'to be in the habit of' and is used only in the present and imperfect tenses:

> Suelen acostarse a las once y media.
> *They go to bed at eleven thirty (usually).*
>
> Aquél era el método que solía emplear.
> *That was the method he used to employ.*

(r) TENER

> tener aspecto de, *to look like*
> tener cuidado, *to be careful; to take care*
> tener en cuenta, *to bear in mind; to take into account*
> tener éxito, *to be successful*
> tener frío (calor), *to be (feel) cold (hot)*
> tener ganas de hacer algo, *to want very much to do s.t.*
> tener (la) intención, *to intend*

tener la suerte de hacer algo, *to have the luck of doing s.t.*
tener miedo de algo (de alguien), *to be afraid of s.t. (s.o.)*
tener (la) ocasión, *to have the chance, opportunity*
tener presente, *to bear in mind*
tener prisa, *to be in a hurry*
tener que hacer algo, *to have to do s.t.*
tener razón, *to be right*
no tener razón, *to be wrong*
tener sed (hambre), *to be thirsty (hungry)*
tener sueño (vergüenza), *to be sleepy (ashamed)*

Aquí tiene usted el billete.
Here is the ticket.

¿Qué tiene usted?
What's the matter with you?

Mi hermana tiene los ojos verdes.
My sister's eyes are green. (My sister has green eyes.)

¿Qué edad tiene usted?
How old are you?

Tengo dieciséis años.
I am 16 years old.

La habitación tiene 20 pies de largo.
The room is 20 feet long.

(s) VALER

i. **Valer,** *to be worth*:

> ¿Cuánto vale el reloj?
> *How much is the watch (worth)?*

> No vale nada.
> *It's worth nothing.*

ii. **Valer la pena,** *to be worth-while*:

> No vale la pena viajar a Murcia.
> *It is not worth-while travelling to Murcia.*

iii. **Valerse de algo,** *to use s.t.*:

> Se valió de mi erudición.
> *He used my knowledge.*

iv. **¡Válgame Dios!,** *Good heavens!*

21 English verbs difficult to translate

(a) TO ASK

i. **Pedir algo,** *to ask for s.t.* (*order s.t. in a restaurant,* etc.):

Pidieron café.
They ordered coffee.

ii. **Pedir algo a alguien,** *to ask s.o. for s.t.:*

Piden limosna a los transeúntes.
They ask passers-by for alms.

iii. **Pedir a alguien que** (followed by a subjunctive), *to ask s.o. to do s.t.:*

Les pedimos que se callen.
We ask them to stop talking (to be quiet).

iv. **Preguntar,** *to ask* (*inquire,* etc.):

– ¿A cuántos estamos? – preguntó el profesor.
'What's the date?' the teacher asked.

v. **Hacer preguntas,** *to ask questions* (see *hacer, 20(j)*).

vi. **Preguntar por alguien,** *to ask after s.o.:*

Preguntamos por la mujer del médico.
We asked after the doctor's wife.

vii. **Rogar,** *to request*:

Rogó que fuéramos a verle.
He requested us to go and see him.

(b) TO BECOME

i. 'To become' followed by an adjective:

a **crecer, hacerse, salir** followed by an adjective imply gradual change:

El trabajo se ha hecho más difícil.
The work has become more difficult.

b **estar** and **ir** followed by *gerundio* and adjective are used for gradual, continuous change:

Se está volviendo cada día más agresivo.
He is becoming more aggressive every day.

NOTE: The adjective is incorporated in verbs such as *anochecer,* to become dark, *amanecer,* to become light, *enriquecerse,* to become rich, *acalorarse,* to become warm, *encanecer,* to become (grow) grey, *enrojecer,* to turn red:

El cielo está enrojeciendo.
The sky is becoming red.

c **ponerse** or **volverse** followed by an adjective imply definite, often sudden, change of state, health, temper, etc.:

> Se han puesto tristes.
> *They have become sad.*

d **quedar(se)** followed by an adjective implies involuntary or accidental change:

> Quedó estupefacto de la noticia.
> *The news left him stupefied.*

> Ha quedado cojo del accidente.
> *He became lame from the accident.*

ii. 'To become' followed by a noun:

a **llegar a ser,** *to become*:

> Llegó a ser alcalde del pueblo.
> *He became mayor of the town.*

b **hacerse** plus noun (personal effort, usually) **convertirse en** plus noun:

> Se ha hecho director (abogado).
> *He has become manager (lawyer).*

> Se ha convertido en profesor.
> *He has become a teacher.*

c **ser de** plus noun (or pronoun) is used to translate *'What's become of?'*:

> ¿Qué ha sido de su amigo Juan?
> *What's become of your friend John?*

iii. To become s.o., (to suit s.o.):

> El traje negro no le sienta bien.
> *The black dress does not suit her.*

(c) TO GET

> *to get angry*, enfadarse
> *to get down*, bajar
> *to get dressed*, vestirse
> *to get drunk*, emborracharse
> *to get lost*, perderse
> *to get into the house*, entrar en la casa

to get into the train (*bus*, etc.), subir al tren (autobús, etc.)
to get out, salir
to get ready, prepararse
to get rich, enriquecerse
to get someone to do s.t., mandar hacer algo a alguien
to get something, conseguir algo
to get something done, mandar hacer algo
to get to know someone, conocer a alguien
to get to the station, llegar a la estación
to get up, levantarse
to get up early, madrugar

(d) TO GO

to go abroad, ir al extranjero
to go away, irse, salir, marcharse
to go back home, volver (regresar) a casa
to go by air (*bicycle*, *car*, *train*, etc.); ir en avión (bicicleta, automóvil, tren, etc.)
to go downstairs, bajar la escalera
to go into the cinema, entrar al cine
to go out into the street, salir a la calle
to go mad, volverse loco, enloquecer
to go on foot (*on horseback*, etc.), ir a pie (a caballo, etc.)
to go on holiday, ir de vacaciones
to go on reading, seguir leyendo
to go out of the room, salir de la sala
to go pale, ponerse pálido, palidecer
to go shopping, ir de compras
to go to bed, ir a la cama, acostarse
to go to his help, ir en su ayuda
to go to sleep, dormirse
to go to Spain, ir a España
to go up in the lift, subir en el ascensor
to go with s.o., acompañar a (ir con) alguien

(e) TO KNOW

i. To have knowledge of, **saber**:

¿Sabe usted la lección?
Do you know your lesson?

ii. To know how to do s.t., **saber hacer algo**:

> ¿Sabe usted nadar?
> *Can you swim?*

iii. To be acquainted with, to meet, **conocer**:

> No conozco a la mujer de mi amigo.
> *I am not acquainted with my friend's wife.*

> Me conocieron en Madrid.
> *They met me (got to know) me in Madrid.*

(f) TO PLAY

i. *To play (games)*, **jugar**:

> jugar (a) un juego, *to play a game*
> jugar al fútbol, *to play football*
> jugar limpio, *to play fair*

ii. *To play (instruments)*, **tocar**:

> tocar un instrumento, *to play an instrument*
> Toca el piano.
> *He is playing the piano.*

iii. *To play (a part)*, **desempeñar**:

> hacer· (representar, desempeñar) un papel, *to play a part*
> La actriz desempeñaba un papel muy largo.
> *The actress played a very long part.*

iv. *To play (a trick, a joke) on s.o.*, **gastar (una broma)**:

> Le gastaron una broma bastante graciosa.
> *They played a rather amusing joke on him.*

(g) TO PUT

i. *To put s.t. somewhere*, **poner**:

> Puso el diario en la mesa.
> *He put the newspaper on the table.*

ii. *To put s.t. in*, **meter**:

> Metió el lápiz en la caja.
> *He put the pencil in the box.*

iii. *To put on a garment*, **ponerse una prenda**:

> Se ponen los guantes.
> *They put their gloves on.*

iv. *To put on (out) lights, switches, etc.*, **encender (apagar):**

> Enciendo la televisión.
> *I put on (switch on) the TV.*

> Apagó la luz.
> *He put out (switched off) the light.*

(h) TO SUCCEED

i. *To succeed in doing s.t.*, **lograr (conseguir) hacer algo:**

> El capitán logró escaparse.
> *The captain succeeded in escaping.*

ii. *To be successful*, **tener éxito:**

> El plan no tuvo éxito.
> *The plan was not successful.*

iii. *To succeed (follow) in office, etc.*, **suceder:**

> ¿Quién sucedió al Presidente Johnson?
> *Who succeeded President Johnson?*

(i) TO TAKE

Here are just a few of the many possible constructions:

i. *To take (consume)*, **tomar algo:**

> Toman el café por la mañana.
> *They take coffee in the morning.*

ii. *To take a bus (a train, etc.)*, **tomar un autobús (un tren, etc.):**

> Tomaré un taxi.
> *I'll take a taxi.*

iii. *To take (carry)*, **llevar:**

> El muchacho llevará la maleta.
> *The boy will carry the suitcase.*

iv. *To take (carry) away*, **llevarse, robar:**

> La muchacha se llevó el paraguas.
> *The girl took the umbrella with her.*

v. To take off:

> a clothes, etc., **quitarse:**

>> Quítese el sombrero y siéntese.
>> *Take off your hat and sit down.*

b aeroplane, **despegar**:

¿A qué hora despegará el avión para Bilbao?
What time will the 'plane take off for Bilbao?

vi. *To take up,* **coger, tomar**:

Cogió (tomó) al niño en brazos.
She took the child in her arms.

vii. *To take (pick) up,* **recoger**:

Recogió el libro que estaba en el suelo.
He picked up the book from the floor.

viii. *To take s.t. out of s.t.,* **sacar algo de algo**:

Sacan la fruta de la cesta.
They take the fruit out of the basket.

ix. *To take photographs,* **sacar (tomar) fotografías**:

Sacaron muchas fotografías de la familia.
They took a lot of photographs of the family.

x. *To take s.t. down,* **bajar, descolgar**:

Vamos a descolgar el cuadro.
We are going to take down the picture.

xi. *To take advantage of s.t.,* **aprovechar algo** or **aprovecharse de algo**:

Nos aprovechamos del buen tiempo.
We took advantage of the fine weather.

xii. *To take after (resemble) s.o.* **parecerse a alguien**:

Me parezco a mi hermana.
I take after my sister.

xiii. *To take into account,* **tener en cuenta**:

Hay que tener en cuenta la fuerza del viento.
The strength of the wind has to be taken into account.

xiv. *To take time to do s.t.* **tardar (mucho, poco) en hacer algo**:

Tardó dos días en leer el libro.
He took two days to read the book.

(j) TO THINK

i. *To think of s.t. (s.o.),* **pensar en algo (en alguien)**:

Pensamos en las próximas vacaciones.
We think of the forthcoming holidays.

ii. *To think of* (*intend to*), **pensar hacer algo**:

Piensa escribir muchos libros.
He is thinking of writing many books.

iii. *To think* (*imagine*) *doing s.t.*, **creer hacer algo**:

Creen hablar bien el español.
They think they speak Spanish well.

iv. Some useful **idioms**:

a Creo que sí (no).
I think so (*not*).

b Me parece que están sonriendo.
I think (*it seems to me*) *that they are smiling.*

c ¿Qué le parece la fotografía?
What do you think of the photograph?

(k) TO TURN

To turn on (*off*) *the light*, encender (apagar) la luz
To turn on (*off*) *the tap*, abrir (cerrar) el grifo
To turn pale (*red, etc.*) (see 'to become', 21(b))
To turn round, volverse
To turn the corner, doblar (dar vuelta a) la esquina
To turn to the right, torcer a la derecha
To turn up (*appear*), aparecer; acudir
It is my turn to speak.
Me toca a mí hablar.

22 Exclamations

¡Adelante!, *Come in!*
¡Adiós!, *Good-bye!*
¡Alto!, *Stop!*
¡Anda!, *Go on!*
¡Caramba!, *Heavens!* (*surprise*)
¡Cuidado!, *Mind!*
¡De nada!, *Don't mention it!*
¡Dios mío!, '*Pon my word!, Goodness me!*
¡Estupendo!, *Marvellous!*
¡Jesús!, *Good heavens!*
¡Maldito sea!, *Curse it!*

¡No hay de qué!, *Don't mention it!*
¡Oiga!, *I say!*, *Listen!*
¡Ojo!, *Look out!*
¡Olé!, *Bravo!*
¡Oye!, *Listen!*, *I say!*
¡Pase!, *Come in!*
¡Perdón!, *Pardon!*
¡Por Dios!, *For Heaven's sake!*
¡Por supuesto!, *Of course!*
¡Puf!, *Phew!*
¡Qué disparate!, *What nonsense!*, *How absurd!*
¡Qué lástima (pena)!, *What a pity!*, *How sad!*
¡Qué lío!, *What a mess!*
¡Qué rico!, *How delicious!*
¿Quién sabe?, *Who knows?*, *Heaven only knows!*
¡Riquísimo!, *Simply delicious!*, *How scrumptious!*
¡Uf!, *Ugh!*
¡Ya lo creo!, *Of course!*
¡Ya voy!, *I'm coming!*

23 Diminutives, Augmentatives and Pejoratives

These derivatives are extremely difficult to use correctly, particularly for students in whose mother-tongue no equivalent use is made of the varied shades of meaning that the different endings provide. Only Spanish-speaking people seem to know what is right and what is wrong – but even they use different endings from time to time, or even from region to region. However, careful study brings out some sort of pattern:

(a) Diminutives, for instance, appear more frequently than augmentatives and pejoratives. The endings **-ito, -ita, -itos, -itas**, and **-illo, -illa, -illos, -illas** usually have the meaning of 'nice', 'dear', 'little', whereas **-ín, -ina, -ines, -inas** often have no sentimental value and refer to small size only:

Espérame, Luisito.
Wait for me, Luis dear.
¡Qué manita tienes! *What a nice little hand you have!*

211

el llavín, *small key*
el maletín, *small suitcase*

(b) Augmentatives are also rather widely used. The main endings
-ón, -ona, -ones, -onas imply large size; other augmentative endings
are: **-ote, -ota, -otes, -otas**:

el nubarrón, *big black cloud*
el niñote, *big clumsy boy*

(c) Pejoratives contain, in varying degrees, an element of scorn or
contempt. The endings **-ucho, -ucha, -uchos, -uchas**, and **-aco,
-aca, -acos, -acas** are the most representative of this group:

la casucha, *hovel*
el cafetucho, *miserable-looking café*

The English-speaking student should refrain from using these endings
until he is confident and conversant with their meaning. It does not
follow, however, that to study them is superfluous, since he will find that
they crop up quite frequently both in speech and in the written word.

Here are lists of words which are fairly common. The student should
enlarge the list as he comes across other words.

Word	Diminutive	Augmentative	Pejorative
el árbol, *tree*	arbolito	arbolazo	arbolejo
el brazo, *arm*	bracito	brazote	brazucho
el burro, *donkey*	borriquillo	borricote	borricucho
la casa, *house*	casita	casona	casucha
el café, *coffee-shop*	cafetín	cafetazo	cafetucho
el chico, *boy*	chiquitín	chicarrón	chiquitajo
la cruz, *cross*	crucecilla	cruzota	cruceja
el frasco, *flask*	frasquito	frascote	frascucho
la hermana, *sister*	hermanita	hermanota	hermanuca
el hilo, *thread*	hilito	hilazo	hilucho
la llave, *key*	llavín	llavota	llavucha
la maleta, *suitcase*	maletín	maletón	maletuca
la moza, *girl*	mocita	mocetona	mozuela
el mozo, *boy*	mocito	mocetón	mozuelo
la mujer, *woman*	mujercita	mujerona	mujerzuela

el niño, *child*	niñito	niñote	niñato
la nube, *cloud*	nubecilla	nubarrón	nubeja
los ojos, *eyes*	ojillos	ojazos	ojuelos
el pájaro, *bird*	pajarito	pajarote	pajarraco
la palabra, *word*	palabrita	palabrota	palabreja
pálido, *pale*	palidito	palidote	paliducho
el papel, *paper*	papelito	papelote	papelucho
el pueblo, *village*	pueblecito	poblachón	pueblucho
la risa, *laughter*	risita	risotada	risuca
el santo, *saint*	santito	santón	santuco
el zapato, *shoe*	zapatito	zapatón	zapatajo

24 Idioms

a

abajo, *downstairs*
¿a cuántos estamos?, *what is the date today?*
al fin y al cabo, *when all is said and done*
al pie de la letra, *word by word, literally*
a mi parecer, *in my opinion*
andar de boca en boca, *to be the talk of the town*
andarse por las ramas, *to beat about the bush*
aquí hay gato encerrado, *there is s.t. fishy here*
arriba, *upstairs*
así es la vida, *that's life*

b

bajo la lluvia, *in the rain*
boca abajo, *face downwards*
boca arriba, *on one's back, upwards*

c

cada vez más, *more and more*
calle abajo (arriba), *down (up) the street*
cantar victoria, *to boast of a triumph*
castizo, *typical; pure-blooded; classical*
charlar por los codos, *to chatter, be a chatterbox*
como de costumbre, *as usual*
como el que más, *like the best*
concurrido, *busy (crowded with people)*
costar trabajo, *to be difficult (painful) to carry out*

creo que sí (no), *I (do not) think so*
cual, *like*
¡cuál no sería su asombro!, *how surprised he was!*
cueste lo que cueste, *cost what it may; at all costs*
¡cuidado!, *be careful*
¡cuidado con . . .!, *beware of . . .!*

ch

charlar por los codos, *to chatter; to be a chatterbox*

d

dar (see *20(b)*)
de al lado, *adjacent, next*
deber (see *20(c)*)
dejar (see *20(d)*)
desempeñar un papel, *to play a part*
dormir a pierna suelta, *to sleep soundly*

e

echar (see *20(f)*)
encogerse de hombros, *to shrug one's shoulders*
en un abrir y cerrar de ojos, *in the twinkling of an eye*
excusado es decir, *needless to say*

g

gana(s) (see *20r*)
ganarse la vida, *to earn one's living*
gastar una broma a alguien, *to play a trick on s.o.* (see *21f*)
gustar (see *20(h)*)

h

hacer (see *20(j)*)
hasta el final de . . , *to the end of . . .*
hasta mañana, *see you tomorrow*
de hito en hito, *staringly*

i

importa, *it is important* (no importa, *it does not matter*)
ir (see *21(d)*)

j

jugar(le) una mala partida a alguien, *to play a nasty trick on s.o.*

l

lavarse las manos de algo, *to wash one's hands of s.t.*
lo mismo me da, *it's all the same to me*
lo mismo que, *just like*

ll

llamar al pan pan y al vino vino, *to call a spade a spade*
llevar la batuta, *to call the tune*
llevarse bien (mal), *to get on well (badly)*
llevarse chasco, *to be disappointed*
llevarse la palma, *to carry off the prize*
llover a cántaros, *to rain cats and dogs*

m

más bein, *rather*
meter, (see *21* (g))
meter gato por liebre, *to swindle, to cheat*
mirar de reojo, *to look out of the corner of one's eye*
mirar de soslayo, *to look askance*
mirar de través, *to look askance*

n

nada más me faltaba eso, *that's the last straw*
no poder con alguien, *unable to control s.o.*
no poder tragar a alguien, *unable to stomach s.o.*

o

ordinario, *ordinary (everyday)*

p

pasar de largo, *to pass by*
pasar las de Caín, *to go through a bad patch*
pasarlo bien (mal), *to have a good (bad) time*
pedir prestado algo a alguien, *to borrow s.t. from s.o.*
pegar a alguien, *to strike s.o.*
pegar algo a . . ., *to stick s.t. on to . . .*
pegar fuego, *to set fire*
pegarle a uno un resfriado, *to give s.o. one's cold*
pese a (a pesar de), *in spite of*
poder (see *20(m)*)
poner (see *20(n)*)

q

quedar en hacer algo, *to agree to do s.t.*
quedarse con algo, *to take (buy, steal, etc.) s.t.*
¿qué le parece?, *what do you think of . . .?*
¿qué mosca te ha picado?, *what makes you angry?*
¿qué quiere decir?, *what does it mean?*
quitarse los guantes, *to remove one's gloves*

r

reír a carcajadas, *to roar with laughter*
reírse de alguien, *to laugh at s.o.; to mock s.o.*

s

saber (see *21(e)*)
saber(se) algo al dedillo, *to know s.t. thoroughly*
se armó la de San Quintín, *there was an awful row*
sí, es posible, *yes, it is possible*
si mal no recuerdo, *if I remember correctly*

t

tarde o temprano, *sooner or later*
tener (see *20(r)*)
tocarle a alguien la vez, *to be s.o.'s turn*
tocarle a uno en suerte, *to be favoured by chance*
tocar en lo vivo, *to touch a tender spot*
tocar un instrumento, *to play a musical instrument*
tomar algo a pecho, *to take s.t. to heart*
tomarle el pelo a alguien, *to pull s.o.'s leg*
tomar por el medio del bosque, *to go through the middle of the wood*
tratarse de, *to be a question of*
trato hecho, *it's a deal*

u

un día sí y otro no, *every other day*
un no sé qué indefinible, *s.t. hard to define*

v

venga lo que venga, *come what may*
viento en popa, *sailing before the wind (with good luck)*
vivito y coleando, *alive and kicking*
volver a hacer algo, *to do s.t. again*
volver en sí, *to regain consciousness*

25 Some misleading similarities

A number of Spanish words should be regarded as false friends: their similarity with English is more apparent than real and the meaning might be quite different. Here follows a selection:

abrasar, *to burn*
abrazar, *to embrace*

actual, *present* (never *actual*)
actualmente, *at the present time, now*
en la actualidad, *at the present time*

el conductor, *driver*
el director de orquesta, *conductor*
el cobrador, *bus conductor*

la confección, *clothes-making*
la confitería, *confectionery*

el conferenciante, *lecturer*
el lector, *reader*
la lectura, *reading*

el corresponsal, *correspondent (letter-writer; journalist)*

crear, *to create*
creer, *to believe; to think*
criar, *to breed*
gritar, *to shout*

el cuento, *story*
la cuenta, *account (financial)*

el dato, *date (information)*
los datos, *data*
el dátil, *date (fruit)*
la cita, *date (appointment)*
la fecha, *date (time)*
el hecho, *fact*

la decepción, *disappointment*
el engaño, *deception*

la desgracia, *misfortune*
desgraciadamente, *unfortunately*
desgraciado, *unfortunate*
la deshonra, *disgrace*

la deuda, *debt*
el deudo, *relative*
dudar, *to hesitate; to doubt*
vacilar, *to hesitate*

embarazada, *pregnant*
turbado, *embarrassed*

el éxito, *success*
tener éxito, *to be successful*
la salida, *exit*
suceder, *to happen; to succeed*
el suceso, *event*

expresar, *to express*
exprimir, *to squeeze out*

los familiares, *relatives*
los parientes, *relatives*
los padres, *parents (father and mother); priests*

la fruta, *fruit (collective)*
el fruto, *fruit (individual); profit, result*

el forastero, *stranger*
el desconocido, *unknown person*
el extranjero, *foreigner*

la herida, *injury*
el daño, *damage*
la injuria, *insult*

ignorar, *to be ignorant of s.t.*
no hacer caso de algo, *to ignore s.t.*

intentar hacer algo, *to try to do s.t.*
tener intención de hacer algo, *to intend to do s.t.*

el jubilado, *pensioner*
el júbilo, *joy*

largo, *long (not large)*

los naturales, *natives*
la naturaleza, *nature*

otro cualquiera, *anybody else*

particular, *private*

el partido, *game (football, rugby, tennis, etc.); political party*
la partida, *game (cards, chess); departure*

la pila eléctrica, *electric battery*
la pila, *holy water-basin; wash-basin*
el nombre de pila, *Christian name*

presentar, *to introduce (socially)*
introducir, *to insert; to admit*

pretender hacer algo, *to try to do s.t.*
el pretendiente, *suitor*
el pretendiente al trono, *pretender to the throne*
fingir hacer algo, *to pretend to do s.t.*

real, *royal; real; 25 cents*
realizar algo, *to achieve s.t.; to realize (assets)*
realmente, *really; actually*

reflejar, *to reflect (lights)*
reflexionar, *to ponder*

el representante, *representative*
representar una obra, *to stage a play*

restar, *to subtract*
sumar, *to add up*

sencillo, *easy; plain; frank*
sensible, *sensitive; noticeable*
simple, *silly*
la simpleza, *foolishness*
sensato, *sensible; prudent*

la sopa, *soup*
el jabón, *soap*

el súbdito, *subject (of a country)*
el sujeto, *topic; subject (grammar)*
el individuo, *person (sometimes used pejoratively)*
el tema, *theme; subject (study)*
la asignatura, *subject (curriculum)*
el asunto, *matter; affair*

últimamente, *recently; lately; finally*
por último, *lastly; at last*

varios, *several*
distintos, *various*

el vasco, *Basque (noun)*
el vascuence, *Basque language*

26 Pitfalls in spelling and accents

(a) Except for **cc**, **ll**, **nn**, **rr** there are no double consonants in Spanish, and the counterpart of a double-consonant English word has usually a single consonant in Spanish: *abadía* (abbey), *adición* (addition), *ofensa* (offence), *bagaje* (baggage), *sumario* (summary), *oponer* (oppose), *asesinar* (assassinate), *atender* (attend). But notice: *acceso* (access), *rollo* (roll), *innovación* (innovation) and *errar* (err).

The following notes, if consulted, should help students to avoid some of the most frequent pitfalls in spelling:

The English ending **-tion** is spelt **-ción** in Spanish:
nación, *la nación*

The English **mm** becomes **nm** in Spanish:

  commotion, *la conmoción*

The equivalent of the English **-ty** is **-dad** or **-tad** in Spanish:

  ability, *la habilidad*
  majesty, *la majestad*

The English **ph** is always **f**:

  photographer, *el fotógrafo*

The **th** of many English words becomes **t** in their Spanish equivalents:

  cathedral, *la catedral*

The English **-que, -qua** has often its Spanish counterpart in **-cue, -ca**
or **-cua**:

  frequent, *frecuente*
  quality, *la calidad, la cualidad*
  quarter, *cuarto*

The English vowel **y** frequently becomes **i**:

  bicycle, *la bicicleta*
  mystery, *el misterio*

(b) The following is a list of Spanish words very similar in meaning to
their English counterparts but differing in spelling:

a

  acelerar, *to accelerate*
  la actitud, *attitude*
  el acueducto, *aqueduct*
  el almirante, *admiral*
  la amenaza, *menace*
  la ansiedad, *anxiety*
  la aprensión, *apprehension*
  la asimilación, *assimilation*
  atacar, *to attack*
  el ataque, *attack*
  atribuir, *to attribute*
  la ausencia, *absence*
  la aventura, *adventure*

b

  la biblia, *bible*
  la botella, *bottle*

c

la cantidad, *quantity*
el carácter, *character*
los caracteres, *characters*
católico, *catholic*
celoso, *jealous*
cero, *zero*
la ciencia, *science*
el científico, *scientist*
el cilindro, *cylinder*
la comprensión, *comprehension*
la conciencia, *conscience*
conectar, *to connect*
confortar, *to comfort*
consagrado, *consecrated*
cristal, *crystal*

d

el descendiente, *descendant*

e

el enemigo, *enemy*
el entusiasmo, *enthusiasm*
escuálido, *squalid, thin*
el escultor, *sculptor*
el estrecho, *strait*
exagerar, *to exaggerate*
excelente, *excellent*

f

la farsa, *farce*
fragante, *fragrant*
la frecuencia, *frequency*

g

el gabinete, *cabinet*
el gigante, *giant*
el guardarropa, *wardrobe*

h

el héroe, *hero*
la heroicidad, *heroism*
la heroína, *heroine* or *heroin*
el himno, *hymn*
el huracán, *hurricane*

i

incomprensible, *incomprehensible*
inimaginable, *unimaginable*
inmediatamente, *immediately*
inmenso, *immense*
el ínterin, *interim*
invencible, *invicible*

j

el jacinto, *hyacinth*
la jerarquía, *hierarchy*
la jeringa, *syringe*
el juez, *judge*

l

leal, *loyal*
la lealtad, *loyalty*
lírico, *lyrical*
el lirismo, *lyricism*

m

manejable, *manageable*
el misterio, *mystery*
la mostaza, *mustard*

n

el navegante, *navigator*
navegar, *to navigate*
la necesidad, *necessity*

o

la objeción, *objection*
la ocasión, *occasion*
ocurrir, *to occur*

el oficial, *officer, official*
oportuno, *opportune*
opuesto, *opposite*
la orquesta, *orchestra*

p

el perfil, *profile*
perjudicar, *to prejudice*
el perjuicio, *prejudice*
la posesión, *possession*

q

el queso, *cheese*
la quilla, *keel*
la química, *chemistry*

r

la rebelión, *rebellion*
reemplazar, *to replace*
regocijar(se), *to rejoice*
el relicario, *reliquary*
la reliquia, *relic*
respetable, *respectable*
el respeto, *respect*
la responsabilidad, *responsibility*
el resultado, *result*
la riqueza, *richness*
rítmico, *rhythmical*
el ritmo, *rhythm*

s

sagrado, *sacred*
la silueta, *silhouette*
el símbolo, *symbol*
el sistema, *system*
sombrío, *sombre, shady*
sorprender, *to surprise*
la sorpresa, *surprise*
sospechoso, *suspicious*

t

el té, *tea*
el teatro, *theatre*
  templado, *temperate, tepid*
el tesoro, *treasure*
  tremendo, *tremendous*
el triunfo, *triumph*
el trofeo, *trophy*

u

  ubicuo, *ubiquitous*

v

el vagón, *wagon*
la vanagloria, *vainglory*
el ventrílocuo, *ventriloquist*
el virrey, *viceroy*

y

el yate, *yacht*
la yuxtaposición, *juxtaposition*

z

el zafiro, *sapphire*
la zona, *zone*

(c) ACCENTS

There is a growing tendency to ignore the use of accents, not only by students but also by Spaniards themselves when writing letters and, more and more, in print on capital letters. It should be remembered that accents have several important uses: (a) to determine stress; (b) to distinguish the meaning of words with identical spellings; and (c) to indicate the interrogative. Here are some examples:

i. él habló, *he spoke*   yo hablo, *I speak*
  el carácter, *character*   los caracteres, *characters*
  el resumen, *résumé*   los resúmenes, *résumés*

ii. mi; tu, *my; thy*   mí; tú, *me; thou*
   si, *if*   sí, *yes; self*
   te, *thee*   el té, *tea*
   de, *of; from*   dé, *give*
   se, *oneself*   sé, *I know*
   mas, *but*   más, *more*
   porque, *because*   ¿por qué?, *why?*
        el porqué, *reason why*
   el, *the*   él, *he; him*
   aun, *even*   aún, *still*
   solo, *alone*   sólo, *only*

iii. como, *as*   ¿cómo?, *how?*
   que, *which; that*   ¿qué?, *which?; what?*
   cuando, *when*   ¿cuándo?, *when?*

NOTE: The accent is used not only on explicit questions but also on words implying a question put to others or to oneself:

No sabemos cuántos vendrán.
We do not know how many will come.

Me pregunto cuándo y cómo nos veremos.
I wonder when and how we shall meet.

226

Appendices A—E

Appendix A

Numerals

1	uno, a	41	cuarenta y uno
2	dos	42	cuarenta y dos
3	tres	50	cincuenta
4	cuatro	60	sesenta
5	cinco	70	setenta
6	seis	80	ochenta
7	siete	90	noventa
8	ocho	100	cien(to)
9	nueve	101	ciento uno
10	diez	102	ciento dos
11	once	110	ciento diez
12	doce	120	ciento veinte
13	trece	200	doscientos
14	catorce	300	trescientos
15	quince	400	cuatrocientos
16	dieciséis or diez y seis	500	quinientos
17	diecisiete or diez y siete	600	seiscientos
18	dieciocho or diez y ocho	700	setecientos
19	diecinueve or diez y nueve	800	ochocientos
20	veinte	900	novecientos
21	veintiuno	1000	mil
22	veintidós	1001	mil uno
23	veintitrés	1010	mil diez
24	veinticuatro	1020	mil veinte
25	veinticinco	1021	mil veintiuno
26	veintiséis	1555	mil quinientos cincuenta y cinco
27	veintisiete		
28	veintiocho	2000	dos mil
29	veintinueve	3000	tres mil
30	treinta	100.000	cien mil
31	treinta y uno	200.000	doscientos mil
32	treinta y dos	1.000.000	un millón
40	cuarenta	2.000.000	dos millones

NOTE:

1. *Ciento* is shortened to **cien** before nouns, ordinary adjectives and **mil**; e.g. *cien casas, cien buenas casas, cien mil hombres.*

2. *Doscientos, trescientos*, etc., have a feminine form for use with feminine nouns; e.g. *trescientas páginas, quinientas ventanas.*

3. **Y** (or **i**) is used only in compound numerals between the tens and the units:

       e.g. 105   ciento cinco
             115   ciento quince
             118   ciento dieciocho (diez y ocho)
             121   ciento veintiuno
             137   ciento treinta y siete
             888   ochocientos ochenta y ocho

Appendix B
Punctuation vocabulary for dictation

The usual Spanish equivalents are:

	el dictado	*dictation*
.	(el) punto (final)	*full stop*
,	(la) coma	*comma*
;	(el) punto y coma	*semicolon*
:	(los) dos puntos	*colon*
. . .	(los) puntos suspensivos	*used instead of the English dash to show unfinished sentences*
..	(la) diéresis	*diaeresis*
-	(el) guión	*hyphen*
—	(la) raya	*dash (for introducing direct speech)*
" "	(las) comillas	*quotation marks*
( )	(el) paréntesis	*brackets, parenthesis*

Just as we have inverted quotation marks in English to show the beginning of a quotation so the Spaniards have inverted question and inverted exclamation marks:

¿	(la) apertura de interrogación	*open the question mark*
?	(el) cierre de interrogación	*close the question mark*

¡	(la) apertura de admiración	*open exclamation mark*
!	(el) cierre de admiración	*close exclamation mark*
	(el) párrafo	*paragraph*
	(el) nuevo párrafo	*fresh paragraph*
	(la) línea siguiente	*next line*
	(la) letra mayúscula	*capital letter*
	(la) letra minúscula	*small letter*
	subrayar algo	*to underline s.t.*

Appendix C

Table of spelling changes in verbs

Verbs ending in	change,	before:	Examples:
-car	c > qu	e	sacar, *to take out* / saqué, *I took out*
-gar	g > gu	e	llegar, *to arrive* / llegué, *I arrived*
-zar	z > c	e	empezar, *to begin* / empecé, *I began*
-guar	gu > gü	e	averiguar, *to verify* / averigüé, *I verified*
-cer, -cir (prec. by consonant)	c > z	a, o	vencer, *to conquer* / venzo, *I conquer*
-cer, -cir (prec. by vowel)	c > zc	a, o	conocer, *to know* / conozco, *I know* / conducir, *to drive* / conduzco, *I drive*
-ger, -gir	g > j	a, o	dirigir, *to direct* / dirijo, *I direct*
-guir	gu > g	a, o	seguir, *to follow* / sigo, *I follow*

Appendix D

List of countries[1] and adjectives of nationality

España	*Spain*	español	{ *Spanish* / *Spaniard*
Inglaterra	*England*	inglés	{ *English,* / *Englishman*
Escocia	*Scotland*	escocés	{ *Scottish,* / *Scot*
(*el* país de) Gales	*Wales*	galés	*Welsh* (*man*)
Gran Bretaña	*Great Britain*	británico	*British*
Irlanda	*Ireland*	irlandés	*Irish* (*man*)
(*el*) Portugal	*Portugal*	portugués	*Portuguese*
Francia	*France*	francés	*French* (*man*)
Italia	*Italy*	italiano	*Italian*
Alemania	*Germany*	alemán	*German*
Bélgica	*Belgium*	belga	*Belgian*
(*los*) Países Bajos	*Netherlands*	holandés	*Dutch* (*man*)
Dinamarca	*Denmark*	danés	*Danish, Dane*
Suecia	*Sweden*	sueco	*Swedish, Swede*
Noruega	*Norway*	noruego	*Norwegian*
Austria[2]	*Austria*	austríaco	*Austrian*
Rusia	*Russia*	ruso	*Russian*
Grecia	*Greece*	griego	*Greek*
Suiza	*Switzerland*	suizo	*Swiss*
Europa	*Europe*	europeo	*European*
(*los*) Estados Unidos EE.UU.	*United States* / *U.S.A.*	estadounidense	*North American*
Filipinas	*Philippines*	filipino	*Philippine*
(*el*) Canadá	*Canada*	canadiense	*Canadian*
(*el*) Méjico[3]	*Mexico*	mejicano[3]	*Mexican*
Costa Rica	*Costa Rica*	costarricense	*Costa Rican*
El Salvador	*Salvador*	salvadoreño	*Salvadorean*
Guatemala	*Guatemala*	guatemalteco	*Guatemalan*
Honduras	*Honduras*	hondureño	*Hondurean*
Nicaragua	*Nicaragua*	nicaragüense	*Nicaraguan*
(*el*) Panamá	*Panama*	panameño	*Panamanian*
Argentina	*Argentina*	argentino	*Argentine*
(*el*) Chile	*Chile*	chileno	*Chilean*

Colombia	*Colombia*	colombiano	*Colombian*
(*el*) Ecuador	*Ecuador*	ecuatoriano	*Ecuadorean*
(*el*) Paraguay	*Paraguay*	paraguayo	*Paraguayan*
(*el*) Perú	*Peru*	peruano	*Peruvian*
(*el*) Uruguay	*Uruguay*	uruguayo	*Uruguayan*
Venezuela	*Venezuela*	venezolano	*Venezuelan*
Australia	*Australia*	australiano	*Australian*
Nueva Zelanda	*New Zealand*	neozelandés	*New Zealand, New Zealander*
China	*China*	chino	*Chinese*
(*el*) Japón	*Japan*	japonés	*Japanese*
África[2]	*Africa*	africano	*African*
India	*India*	indio	*Indian*
Antillas	*West Indies*	antillano	*West Indian*
Jamaica	*Jamaica*	jamaicano	*Jamaican*
Cuba	*Cuba*	cubano	*Cuban*
Trinidad	*Trinidad*	trinitario	*Trinidadian*

[1] All have a feminine gender except those which are indicated to the contrary.
[2] Although feminine, *el* Austria and *el* África (see 2(b)).
[3] In Mexico these are written *México* and *mexicano*.

Appendix E

Verb Tables

Infinitive and Meaning	Gerundio and Past Participle	Present Indicative		Present Subjunctive and Polite Imperative		Familiar Imperative
Models Hablar, *to speak*	hablando hablado	hablo hablas habla	hablamos habláis hablan	hable hables hable	hablemos habléis hablen	habla hablad
Comer, *to eat*	comiendo comido	como comes come	comemos coméis comen	coma comas coma	comamos comáis coman	come comed
Vivir, *to live*	viviendo vivido	vivo vives vive	vivimos vivís viven	viva vivas viva	vivamos viváis vivan	vive vivid
Radical Changing Pensar, *to think*	pensando pensado	**pienso** **piensas** **piensa**	pensamos pensáis **piensan**	**piense** **pienses** **piense**	pensemos penséis **piensen**	**piensa** pensad
Volver, *to return*	volviendo **vuelto**	**vuelvo** **vuelves** **vuelve**	volvemos volvéis **vuelven**	**vuelva** **vuelvas** **vuelva**	volvamos volváis **vuelvan**	**vuelve** volved
Sentir, *to feel,* or *to be sorry*	**sintiendo** sentido	**siento** **sientes** **siente**	sentimos sentís **sienten**	**sienta** **sientas** **sienta**	**sintamos** **sintáis** **sientan**	**siente** sentid
Dormir, *to sleep*	**durmiendo** dormido	**duermo** **duerme** **duerme**	dormimos dormís **duermen**	**duerma** **duermas** **duerma**	**durmamos** **durmáis** **duerman**	**duerme** dormid
Pedir, *to ask for*	**pidiendo** pedido	**pido** **pides** **pide**	pedimos pedís **piden**	**pida** **pidas** **pida**	**pidamos** **pidáis** **pidan**	**pide** pedid
Irregular Andar, *to go, walk*	andando andado	ando andas anda	andamos andáis andan	ande andes ande	andemos andéis anden	anda andad
Caber *see p.* 231	cabiendo cabido	**quepo** cabes cabe	cabemos cabéis caben	**quepa** **quepas** **quepa**	**quepamos** **quepáis** **quepan**	cabe cabed
Conducir *to drive, lead*	conduciendo conducido	**conduzco** conduces conduce	conducimos **conducs** conducen	**conduzca** **conduzcas** **conduzca**	**conduzcamos** **conduzcáis** **conduzcan**	conduce conducid

The parts that are irregular are printed in bold type.

	Preterite or Past Historic	Past Subjunctive	Future Indicative	Imperfect
hablé	hablamos	hablara or	hablaré, etc.	hablaba, etc.
hablaste	hablasteis	hablase, etc.		
habló	hablaron			
comí	comimos	comiera or	comeré, etc.	comía, etc.
comiste	comisteis	comiese, etc.		
comió	comieron			
viví	vivimos	viviera or	viviré, etc.	vivía, etc.
viviste	vivisteis	viviese, etc.		
vivió	vivieron			
pensé	pensamos	pensara or	pensaré, etc.	pensaba, etc
pensaste	pensasteis	pensase, etc.		
pensó	pensaron			
volví	volvimos	volviera or	volveré, etc.	volvía, etc.
volviste	volvisteis	volviese, etc.		
volvió	volvieron			
sentí	sentimos	**sintiera** or	sentiré, etc.	sentía, etc.
sentiste	sentisteis	**sintiese**, etc.		
sintió	**sintieron**			
dormí	dormimos	**durmiera** or	dormiré, etc.	dormía, etc.
dormiste	dormisteis	**durmiese**, etc.		
durmió	**durmieron**			
pedí	pedimos	**pidiera** or	pediré, etc.	pedía, etc.
pediste	pedisteis	**pidiese**, etc.		
pidió	**pidieron**			
anduve	**anduvimos**	**anduviera** or	andaré, etc.	andaba, etc.
anduviste	**anduvisteis**	**anduviese**, etc.		
anduvo	**anduvieron**			
cupe	**cupimos**	**cupiera** or	**cabré**, etc.	cabía, etc.
cupiste	**cupisteis**	**cupiese**, etc.		
cupo	**cupieron**			
conduje	**condujimos**	**condujera** or	conduciré, etc.	conducía, etc.
condujiste	**condujisteis**	**condujese**, etc.		
condujo	**condujeron**			

Verb Tables (*continued*)

Infinitive and Meaning	Gerundio and Past Participle	Present Indicative		Present Subjunctive and Polite Imperative		Familiar Imperative
Dar, *to give*	dando dado	**doy** das da	damos dais dan	**dé** des **dé**	demos deis den	da dad
Decir, *to say, tell*	**diciendo** **dicho**	**digo** **dices** **dice**	decimos decís **dicen**	**diga** **digas** **diga**	**digamos** **digáis** **digan**	**di** decid
Estar, *to be*	estando estado	**estoy** estás está	estamos estáis están	esté estés esté	estemos estéis estén	está estad
Haber, *to have*	habiendo habido	**he** **has** **ha**	**hemos** habéis han	**haya** **hayas** **haya**	**hayamos** **hayáis** **hayan**	**he** habed
Hacer, *to do, make*	haciendo **hecho**	**hago** haces hace	hacemos hacéis hacen	**haga** **hagas** **haga**	**hagamos** **hagáis** **hagan**	**haz** haced
Ir, *to go*	**yendo** ido	**voy** vas va	**vamos** vais van	**vaya** **vayas** **vaya**	**vayamos** **vayáis** **vayan**	**ve** id
Oír, *to hear*	**oyendo** oído	**oigo** **oyes** **oye**	oímos oís **oyen**	**oiga** **oigas** **oiga**	**oigamos** **oigáis** **oigan**	**oye** oíd
Poder, *to be able*	**pudiendo** podido	**puedo** **puedes** **puede**	podemos podéis **pueden**	**pueda** **puedas** **pueda**	podamos podáis **puedan**	**puede** poded
Poner, *to put*	poniendo **puesto**	**pongo** pones pone	ponemos ponéis ponen	**ponga** **pongas** **ponga**	**pongamos** **pongáis** **pongan**	**pon** poned
Querer, *to wish, love*	queriendo querido	**quiero** **quieres** **quiere**	queremos queréis **quieren**	**quiera** **quieras** **quiera**	queramos queráis **quieran**	**quiere** quered
Saber, *to know*	sabiendo sabido	**sé** sabes sabe	sabemos sabéis saben	**sepa** **sepas** **sepa**	**sepamos** **sepáis** **sepan**	sabe sabed

The parts that are irregular are printed in bold type.

	Preterite or Past Historic	Past Subjunctive	Future Indicative	Imperfect
di diste dio	dimos disteis dieron	diera *or* diese, etc.	daré, etc.	daba, etc.
dije. dijiste dijo	dijimos dijisteis dijeron	dijera *or* dijese, etc.	diré, etc.	decía, etc
estuve estuviste estuvo	estuvimos estuvisteis estuvieron	estuviera *or* estuviese, etc.	estaré, etc.	estaba, etc.
hube hubiste hubo	hubimos hubisteis hubieron	hubiera *or* hubiese, etc.	habré, etc.	había, etc.
hice hiciste hizo	hicimos hicisteis hicieron	hiciera *or* hiciese, etc.	haré, etc.	hacía, etc.
fui fuiste fue	fuimos fuisteis fueron	fuera *or* fuese, etc.	iré, etc.	iba, etc.
oí oíste oyó	oímos oísteis oyeron	oyera *or* oyese, etc.	oiré, etc.	oía, etc.
pude pudiste pudo	pudimos pudisteis pudieron	pudiera *or* pudiese, etc.	podré, etc.	podía, etc.
puse pusiste puso	pusimos pusisteis pusieron	pusiera *or* pusiese, etc.	pondré, etc.	ponía, etc.
quise quisiste quiso	quisimos quisisteis quisieron	quisiera *or* quisiese, etc.	querré, etc.	quería, etc.
supe supiste supo	supimos supisteis supieron	supiera *or* supiese, etc.	sabré, etc.	sabía, etc.

235

Verb Tables (*continued*)

Infinitive and Meaning	Present and Past Participle	Present Indicative		Present Subjunctive and Polite Imperative		Familiar Imperative
Salir, *to go out*	saliendo salido	**salgo** sales sale	salimos salís salen	**salga** **salgas** **salga**	**salgamos** **salgáis** **salgan**	**sal** salid
Ser, *to be*	siendo sido	**soy** eres es	**somos** **sois** **son**	**sea** **seas** **sea**	**seamos** **seáis** **sean**	**sé** sed
Tener, *to have*	teniendo tenido	**tengo** **tienes** tiene	tenemos tenéis **tienen**	**tenga** **tengas** **tenga**	**tengamos** **tengáis** **tengan**	**ten** tened
Traer, *to bring*	**trayendo** **traído**	**traigo** traes trae	traemos traéis traen	**traiga** **traigas** **traiga**	**traigamos** **traigáis** **traigan**	trae traed
Valer, *to be worth*	valiendo valido	**valgo** vales vale	valemos valéis valen	**valga** **valgas** **valga**	**valgamos** **valgáis** **valgan**	**val(e)** valed
Venir, *to come*	**viniendo** venido	**vengo** **vienes** viene	venimos venís **vienen**	**venga** **vengas** **venga**	**vengamos** **vengáis** **vengan**	**ven** venid
Ver, *to see*	viendo **visto**	**veo** ves ve	vemos veis ven	**vea** **veas** **vea**	**veamos** **veáis** **vean**	ve ved

The parts that are irregular are printed in bold type.

	Preterite or Past Historic	Past Subjunctive	Future Indicative	Imperfect
salí saliste salió	salimos salisteis salieron	saliera *or* saliese, etc.	**saldré**, etc.	salía, etc.
fui fuiste fue	fuimos fuisteis fueron	fuera *or* fuese, etc.	seré, etc.	**era**, etc.
tuve tuviste tuvo	tuvimos tuvisteis tuvieron	tuviera *or* tuviese, etc.	**tendré**, etc.	tenía, etc.
traje trajiste trajo	trajimos trajisteis trajeron	trajera *or* trajese, etc.	traeré, etc.	traía, etc.
valí valiste valió	valimos valisteis valieron	valiera *or* valiese, etc.	**valdré**, etc.	valía, etc.
vine viniste vino	vinimos vinisteis vinieron	viniera *or* viniese, etc.	**vendré**, etc.	venía, etc.
vi viste vio	vimos visteis vieron	viera *or* viese, etc.	veré, etc.	**veía**, etc.

237

Vocabulary

Spanish–English

This vocabulary contains most of the Spanish words in the book which might not be known by the majority of 'O' Level students. However, words which are the same in both languages (e.g. *idea*) are excluded. The meanings given are not always the usual ones, but rather the meanings of the words in their particular context.

Radical-changing verbs are indicated in the usual way: (ue), (ie) (i), (i).

el **abanico**, fan
abarcar, to include; take in
las **abarcas**, sandals
abatido, mean; dejected
abatir, to knock down
abrazar, to embrace
el **abrigo**, overcoat
abuchear, to boo; hiss
el **abuelo**, grandfather
abundar, to abound; have in abundance
aburrido, boring
acabar, to terminate
acalambrado, stiff (with cramp)
acalorarse, to become excited
acaparar, to monopolize
acariciar, to caress, stroke
acarrear, to carry
acaso, perhaps
acceder, to accede
el **aceite**, oil
la **acera**, pavement, sidewalk
acertar (ie), to succeed; guess correctly
aclararse, to become clear
acometer, to attack
acomplejado, having a complex, mixed up
acordarse (ue), to remember
acostumbrar, to be accustomed
acre, sharp; acrid
acrecentar (ie), to increase
acudir, to go to; answer a summons to
achampanado, sparkling (like champagne)

adecuado, adequate
adelante, forward, ahead
el **ademán**, gesture, attitude
además, besides
adentrarse, to enter
adherir (ie) (i), to stick
adosado, with its back to; addorsed
adquirir, to acquire
adular, to flatter
advertir (ie) (i), to notice
el **afán**, eagerness
afanarse, to plod, peg away
afeitar, to shave
aferrarse, to grip
las **afueras**, outskirts
agachar(se), to bend
agarrar, to grasp
agasajado, regaled, welcomed
aglomerar, to collect, gather
agradecer, to be grateful
agregar, to add
agresor, of the assailant; aggressive
aguantar, to endure
aguardar, to wait
el **aguardiente**, brandy
el **águila** (*f*), eagle
la **aguja**, needle
ahitarse, to weary, get tired
ahogarse, to drown
ahormar, to break in (shoes); give shape to
ahorrar, to save
ahuyentar, to scare away
aislado, isolated

239

el **ajenjo**, absinth
ajeno, other people's
ajetrearse, to bustle about
ajironado, colour-patched
el **ala** (*f*), wing
alabarse, to boast
el **alambre**, wire
alargar, to lengthen, extend
el **alarido**, scream
el **alazán**, sorrel horse
el **alba** (*f*), dawn
la **albacea**, executor (of a will)
alborotado, impetuous; agitated
el **alboroto**, din, disturbance
el **alcalde**, mayor
alcanzar, to reach
la **alcantarilla**, drain, culvert
la **alcoba**, bedroom
alegre, happy
la **alegría**, happiness
alejarse, to move away
alemán, German
la **alfombra**, carpet
alfombrado, carpeted
la **algarabía**, gabble
la **alianza**, alliance
alineado, lined up
el **alivio**, comfort
el **alma** (*f*), soul
el **almacén**, department store
el **almirante**, admiral
el **almuerzo**, lunch
alojarse, to lodge
alquilar, to hire
alrededor de, around
altanero, high-flying
el **altavoz**, loudspeaker
el **altozano**, hill; height
la **altura**, height
aludir, to refer
alusivo, allusive
alzar(se), to rise, get up
allegar, to collect; bring together
amanecer, to dawn
amansar, to tame
amargo, bitter
ambos, both
la **amenaza**, threat
amenguar, to diminish
la **ametralladora**, machine-gun

la **amistad**, friendship
amoratado, purple
análogo, similar
ancho, broad
la **andanza**, wandering; excursion
angosto, narrow
el **ángulo**, angle
angustiado, anxious
el **anhelo**, yearning, desire
animar, to encourage
animarse, to pluck up courage
el **ánimo**, mind
anochecido, dark
ante, in the face (presence) of
la **antinomia**, antinomy; conflict
antojarse, to take a fancy
anunciar, to announce
añadir, to add
apacible, peaceful
apagar, to put out; extinguish
apalcuachar(in Mexico), to smash
apartar, to draw back
el **apellido**, surname
apenas, hardly
apeñuscado, clinging; grouped
together
el **aperador**, steward (of an estate)
apesadumbrar, to sadden; grieve
apetecer, to long for
el **ápice**, trifle
apilar, to pile up, heap
apiñado, crowded together
aplastar, to crush, squash
el **aplazamiento**, postponement
aplicado, industrious
el **aplomo**, assurance
el **apocado**, coward
apoderarse, to take possession
el **apodo**, nickname
apoyarse, to lean upon, rest
apretar, to squeeze, press
aprisa, quickly
apropiarse, to take possession
el **aprovechamiento**, utilization
aproximar(se), to approach
apurarse, to worry
las **arcadas**, retching; arcade(s)
el **arco**, arch
armar, to arm; break out
arquear, to arch

arrancar, to tear out (away)
arrastrar, to drag
arrebatar, to seize
el arrechucho, fit (of anger, etc.)
el arreglo, order, adjustment
arriba, up, upstairs
el arriero, muleteer; driver
arriesgar, to risk
arrimar(se), to lean against
arrojar, to throw
el arroyo, stream
el arroz, rice
el asco, disgust
el aseo, cleanliness; wash-room
asiduo, assiduous
el asiento, seat
el asistente, helper, attendant; someone present
asistir, to be present at; attend
asomarse, to lean out
asombroso, marvellous; astonishing
el asta (f), flagstaff
la astilla, splinter, chip of wood
el asunto, matter; business
asustar, to frighten
atar, to attach, fix
el atardecer, evening
atareado, busy
ateniense, Athenian
aterciopelado, velvety
atestado, stubborn; witnessed
atrapar, to catch
atreverse, to dare
atribulado, troubled; vexed
atropelladamente, hastily
aumentar, to increase
aunque, although
la ausencia, absence
avaricioso, avaricious, miserly
el ave (f), bird
avecindar, to admit as a citizen
avenirse, to conform
avergonzarse, to be ashamed
averiguar, to verify
avisar, to warn
ayudar, to help
el ayuno, fasting, fast
por azar, by chance
azarado, confused

el azote, whip, scourge
la azotea, flat roof
el azucarero, sugar-basin

el bailador, dancer
el bailarín, dancer
el baile, dance
la baja, setback; fall; casualty
bajar, to descend
bajo, short
la bala, bullet
balbuciente, stammering
el bálsamo, balm
bambolearse, to wobble
el banco, bench; bank
la bandera, flag
la banqueta, stool; (in Mexico) sidewalk
la barba, chin; beard
el barbero, barber
la barra, bar
la (el) barranca (-o), ravine
barrer, to sweep
la barriada, district
el barrio, district
el barro, mud; earthenware
bastar, to suffice
la basura, refuse, trash, rubbish
el batiente, doorpost
de belenes, in confusion
la belleza, beauty
benéfico, beneficent
berrear, to low, bleat
besar, to kiss
el bien, good
bien, well; -a-, certainly; no-, no sooner; o-, or else
el bienestar, well-being
el bigote, moustache
el biógrafo, biographer
bizquear, to squint
blando, soft
blanquear, to whiten
la boda, wedding
el boj, boxwood
la bola, ball, globe
el bolero, bolero (Andalusian dance)
el bolígrafo, ball-pointed pen
la bolsa, bag; -de la plaza, shopping bag

la **bombilla**, light bulb
la **bondad**, kindness
en **borbollas**, bubbling
borracho, drunk
la **bota**, boot
el **botones**, page(boy)
el **bragazas**, man who is easily led
la **brazada**, stroke (of swimmer)
el **brinco**, jump; caper
en **broma**, as a joke, jokingly
brotar, to gush, issue forth
la **bruja**, witch
la **bufanda**, scarf
el **bulto**, shape; bulk
bullir, to boil; give signs of existence
buscar, to look for

la **cabalgadura**, mount
el **caballero**, gentleman; -**andante**, knight-errant
el **cabello**, hair
caber, to hold (20a)
el **cabo**, end
la **cabra**, goat
la **cacerola**, saucepan
el **cacique**, chief
el **cadáver**, corpse
la **cadencia**, cadence, rhythm
caer, to fall
la **cafetera**, coffee-pot
la **caída**, fall
la **caja**, case, box, chest
el **cajón**, large box
la **calabaza**, pumpkin
el **calabozo**, cell, dungeon
calentar, to heat
la **calidad**, quality
calumnioso, slanderous
los **calzones**, breeches
callar, to be silent
el **callejón**, alley
la **cama**, bed
el **cambio**, change
la **camisa**, shirt
caminar, to travel (along)
la **caminata**, long walk
la **campana**, bell
el **campesino**, countryman
el **campo**, ground, field; country

la **canilla**, shinbone
el **cansancio**, weariness
la **cantidad**, quantity
la **capa**, cloak
el **capricho**, whim
la **cara**, face
el **caracol**, snail; **de-**, spiral
el **carácter**, character
el **carbón**, charcoal
la **carga**, loading
cargar, to load; charge
el **cargo**, charge; load
la **caricia**, caress
el **cariño**, affection, love
la **carne**, flesh
la **carrera**, career; race
el **carrete**, coil, reel, roll
la **carretera**, road
el **carro**, cart; (in L.Am.) car; wagon
la **cartera**, wallet, brief-case, satchel, handbag
el **cartón**, cardboard
la **casaca**, dress-coat
casarse, to marry
el **cascabel**, little bell
cascado, broken; effete
casi, almost
en **caso de**, in case of
la **casta**, caste; lineage
castaño, chestnut, brown
castigar, to punish
el **castigo**, punishment
el **castillo**, castle
la **casualidad**, chance
la **catadura**, aspect
el **catedrático**, professor
cavilar, to cavil; criticize
el **cazador**, hunter
cazar, to hunt
la **cecina**, salted meat
ceder, to yield; give way
cegado, blinded
cegador, blinding
la **ceguera**, blindness
el **cementerio**, cemetery
la **cena**, supper
el **centón**, patchwork quilt; — **de conocimientos**, widely based knowledge
ceñudo, frowning

el **cerebro**, brain
cerrado, compact; heavy
la **ciencia**, knowledge; science
el **cierre**, closing
la **cifra**, figure
cimbrarse, to shake; tremble
el **cine**, cinema
la **cinta**, ribbon
la **cintura**, belt; waist
el **círculo**, club; circle
el **cirujano**, surgeon
claro, clear, light; el —, clearing
clavar, to pierce
la **clientela**, clientele
el **cobrador**, conductor (bus); collector of money
cobrar, to collect
la **cocinera**, cook
el **cochero**, coachman
codiciar, to covet; envy
la **coladera**, colander
el **colega**, colleague
la **cólera**, anger
colgar (ue), to hang
la **colina**, hill
colmado, heaped up
colocación, job
colocar, to place
el **coloquio**, conversation
la **comedera**, market; food
la **comitiva**, suite; followers
la **comodidad**, comfort
cómodo, handy; comfortable
el **compadre**, pal; crony
el **compañero de armas**, comrade-in-arms
el **compás**, rhythm; step (military)
complejo, complex
componerse, to consist
comportarse, to behave
comprimir, to repress, restrain
la **compuerta**, sluice, lock
la **conciencia**, conscience, knowledge
el **concierto**, harmony; concert
concluir, to conclude
concurrido, crowded; busy
condenar, to condemn
confeccionar, to concoct
la **confianza**, trust

el **confinamiento**, confining; detention
confundir, to confuse
la **congoja**, anguish; distress
la **conjuración**, plot
el **conquistador**, conqueror
conseguir, (i) to obtain; succeed
el **consejo**, advice; counsel
consulta, consultation
contado, rare; infrequent
contar (ue), to relate, to count
contraer, to contact
contrariar, to annoy
la **contrariedad**, opposition; vexation
convecino, neighbour
convenir, to agree
la **copa**, glass
el **copo**, snow-flake
la **coraza**, armour-plating
el **corazón**, heart
la **corbata**, tie
el **corcovado**, humpbacked; humped
la **cordillera**, mountain range
el **cordonero (de jarcia)**, maker or seller (of rigging)
la **corneta**, bugle; cornet
en coro, together, in chorus
la **corona**, crown
el **coronamiento**, crowning; completion
la **coronilla**, top, crown
la **correría**, raid, incursion
el **corsario**, pirate
la **corte**, Court; Madrid
el **cortejo**, lover
el **cortijo**, estate
la **cortina**, curtain
el **coscorrón**, cuff, blow on the head with the knuckles
la **costa**, coast
la **costilla**, rib; money
la **coyuntura**, joint
crear, to create
crecer, to increase; grow
el **crepúsculo**, dusk
criar, to bring up
el **criollo**, Creole
la **cripta**, crypt

243

el **cristal,** glass
crujir, to crackle, creak
la **cruz,** cross
cruzar, to cross
cuadrado, square
cuajado, dumbfounded; immobile
cual, like
en **cuanto,** as soon as
el **cuartel,** barracks
los **cuartos,** money
el **cucurucho,** paper cornet
la **cuchara,** spoon
el **cuchillo,** knife
el **cuello,** neck; collar
la **cuenta,** account
el **cuerno,** horn
el **cuero,** leather
el **cuerpo,** body
la **cuesta,** slope, hill
el **cuidado,** care
cuidar, to look after
la **culebra,** snake
culpable, guilty
culpar, to blame
cumplir, to fulfil
la **cuneta,** ditch
el **curso,** course of study; term
la **cúspide,** summit, top

la **chaira,** steel (for sharpening)
chamuscar, to scorch
chapotear, to splash
el **charco,** puddle
la **chirimía,** flageolet
la **chispa,** spark
el **chorro,** gush, stream
chupetear, to suck

darse cuenta, (20b) to realize
dar oídos a, to listen to
débil, weak
decaer, to languish
la **decepción,** disappointment
decretar, to decree
dedicar, to dedicate; give pay
el **dedo,** finger
deglutir, to swallow

delgado, thin
los **demás,** the remainder
demasiado, too much
demoledor, destructive
demostrar (ue), to demonstrate
el **derecho,** right
derrumbado, bent down
desabrochado, undone
desalojar, to empty
el **desarrollo,** development
desasirse de, to break away from
desasosegado, disturbed
el **desasosiego,** restlessness
el **desayuno,** breakfast
la **desazón,** displeasure
descalzo, barefooted
el **descanso,** rest; landing
descargado, unloaded
el **descarrilamiento,** derailment
descifrar, to decipher
descollar (ue), to stand out
descomponerse, to go wrong
desconcertado, baffled
la **desconfianza,** mistrust
desconfiar de, to mistrust
desconocido, unknown
el **descubridor,** discoverer
desdeñar, to disdain, scorn
desechar, to reject
desenrollarse, to unroll
desensillar, to unsaddle
el **desfile,** march past; procession
desgarrar, to tear
por **desgracia,** unfortunately
desgraciado, unfortunate
desigual, unequal, uneven
desleal, disloyal
desmesurado, excessive
desnudo, naked
desollar (ue), to flay
desordenado, untidy, in disorder
desparramar, to scatter; cast
despegar, to detach; take off (plane); get out of
despeñar, to precipitate
despertar (ie), to awaken
desplazarse, to move about
destacable, prominent
el **desprecio,** scorn

desprevenido, unprepared
desteñido, faded
el detalle, detail
detenerse, to stop; pause
el deudo, relative
el diablo, devil
diáfano, transparent
el diario, daily newspaper
dibujar, to sketch, draw
la dicha, happiness
digno, worthy
el dineral, fortune
el dinero, money
dirigir, to direct, control
disculpar, to pardon, forgive
discutir, to discuss
el disfraz, disguise
disfrazar, to disguise
disfrutar, to enjoy
disimular, to misrepresent
disminuir, to diminish
dispar, different
disparar, to shoot, fire
el disparate, nonsense
el dispendio, extravagance
dispuesto, ready, disposed
distinto, different
la diversión, amusement
divertido, amusing
divertirse (ie) (i), to amuse (oneself)
doble, double
doler (ue), (20e) to ache; grieve
el dolor, pain, grief
el dominio, to control
el don, gift
la doncella, maid
dorar, to gild
la duda, doubt
dudar, to hesitate; doubt
la dueña, mistress
durar, to last
el duro, five pesetas

echar, (20f) to throw; **sin — en saco roto,** not forgetting
la edad, age
edificar, to build
el efecto, effect, **en-,** in fact

efectuado, carried out, played
eficaz, efficacious
el ejemplo, example
ejercer, to exercise; carry out
el ejército, army
elaborar, to prepare
emanar, to emanate
embadurnar, to smear
embarcarse, to embark
sin embargo, nevertheless
embarullar, to muddle
la embocadura, entrance; mouth of a river
embustero, deceitful
empalagoso, wearisome; cloying
empapar, to soak
empeñar, to pawn; **-se en,** persist in
el empeño, insistence
la emperatriz, empress
empezar (ie), to begin
la empresa, undertaking, enterprise
empuñar, to grip, seize
encabezar, to lead; head
el encaje, lace
el encanto, charm
encaramarse, to rise; climb
encargarse, to take charge; order
encender (ie), to light
encerrar (ie), to enclose
encogerse, to shrug; shrink
encomendar (ie), to entrust; commend
encorvarse, to bend down
el encuentro, meeting
encharcado, with puddles
enderezar, to guide, manage
el enemigo, enemy
el energúmeno, person possessed of the devil
la enfermedad, illness
la enfermera, nurse
el enfermo, patient
enfrentarse, to face up to
enfriarse, to get cold
engalanar, to adorn, deck
el engaño, deception
el enjambre, swarm
enjuto, thin; wizened

el **enlace,** link; marriage
enlutado, in mourning
enredar, to surround
ensayar, to try out, test
la **enseñanza,** instruction
enseñar, to teach
ensillar, to saddle
ensombrecido, hidden
entablar, to begin
el **ente,** entity; being
enterarse, to find out; become
por **entre,** through
entregar, to give; deliver
el **entrenamiento,** training
entrenar, to train
entusiasmar, to delight
envenenado, poisoned
enviar, to send
envidiar, to envy
envuelto, wrapped, enveloped
la **época,** epoch; age
el **equipo,** team
la **equis,** X (letter of alphabet)
equivocarse, to be wrong
erguirse (i), to stand up
erizar, to bristle
errar, to miss; wander
la **erre,** R (letter of alphabet)
escabroso, uneven; craggy
la **escala,** scale; ladder
la **escalera,** staircase; ladder;
steps
el **escalón,** step
el **escaño,** bench
el **escaparate,** shop-window
el **escardador,** weeder; picker
escarpado, steep
escaso, niggardly
la **escenificación,** picture; making
of a scene
el **escobón,** broom
escoger, to choose
la **escolta,** escort
el **escondite,** hiding place
el **escultor,** sculptor
la **escupida,** spitting
escupir, to spit
esforzarse (ue), to make an
effort
esmerar, to polish; take pains

espaciarse, to diffuse
la **espada,** sword
la **espalda,** back
espantar, to frighten
el **espejo,** mirror
la **espeleología,** pot-holing
la **esperanza,** hope
esperar, to wait; hope
espeso, thick
la **espesura,** density, thickness
espiar, to spy
espiritarse, to be partial to; fret
el **espíritu,** soul; spirit
la **espuela,** spur
la **espuma,** foam, froth
el **esqueleto,** skeleton
la **esquina,** corner
la **esquirla,** splinter
el **estado,** state; condition
estafar, to swindle, defraud
estallar, to burst out, break out
la **estatua,** statue
estezado, dressed up for riding,
hunting; tanned
el **estiércol,** dung
estimar, to judge; value
el **estrago,** ruin, destruction
estrecho, tight; narrow
la **estrella,** star
estrellarse, to be smashed; crash
estremecer (se), to shake; ripple
estrenar, to wear for the first
time
estrepitoso, noisy
la **estridencia,** screech, din
el **estropajo,** rubbish
estropeado, maimed
evitar, to avoid, prevent
las **exigencias,** demands
exigir, to demand
expresivo, expressive
extemporáneo, inopportune
el **exterminio,** extermination
extraer, to extract, take out
extranjero, foreign
extraño, strange
extremar, to carry to an extreme

la **fábrica,** factory
las **facciones,** features

la falda, skirt; slope (of a hill)
    faldear, to skirt, go round
    falta, lack; **hacer —,** to be
      necessary
    faltar, (*20g*) to be missing, lack
    fallecido, dead
    familiar, family (adj.)
la fecha, date
    feo, ugly
    fiel, faithful
el fieltro, felt
la fiera, wild animal
    fiero, wild, cruel; furious
la fiesta, fete, holiday
    figurar, to figure, imagine
    fijarse (en), to notice
    fijo, fixed
    firmar, to sign
la fisga, banter, raillery
el flaco, weakness
la flaqueza, weakness
la flecha, arrow
    fletar, to charter
    flojo, weak; lazy; loose
a flor de, level with; on the sur-
    face
    floreado, with a pattern of
    flowers
    florecer, to bloom; open
la fogata, blaze, bonfire
el fogón, fire-place; stove
el follaje, foliage
el folletín, serial story
el fondo, depth
    fornido, strong; lusty
la fortaleza, strength; fortress
    fosco, angry
el fósforo, match
    fracasar, to fail
el fregado, complicated affair
    fregar (ie), to scour, clean
el frente, front; **la-,** brow
el fresco, coolness
el fresno, ash (tree)
    frito, fried
    frívolo, frivolous
    frotar, to rub
la fruición, delight
el fuego, fire
la fuente, dish; fountain

fuera, outside; away; **-de,** apart
    from
    fugaz, fleeting
el funcionario, official
    fundar, to found
    funesto, fatal
la fusta, whip

la gallardía, elegance
    gallardo, gallant
la galleta, biscuit; cooking pot
la gana, wish, desire, longing
    ganar, to win; earn
el gañán, (day) labourer
la gasa, gauze
    gastar, to spend; **-una broma,**
    play a trick
los gemelos, twins
el gemido, groan, whine
    gemir, to groan, whine
el genio, temper, character, type
la gente, people
el gentío, crowd
el gesto, gesture; expression
    gimotear, to whine
    girar, to girate
el gitano, gipsy
el gobierno, government
el gol, goal
el golpe, blow; **de-,** at one go;
    suddenly
    golpear, to strike, hit
    gordo, fat
la gorra, cap
el gorrito, cap
la gota, drop
    gozar, to enjoy
el gozo, joy
la gracia, wit; gracefulness
    gracias a, thanks to
el granizo, hail
el grano, grain, seed
    grasiento, greasy, fatty
    grávido, pregnant
el graznido, cry, shriek
el grito, shout
    gruñir, to growl
el guante, glove
    guapo, pretty

el **guarda**, keeper
guardar, to keep
el **guardián**, keeper, custodian
la **guerra**, war
la **guerrera**, tunic (military)
a **gusto**, (*2oh*) happy

el **haba** (*f*), bean
hábil, clever
la **habilidad**, skill
el **hacha** (*f*), axe, hatchet
el **hachazo**, axe blow
el **hada** (*f*), fairy
el **hambre** (*f*), hunger
la **harina**, flour
harto, fed up: enough
hasta, even; as far as
el **hechizo**, charm
el **hecho**, fact
hediondo, pestilent; smelly
helar (ie), to freeze
la **hélice**, propeller
la **herida**, wound
hervir (ie) (i), to boil
el **hidalgo**, noble
la **hierba**, grass
el **hierro**, iron
hinchar, to swell
el **hipo**, gurgle
hirsuto, hairy
el **hocico**, snout
el **hogar**, hearth, home
la **hoja**, leaf; page; blade
holgado, comfortable; commodious
el **hombre**, shoulder
el **homenaje**, homage
el **hongo**, mushroom
la **honradez**, honesty
horadante, piercing
hosco, grim, severe
hospedarse, to stay, sojourn
la **hucha**, money-box
hueco, empty; hollow
la **huelga**, strike; party
la **huella**, track
el **hueso**, bone
el **huevo**, egg
huir, run away
el **hule**, rubber

la **humedad**, humidity
hundido, dilapidated; sunk; collapsed
hundir (se), to sink, plunge
el **huracán**, hurricane
huraño, unsociable

el **idioma**, language
la **iglesia**, church
ignorar, not to know
igual, equal; same
impedir (i), to impede
el **imperio**, empire
imponer, to inspire, impose
improvisado, improvised
de **improviso**, unexpectedly
el **impudor**, shamelessness; cynicism
incaico, of the Incas
el **incendio**, fire
incitar, to incite; induce; spur on
incomprensible, incomprehensible
incorporarse, to sit up straight
el **indicio**, indication; sign; token
la **indirecta**, insinuation
indudablemente, undoubtedly
inédito, unpublished
inesperadamente, unexpectedly
inferir (ie) (i), to deduce; infer
influir, to influence
inimaginable, unimaginable
la **injuria**, insult
inolvidable, unforgettable
inopinadamente, unexpectedly
la **inoportunidad**, untimeliness
la **inquietud**, anxiety
inseguro, uncertain
insensato, senseless
inservible, useless; of no use
la **instancia**, plea
integrar, to join
intentar, to try
el **intento**, effort
la **isla**, island

jactarse, to boast, brag
la **jaculatoria**, short prayer

el jadeo, panting, gasping
la jaquita, pony
jaro, ginger-coloured
el jarrón, large jar; flower vase
la jauría, pack of hounds; kennel
la jedentina, stench
la jerarquía, hierarchy
la jeta, face
la jornada, journey; day
el jornalero, day-labourer
la joya, jewel
jubilar, to pension off, retire
judío, Jewish
el juego, play, game
el juez, judge
la jugada, play
el jugador, player
el juicio, judgement
jurar, to swear
la juventud, youth
juzgar, to judge

el labio, lip
el labriego, farm labourer
ladeado, tilted, inclined
el ladrillo, brick
el lago, lake
la lágrima, tear
la laguna, lagoon, small lake
lamer, to lick
la lana, wool
el lance, event, incident
lanzarse, to throw (oneself)
largarse, to go away
largo, long; **a lo -de,** along
laríngeo, throaty, laryngeal
el lateral, side
el latigazo, lash
el látigo, whip
latir, to beat
la laya, type, kind, class
el lazo, loop
leal, loyal
el lecho, bed
la lechuga, lettuce
la lectura, reading
lejano, distant
lejos, far away
la lengua, tongue

la lentitud, slowness
la leña, firewood
la letra, words (of a song)
las letras ultramarinas, overseas money drafts
la leyenda, legend
la librería, bookshop; book-case
la liebre, hare; **dar gato por —,** to cheat
el lienzo, linen cloth; canvas
limpiar, to clean
la línea, line
lindo, pretty
linfático, lymphatic
liso, smooth; even
listo, ready
el listón, ribbon
loco, crazy, mad
la locura, madness
lograr, to succeed
el lomo, back (animal)
lucir (se), to shine; excel; exhibit
la lucha, struggle
luchar, to struggle
luego, then
el lugar, place
la lumbre, fire
la luna, moon
lustrado, polished
la luz, light

la llamarada, flare-up; flash
llameante, aflame
la llamita, little flame
la llave, key
el llavín, door key
llenar, to fill
llevar, to bring; carry; have; **— se chasco,** to be disappointed
llover (ue), to rain
la lluvia, rain

la maceta, flower-pot
la madera, wood
la madrina, godmother
la madrugada, early morning
madrugar, to get up early

la madurez, maturity
maduro, mature; ripe
majo, flashy
el mal, evil
la maleta, suitcase
malgastar, to squander
malhumorado, ill-tempered
la mancha, stain, spot
manchar, to stain
la mandíbula, jaw
manejar, to handle; operate
el mango, long handle
la manía, mania
maniatado, handcuffed
el manicomio, mental home
manoseado, well-worn, handled
manso, gentle
la mantequilla, butter
la maña, astuteness
la máquina, engine
maquinal, mechanical
maravillarse, be surprised
mareado, bothered, annoyed
el marido, husband
la marmita, cooking-pot; boiler
marmóreo, marble
de marras, aforementioned
mas, but
más bien, rather
masticar, to masticate; chew
el mástil, mast
matar, to kill, murder
el matrimonio, married couple
el mayorazgo, first-born son
mayordomo, steward
la mayoría, majority
mayúsculo, huge
mediante, by means of
mediar, to mediate
las medias, stockings
el medicamento, medicine
la medicina, medicine
el médico, doctor
mejorar, to improve
la melenilla, flowing hair
los menjurjes, medicinal mixtures
el mensaje, message
la mente, mind
el mentón, chin
menudo, small

el merendero, tea-room
el meridiano, noon
la merienda, tea, snack
la meta, goal
meter, put (in)
la mezcla, mixture
mezclar, to mix
el miedo, fear
las mientes, thought; mind
mientras (que), while
el milagro, miracle
el mimbre, osier; **tener —,** to be resourceful
el minero, miner
la mirada, glance; look
la miseria, poverty, wretchedness
el mitin, meeting
los modales, manners
el modo, way
mohino, peevish; sad
mohoso, musty, mouldy
mojar, to moisten
el moka, coffee
el molde, model
moldeable, easy to mould
molestar, to trouble
molesto, worried
la moneda, coin
la monja, nun
el mono, jersey
el monte, mountain; hill
la montera, cap
el montón, pile, heap
el montoncito, little pile
morado, purple
moreno, dark-haired
morir (ue) (u), to die
la mosca, fly
el mote, nickname
el motivo, reason
la moto, motor-cycle
la mozuela, young girl
la muchedumbre, crowd
mudo, dumb; silent
la muerte, death
el muerto, dead man
la muestra, sample; indication
a mujeriegas, side-saddle
el muslo, thigh

nacer, to be born
naciente, budding
nada, nothing; not at all
nadar, to swim
los **naipes,** cards
la **nariz,** nose, nostril
el **natural,** native
la **naturaleza,** nature
el **navegante,** navigator
el **navío,** ship
nebuloso, nebulous, vague
la **nena,** girl
neto, pure
el **nieto,** grandchild
la **nieve,** snow
la **niñez,** childhood
la **nodriza,** wet-nurse
la **norma,** standard
la **noticia,** news
la **novedad,** novelty
la **novia,** girl friend
la **nube,** cloud
el **nudo,** knot

obeso, fat
el **obispo,** bishop
la **obra,** work
no **obstante,** notwithstanding
obstinarse, to insist
ocioso, idle; fruitless; needless
oculto, hidden
ocuparse de, to worry about
ocurrir, to happen, occur
odiar, to hate
el **oficio,** job
ofuscar, to dazzle, confuse
los **oídos,** ears
la **ola,** wave
el **óleo,** oil (painting)
olfatear, to sniff out
el **olor,** odour, smell
olvidar, (20k) to forget
opaco, dark, opaque
operar, to operate on
oportuno, opportune
ora, now
el **orgullo,** pride
orgulloso, proud, haughty
orientar, to direct

la **orilla,** bank
oscilar, to move, oscillate, range
oscurecerse, to become obscure;
darken
otoñal, autumnal

el **padrino,** patron, godfather
el **país,** country
el **paisaje,** countryside
la **paja,** straw
el **pájaro,** bird
la **pala,** shovel
pálido, pale
la **palmeta,** cane; caning
el **palmetazo,** caning; slap
el **palo,** stick; mast; shaft (of cart)
palpar, to feel
la **panza,** belly
el **paño,** cloth
los **paños,** clothes, clothing
el **pañuelo,** handkerchief
el **par,** pair; couple
el **parabrisas,** windscreen
la **parada,** stopping place; (football)
save
parar, to stop
pardo, dark grey, brown
al **parecer,** apparently; el **—,**
similarity; opinion
parecido, similar
la **pared,** wall
la **pareja,** couple
el **paréntesis,** bracket
el **pariente,** relative
parodiar, to parody
la **parroquia,** clientele, customers
el **partícipe,** participant
particular, private
el **partido,** game; match; party
(political)
partir, to split; share out
el **pasadizo,** narrow half-way
pasajero, transitory
pasar, (20l) to happen; pass; spend
el **paseo,** walk
el **pasillo,** corridor, passage
pasmar, to stun; amaze
el **paso,** pace, step
la **pasta,** paste

la pata, leg (of animals, furniture, etc.)
la patata, potato
el pato, duck
el patrimonio, inheritance
pavimentado, paved
el pavo, turkey (cock)
la paz, peace
el pecho, breast, chest
el pedazo, piece, **hacer -s**, to smash
pedregoso, rocky
pegar, to stick, affix; beat
el pegote, sticking-plaster (sponger)
pelar, to peel
pelear, to struggle, fight
la película, film
el peligro, danger
el pelmazo, nuisance, bore
el pelo, hair
la pelota, ball **-de hule**, rubber ball
peludo, hairy
la pena, trouble
pender, to hang
la pendiente, slope
el pensamiento, thought
la penumbra, half-light
percatarse (de), to take notice (of)
perdurar, to last
perecerse, to crave
de perfil, from the side; in profile
perjudicar, to prejudice
permanecer, to remain
la perplejidad, perplexity
el perseguidor, pursuer
perseguir (i), to pursue
la personilla, ridiculous, petty character
pertenecer, to belong
pesado, heavy
el pesar, grief; regret
a pesar de, in spite of
el pescuezo, neck
el peso, weight
petrificar, to petrify
peyorativo, depreciatory; pejorative
el picacho, peak
el picadillo, minced meat

picar, to prick; **— la cresta**, hurt badly
la piedad, pity
la piedra, stone
la piel, skin
la pifia, blunder
la píldora, pill
el pincel, brush
el pino, pine; deal
el piropo, compliment
pisar, to tread, walk on
el piso, flat, apartment
el placer, pleasure
a placer, at will, pleasure
la planta, bottom; floor; building site
la plata, silver; money
platicar, to converse, talk
el plato, plate; dish
la playa, beach
la plaza, square
la población, town
el poblado, village
la pobreza, poverty
los podencos, hounds
poderoso, powerful
el poema, poem
el policía, policeman
el polvo, powder; dust
polvoriento, dusty
polvoso, dusty
el pollino, donkey
el ponche, punch
el portal, street door
el portero, (football) goalkeeper
en pos de, behind
postizo, false
postular, to postulate
el pote, pot, jar
el potro, foal, colt
precisamente, precisely
preciso, necessary
precoz, early
la predilección, preference
pregonar, to proclaim
la prenda, garment
prender, to fix; stick
la presa, dam; weir
prescindir, to do without; disregard

presentar, to introduce
el presidio, prison
preso, seized, captured
el preso, prisoner
prestar, to lend
pretender, to claim; attempt
pretérito, past
el pretil, parapet (bridge)
prever, to foresee
previo, previous, prior
el primo, cousin
el principio, beginning; principle
la prisa, speed
privar, to deprive
probar (ue), to try, test
procedente de, coming from
el procedimiento, procedure
procurar, to try
profundizar, to go hard, deep
la prole, offspring, family
propalar, to divulge; publish
propender, to incline, tend
propenso, prone
la propina, tip
propio, of its own
proponer, to propose
el provecho, profit
proveer, to provide; equip
provenir, to come from
el proyecto, project
la prueba, proof; test
el puesto, post; stall
pulir, to polish
la punta, tip; de —, sharp end
    first
de puntillas, on tip-toe
el puñetazo, punch, bang with fist
el puro, cigar

quedar, to remain
quejarse, to complain
quemar, to burn
el quicio, hinge; fuera de —,
    unhinged; mad; out of one's
    wits; sacar de —, to exasperate
la química, chemistry
las quinielas, 'pools'
quitar, to remove, take away;
    forbid

quizá(s), perhaps
la rabia, rage
rabiar, to rage, be furious; a-,
    furiously
el rabo, tail
la racha, burst
la ráfaga, flash; squall; gust (of
    wind)
la rama, branch
la rana, frog
rapar, to crop
el rapaz, youngster
el ras, level
el rasgo, quality; character
raspar, to scratch; steal
el rato, time; space of time; while
el rayo, flash of lightning
la raza, race
la razón, reason
reaccionar, to react
reanudar, to renew
rebasar, to overflow
la rebeldía, disobedience
el recado, message; note
el recelo, mistrust; fear; suspicion
receloso, apprehensive
recobrar, to recover
recoger, to pick up, gather
el reconocimiento, recognition
recordar (ue), to remember
recostar (ue), to repose, rest
el recreo, recreation
la rectitud, soundness
el recuerdo, remembrance, memory
recurrir, to fall back on
rechazar, to reject
la redondela, ring, circle
en redor (rededor), around
la reencarnación, reincarnation
referir (ie) (i), to refer; relate
el reflejo, reflection
refrenar, to control
la refundición, remaking
refunfuñar, to mumble; growl
regalar, to give
regar (ie), to water; scatter;
    strew
regir (i), to rule; prevail
regreso, return; de —, on the
    way back

reír a carcajadas, to laugh heartily
relampaguear, to lighten, flash
el **reloj,** watch; clock
reluciente, gleaming
de **remate,** utterly, completely
el **remedio,** remedy, recourse
el **remedo,** copy
el **remero,** rower, oarsman
el **remo,** oar
el **remolino,** eddy
la **rendija,** crack
la **renta,** income
reñir (i), to quarrel
el **reo,** condemned man; criminal
el **reparto,** delivery; distribution
repentino, sudden
repetidamente, repeatedly
replicar, to reply
reportarse, to refrain
la **repostería,** pastry
reprobar, to condemn
resbaladizo, slippery
resbalar, to slip
el **resbalón,** slip
rescatar, to rescue
resonar (ue), to resound; ring
resoplar, to puff; snort
respingón, reluctant; snub (nose)
resplandecer, to shine
responder, to reply
restallar, to crack, (whip)
resuelto, determined
retemblar (ie), tremble; shudder, shake
reunir (se), to rejoin
la **reunión,** meeting
revelador, revealing
el **revés,** back
el **revuelo,** disturbance
la **revuelta,** revolt
revuelto, in disorder
el **rey,** king
rezar, to pray
la **ribera,** bank
rico, rich; delicious
el **riel,** rail
la **rienda,** rein
el **rincón,** corner
la **riña,** quarrel

la **risa,** laugh; laughter
el **ritmo,** rhythm; **al — de,** in tune with
el **robo,** robbery, theft
el **roce,** touch, rubbing
rodar (ue), to roll
rodear, to surround
las **rodillas,** knees
rogar (ue), to ask; beg
roncar, to snore
ronco, hoarse
la **ropa,** clothing
el **rostro,** face
roto, torn, broken
ruidoso, noisy
sin **rumbo fijo,** at random
la **ruta,** route; way

saber, to know; taste
sabio, wise
el **sabor,** taste; flavour
sabroso, tasty
sacar de quicio, to exasperate
el **sacerdote,** priest
el **saco,** coat; sack
sacudir, to shake
sagaz, astute; sagacious
la **sal,** wit; salt
saltar, to leap
el **salto,** leap; jump
la **salud,** health
saludable, healthy
saludar, to greet
salvar, to save
salvo, except; safe
la **sangre,** blood
sanguinolento, blood-stained
el **sapo,** toad
el **sastre,** tailor
sea . . . sea, whether . . . or
seco, dry
la **sed,** thirst, **sedante,** soothing; sedative
en **seguida,** at once
seguir (i), to follow
según, according to
la **seguridad,** safety, security
seguro, confident, firm
la **selección,** team (selected)

sencillo, simple
sensato, sensible, wise
sensible, sensitive
el **sentido,** sense, meaning
sentir (ie) (i), to feel; be sorry
la **señal,** signal
señalar, to show
señorial, noble
el **séquito,** suite
la **servidumbre,** servants
la **servilleta,** napkin
el **seto,** fence; hedge
la **sidra,** cider
siempre, always
las **sienes,** temples
la **sierra,** mountain range
el **siglo,** century
el **significado,** meaning
siguiente, following
la **sílaba,** syllable
el **silbato,** whistle
la **silla,** chair; saddle
simpático, kind
sino, but
el **síntoma,** symptom; sign
ni **siquiera,** not even
la **sirvienta,** maidservant
el **sitio,** place
de **sobra,** in addition
sobremanera, excessively
el **sobresalto,** shock
la **sobriedad,** sobriety
el **sobrino,** nephew
el **socio,** member
el **socorro,** help
la **soga,** halter; rope
solapado, sly; deceitful
el **soldado,** soldier
soler (ue), (20q) to be accustomed to
soltar (ue), to let loose
el **soltero,** bachelor
la **solterona,** spinster
la **sombra,** shadow; shade; ghost
sombrío, dismal, sombre
someter, to submit
sonar (ue), to sound
el **sonido,** sound
sonreir (i), to smile
el **sonsonete,** monotonous sing-song

soñar (ue), to dream
la **sopa,** soup
soportar, to bear; support
la **sordera,** deafness
sordo, deaf; muffled
la **sorpresa,** surprise
el **sorteo,** draw, drawing of lots
sosegar (ie), to calm
sospechar, to suspect
sospechoso, suspicious
sostener, to support
el **soto,** grove, copse
suave, smooth
suceder, to happen
lo **sucedido,** what happened
sudar, to sweat
el **sudor,** sweat
el **suelo,** floor
el **sueño,** sleep, dream
la **suerte,** kind; chance; **tener —** to be lucky
sufrir, to suffer
sugerir (ie) (i), to suggest
sujetar, to hold fast
sumamente, extremely
sumar, to add up
el **suministro,** supply
a lo **sumo,** at most
la **superficie,** surface
el **suplicio,** torture; agony
surcado, lined; wrinkled
surgir, to spring from, issue forth
suspirar, to sigh
sutil, subtle; shrewd

la **tabla,** board; plank
el **tablazo,** blow with a piece of board
el **tacón,** heel (of shoe)
tal vez, perhaps
el **talón,** heel (of foot)
el **tamaño,** size
el **tambor,** drum
tampoco, neither
tantito antes, shortly before
el **tanto,** bit; **por —,** therefore
tardar (en), take (time); to delay in

la **tarea**, task
teatral, theatrical
el **techo**, ceiling
la **tela**, cloth
temblar (ie), to tremble
el **temblor**, trembling
temer, to fear
temeroso, timorous; terrible
el **tendajón**, shop
tendido, stretched out
el **tenedor**, fork
teñir (i), to tinge; tone down
terminante, conclusive
la **terraza**, terrace
el **terrón**, clod of earth
la **tesis**, thesis
el **tesoro**, treasure
el **testigo**, witness
el **testuz**, brow or nape of the neck
(animals)
tétrico, gloomy
la **tienda**, shop
tierno, tender; soft
tieso, stiff
las **tijeras**, scissors; trestles
el **tinglado**, shed
las **tinieblas**, darkness
tirar, to shoot; throw
tiritar, to shiver
el **tiro**, shot
tironear, to tug
tirotear, to fire; shoot at
titilar, twinkle
el **tocadiscos**, record-player
tocar, to play (instrument)
la **tontería**, nonsense
el **tonto**, fool
topar, to meet; find; knock
torcer (ue), to twist; turn
en **torno**, around
torpe, difficult; clumsy
la **torre**, tower
el **tortel**, flat cake
tosco, crude; coarse; rough
el **trabajo**, work; job; trouble
trabar, to strike up
traducir, to translate
traer, to bring
tragar, to swallow
el **trago**, drink

el **traidor**, traitor
el **traje**, dress; suit
el **tramo**, stretch; distance
transcurrir, to pass (of time)
el **transcurso**, course (of time)
el **transeúnte**, passer-by
el **trapicheo**, contriving
tras, after
trasero, back (*adj.*)
los **trastes**, utensils
el **trastorno**, upheaval
tratar, to try; treat; —**se de**, to be
about
a **través de**, through
de **través**, sideways; athwart
la **travesía**, crossing
la **traza**, aspect
el **trecho**, distance
la **tregua**, truce
trémulo, trembling
trepar, to climb
el **trigo**, wheat
el **trinchante**, carving-knife
el **trino**, chirping
la **tristeza**, sadness
el **triunfador**, victor
las **trizas**, pieces; **hacer** —, to
smash, break up
tronar (ue), to thunder
el **tronco**, trunk (tree)
la **tropa**, troop
el **trote**, trot
el **trozo**, extract; piece
el **truco**, gimmick
tuerto, one-eyed
tumbarse, to fall

por **último**, finally
únicamente, solely, only
las **uñas**, finger-nails
la **urbanidad**, courtesy
las **útiles**, utensils, — **de aseo**,
cleaning equipment

la **vaca**, cow
vaciar, to empty
el **vacío**, space

valer, (20s) to be worth
el valor, valour; value
vanaglorioso, vainglorious
vasco, Basque
el vascuence, Basque language
a veces, sometimes
la vecindad, neighbourhood; casa de — tenement house
el vecindario, neighbourhood
el vecino, inhabitant; neighbour
la vela, sail
el velocímetro, speedometer
la vena, vein
vencer, to conquer
la venganza, revenge
la ventaja, advantage
el ventero, innkeeper
de verdad, really
la verdura, green(ness)
vergonzoso, ashamed
la vergüenza, shame
vertiginoso, dizzy
el vestido, dress; suit
vestir (i), to dress, to wear
una vez, once; de — en cuando, occasionally
la vía, way; route; line
la víbora, viper
el vicio, vice
vidriado, glazed
vienés, Viennese
vigilar, to watch (over)
en vinagre, bitter; sour

el viñedo, vineyard
vislumbrar, to guess, conjecture
la víspera, eve, day before
la vista, view
la viuda, widow
vivo, bright
vocear, to shout, cry, proclaim
el vocerío, shouting
el volador, flying man
el volante, steering-wheel
volar (ue), to fly
el volumen, volume; size
la voluntad, will
volverse (ue), to turn round
la voz, voice
a vuelo, flying
la vuelta, turn, twist, curve; de — back again; dar la — a, to go round
vulgar, common, vulgar

yacer, to lie
la yegua, mare
yermo, uncultivated; bleak

zambullir, to immerse, submerge
el zapatero, shoemaker
de zoco en colodro, from bad to worse
el zorro, fox
la zozobra, worry

Vocabulary

English–Spanish

This vocabulary should be comprehensive enough to satisfy the needs of most ex-'O' Level students. As in the Spanish—English vocabulary, the meanings given are adapted, or adaptable, to the text of the passages or exercises provided. In fact, it is designed to give as much immediate help as possible and occasionally it has been considered advisable to sacrifice strict consistency on the altar of clarity and simplicity.

Radical-changing verbs are indicated in the usual way: (ue), (ie), (i), (i). The numbers in brackets refer to the paragraphs in the Grammar section.

abbey, la abadía
to abound, abundar
about, respecto a; acerca de; alrededor de; sobre
to be about to, estar a punto de
absence, la ausencia
acacia, la acacia
accident, el accidente; **by —,** por casualidad
to accompany, acompañar
accord, la voluntad
accordingly, así pues
to account for, explicar
to accumulate, acumular
to achieve, lograr
achievement, la realización
acquaintance, el conocido
to acquire, conseguir (i)
acquisition, la adquisición
across, al otro lado de
Act, el Acta
action, la acción
to add, añadir; agregar
address, la dirección; las señas
admiral, el almirante
to admit, admitir
to adore, adorar
adventure, la aventura
adverse, adverso
to advertise, anunciar
advice, el consejo
affable, afable
affair, el asunto
affectionate, cariñoso

afterwards, más tarde; después
age, la edad; la época; **dark — s,** la época del oscurantismo
to agree, convenir; estar de acuerdo
agreeable, agradable
aid, la ayuda
to be aimed at, estar destinado a
air, el aire; el aspecto
alarming, alarmante
alas!, ¡ay!
alert, alerta
alike, tanto . . . como
Allah, Alá
to allow, dejar (20 d)
allowance, la bolsa (la asignación); **to make — for,** atribuir
allowed for, dejado a un lado
almost, casi
alone, solo
although, aunque
always, siempre
amazed, sorprendido
ambassador, el embajador
ammunition, las municiones
analytic, dado a analizar
ancestor, el antepasado
to anchor, anclar
angel, el ángel; **Holy — s,** los Sagrados Ángeles

anger, la furia; la ira
anglophile, anglófilo
angrily, con ira
to **annex,** anexionar
to **announce,** anunciar
annoyed, enfadado; furioso
to **answer,** contestar
anticipated, esperado; anticipado
anti-climax, la decepción
anxiety, la ansiedad
anxious, preocupado; **to be — to,** querer
any, cualquiera; **— one,** cualquiera; **— time (that),** siempre (que)
apart (from), aparte (de)
apartment, el piso; el aposento; el recinto
to **apologize,** excusarse
apology, la excusa
appalling, espantoso
apparently, según parece
to **appear,** parecer; **(before court, etc.),** comparecer
applause, el aplauso
apple, la manzana; **— tree,** el manzano
to **appreciate,** apreciar
to **approach,** acercarse a; aproximarse a
arm, el brazo; **— chair,** el sillón
arms (weapons), las armas
army, el ejército
to **arrest,** detener
to **arrive,** llegar
art, el arte
to **ascend,** subir; **— a river,** navegar río arriba
to **ask** (21 a), preguntar; pedir (i); **— questions,** hacer preguntas
asleep, dormido
assimilation, la asimilación
to **assure,** asegurar
astonishment, el asombro
to **attach,** ligar
to **attain (the age of),** cumplir (años)

attempt, el intento
attended by, acompañado de
to **attract,** atraer
author, el autor
automatic, automático
avenue, la avenida
to **avoid,** evitar
awakening, el despertar
to be **aware of,** darse cuenta de

back, la espalda; (*adj.*) trasero; (*adv.*) atrás; **to turn one's —,** dar la espalda (20 b); **to — up,** estar del lado de; **to go —,** volver (ue), regresar
bacon, el tocino
badly, malamente
baggage, el equipaje
ball-pointed pen, el bolígrafo
bandaged, vendado
bank (river, etc.), la orilla; **— manager,** el director, (gerente) de banco
bark(ing), el ladrido
base, la base
basket, la cesta
Basque, vasco
with **bated breath,** en voz baja
battered, magullado
battleground, el campo de batalla
bay, la bahía
beach, la playa
to **bear (the name of),** llevar (el nombre de)
beard, la barba
beaten; vencido; derrotado
because, porque; como; **— of,** por culpa de
to **become** (21 b), ponerse a; volverse (ue); **— part of,** formar parte de
bed, la cama; **(of river),** el lecho
bedroom, el dormitorio
at the **bedside,** al lado de la cama; a la cabecera de la cama

before (9e), antes; (adj.) anterior

to begin, empezar (ie); (war) estallar

in the beginning, al principio

on his behalf, por él

to behave, comportarse

behind (9 g), atrás

to believe (21j), creer

bell (large), la campana

to belong, pertenecer; ser lo de uno

beneath (9i), bajo

to bend down, inclinarse; agacharse

besides, además; así como

better, mejor; **to get —,** mejorarse

between, entre (dos); a medio camino de

beyond, más allá de; **— words,** en un grado indecible

to bid, rogar (ue)

Bill, la bula

at birth, al nacer

bitter, amargo

bitterly, con amargura

bleak, adusto

to bless, bendecir

blessing, la bendición

blind, ciego

blood, la sangre

bloody, sangriento

to blow, soplar; **— out of,** volar por

on board, a borde de

boat, el bote; el barco

bomb, la bomba

bondage, la sumisión

booty, el botín

to borrow, pedir (i) prestado

both . . . and (8), tanto . . . como

to be bothered about s.t., importarle a uno algo

bottle, la botella

bottom, el fondo

to bound, saltar

bowed, inclinado

bowl, la fuente; **(of spoon),** el cuenco

box, la caja; (dim.) la cajita

branch, la rama; **— (of bank, office, etc.)** la sucursal

brain, los sesos; la inteligencia

a brand of, una especie (marca) de

brandy, el coñac

bravery, el valor

break, la interrupción

to break a record, superar un record

breakfast, el desayuno

to breathe, respirar

breeze, la brisa

to bribe, sobornar

bribery, el soborno

bridge, el puente

briefly, por breve espacio

bright, alerta

to bring back (with oneself), traer (consigo)

British, británico

broad, ancho; **— brimmed,** de ala ancha

brush (painter's), el pincel

brusque, brusco

to build, construir

building, el edificio

bulged with, cargado de

bull, el toro; **— fight,** la corrida; **— ring,** la plaza de toros

bunk, el camastro

burden, la carga

burglar, el ladrón

to bury, enterrar (ie)

bus, el autobús

busy, ocupado; **(crowded),** concurrido

butterfly, la mariposa

by, por; **— means of,** mediante

to call, llamar; **— a halt,** contener; **— the tune,** llevar la batuta

camion, el camión
candle, la vela
canvas (artist's), el lienzo
cape, la capa; (*geog.*) el cabo
captain, el capitán
to capture, capturar
car, el automóvil; el coche
card, la tarjeta
care, el cuidado; **under the
   —,** bajo la tutela
to care about, importarle a
   uno
career, la carrera
to carry (away), llevar (se)
carrying, cargado de
case, el caso; **jewel —,** la
   cajita; el joyero
casualty, la baja
catastrophe, la catástrofe
cat-call, el silbido
to catch, coger; **— a train,**
   tomar un tren; **— sight
   of,** vislumbrar
catholicism, el catolicismo
cell, la celda
cellar, el sótano
centre, el centro
century, el siglo
certainly, desde luego
chagrin, la mortificación
chair, la silla; el asiento
chance, la posibilidad
change, el cambio
the Channel, el Canal de la
   Mancha
chap, el amigo
chapel, la capilla
chauffeur, el conductor
cheer (good), el buen
   humor
cheese, el queso
to chew, masticar
chief, el jefe; (*adj.*) principal
to choose, escoger
to christen, bautizar
christening, el bautizo
Christian, el cristiano
Christianity, el cristianismo
Christmas Day, el Día de
   Navidad

church, la iglesia
cigarette, el cigarrillo
circle, el círculo
citadel, la ciudadela
citizen, el ciudadano
civil guard, el (la) guardia
   civil
to claim, reclamar
clamour, el estrépito
cliff, el acantilado
to climb (up), subir
clink, el tintineo; **to —,**
   tintinear
clock, el reloj; **travelling
   —,** el reloj de viaje
clod (of earth), el terrón
to close, cerrar(ie); **— in on,**
   apoderarse de
closely, de cerca
clothes, la ropa
cloud, la nube
coast, la costa
coat (jacket), la chaqueta;
   check-, el abrigo a cua-
   dros
to cock (a gun), montar el
   gatillo (de una escopeta)
cognac, el coñac
collapse, el derrumbamiento
colleague, el colega
to collect, recoger
college, el colegio
colloquy, el coloquio
colonel, el coronel
colour, el pigmento
colourless, descolorido
combination room, la sala
   de profesores
to come, venir; **— across,**
   descubrir; **— back,** volver
   (ue), regresar; **— for,**
   venir a buscar; **— down,**
   bajar
comfortably, cómodamente;
   — off, (bien) acomodado
to command, mandar; capi-
   tanear
commerce, el comercio
common, (*adj.*) corriente;
   in —, en común

communicative, comunicativo

companion, el compañero

company, la compañía

to complain, quejarse

concern, la preocupación

condition, la condición

to confer, conferenciar

confidence, la confianza; **whispered —,** cuchicheos en confianza

conflict, el conflicto

to confront, presentar

confusing, desconcertante

congealed, coagulado

conquest, la conquista

constable, el guardia; **chief —,** el comisario

to construct, construir

to consult, consultar

to contain, contener

contents, el contenido

conversational, hablador

to convert, convertir (ie) (i)

cook, el cocinero

cool, fresco; tranquilo

cordiality, la cordialidad

to corner, acaparar

correspondent, el corresponsal

corridor, el pasillo

cost, el costo

to cough, toser

counsellor, el consejero

countless, incontable

country, el país; **— man,** el paisano; **— station,** la estación de pueblo; **mother —,** la madre patria

couple, la pareja

courage, el valor

of course, naturalmente; desde luego; **in due —,** a su debido tiempo

court (royal), la corte; **(college),** el patio

courtyard, el patio

cousin, el primo

cover, el amparo

covered with, cubierto de

covering (hiding), ocultando

cradle, la cuna

crash, la explosión

to create, crear

crime, el crimen, el delito

to cross off as a failure, dar por fracasado

crossbow, la ballesta

crowd, la muchedumbre; los grupos; **to — around,** apiñarse alrededor

crude, burdo

to cry (weep), llorar; **(shout),** gritar

cup, la taza

custom, la costumbre

customer, el cliente

to cut, cortar; **— the throat,** degollar (üe)

daily, a diario

damnation, la condenación

danger, el peligro

dark, oscuro; *(noun)* la oscuridad

Dark Ages, la época del oscurantismo

dark-skinned, de tez morena

to date back, datar de

dawn, el amanecer

dead, muerto; **illustrious —,** los difuntos ilustres

deal table, la mesa de pino

to deal with, tratar con

death, la muerte

decency, la decencia

deck, la cubierta (de un barco)

defeat, la derrota; **to —** vencer

defence, la defensa

to defend, defender (ie)

definite, determinado

to defray, sufragar

delightful, encantador

degree (honours), la matrícula de honor

to **deny,** negar (ie)
departure, la partida; la salida; la marcha
descendant, el descendiente
deserted, desierto
to **deserve,** merecer
desire, el afán
desk, la mesa; el escritorio
desparado, el bandido
desperate, desesperado
detachment, el destacamento
to **determine,** decidir
to **devise,** concebir (i) (un plan)
devoutness, la devoción
different, distinto
to **dig,** cavar
diplomacy, la diplomacia
to **direct,** orientar; **(command),** estar a cargo de
to **disappear,** desaparecer
to be **disappointed,** llevarse chasco
to **discourage,** desalentar (ie); deprimir
discourteous, desconsiderado
to **discover,** descubrir
to **discredit,** desacreditar
to **discuss,** discutir
to **disguise,** disfrazar
disillusionment, la desilusión
disloyalty, la deslealtad
in **dismay,** en desesperación
dismembered, desmembrado
to **disown,** repudiar
disposition, la aptitud
dispute, la disputa
dissipated, disoluto
to **distinguish,** distinguir
distraught, desorientado; confuso
distressed, afligido
district, el distrito
to **disturb,** interrumpir; molestar
divergence, la variación
to **divide,** separar

to **do (suffice),** bastar
dock, la dársena; el muelle
donkey, el burro
door, la puerta; **— way,** el portal
doubtful, dudoso
dozen, la docena
to **drag off,** llevarse a rastras
to **draw,** trazar; **— the curtain,** correr la cortina
drawing-room, el salón
dreadfully, sumamente
dream, el sueño; **to — (of),** soñar (con)
dress, el vestido
to **dress wounds,** vendar las heridas
dressed, vestido; ataviado
drink, la bebida; **to —,** beber; **to — the health of,** brindar a la salud de
to **drive (a car),** conducir (un automóvil): **— away (in a car),** alejarse (en automóvil); **— a hard bargain,** hacer un buen trato
driver, el conductor
to **drop,** caer; dejar caer; rezagarse; **to — back, (to lessen),** amainar
to **drown,** ahogar (se)
drunk, borracho; **to get —,** emborracharse
to **dry,** secar
ducat, el ducado
dull, aburrido
dulled (sound), amortiguado
dusk, el crepúsculo
dusty, polvoriento
on **duty,** de servicio

early, temprano; primero
easel, el caballete
east, el este; (*adj.*) oriental
easy, natural
ebullience, la algazara
economy, la economía

edge, la orilla; el borde
to educate, educar
education, la educación; los estudios
effectively, eficazmente
effectually, efectivamente
effort, el empeño
egg, el huevo
eighth, octavo
embarrassment (shame), la vergüenza
emergency, la campaña; la emergencia
empire, el imperio
employee, el empleado
employer, el jefe; el patrón
emptiness, la oquedad
empty, vacío
enchantedly, como por ensalmo
enclosed, recogido
enclosure, el recinto
to encourage, animar
end, el fin; **at the — of,** a fines de
enemy, el enemigo
engaged, contratado
to enjoy, disfrutar
enough, bastante, suficiente
enterprise, la empresa
entertainments, las diversiones
enthusiasm, el entusiasmo
era, la era; la época
escape, la huida; **to —,** escaparse
to escort, acompañar
to establish, establecer
to be estimated, ser objeto de juicio
estuary, el estuario
eternal, eterno
explorer, el explorador
eve, la víspera
even, hasta (*9h*); **— if,** incluso si; **— more,** más aún (*26*); **not —,** ni siquiera (*16*)
evening, la noche; la tarde

eventually, finalmente; por fin
everybody else, todos los demás
examination, el examen
example, el ejemplo; **for —,** por ejemplo; **(model),** el modelo
except, a excepción de
excessive, exagerado; excesivo
exchange (telephone), la central
excited, emocionado; agitado; alborotado
excitement, la agitación
exhausted, agotado
to exist, existir
to expect, esperar
to expel, expulsar; desterrar (ie)
expense, el gasto
experiment, el experimento
to explain, explicar
exploits, las andanzas
explorer, el explorador
eye, el ojo; **— wiping,** el deslumbrar; **in the —s of,** a ojos de

face, la cara; el rostro; el semblante
to face, hacer frente a
fact, el hecho
to fail, faltar; dejar de
failure, el no lograr; el fracaso
fair (haired), rubio
fairy story, el cuento de hadas
faith, la fe; la confianza
to fall, caer (se); **— in love,** enamorarse; **— to pieces,** el desmoronamiento
fame, la fama
familiar, familiar
fan, el abanico; **to —,** abanicar(se)

as far as, tan lejano como
  far from, lejos de; — away,
    lejano
  farewell, la despedida
  fastness, la seguridad
  fast train, el rápido
  fat, rechoncho; gordo
  fated, destinado
  favourite, el favorito
  fear, el temor
  feat, la hazaña
to feel, sentir (ie) (i); parecér-
    sele a uno
  feelings, los sentimientos
a few, unos (cuantos)
  fierce, tenaz; feroz
  fiesta, el día de fiesta
to fight, luchar; librar combate
to figure, imaginarse
  filled, lleno
  film, la película
to find, encontrar (ue)
  finger, el dedo
to finish, concluir
  fireplace, la chimenea
  first, primero; antes; at —,
    al principio
  fish, el pez
  fishing village, el pueblo
    de pescadores
to fix, fijar
  flag-ship, la nave capitana
  flank, el flanco
to flash, iluminar (se)
  flask, el frasco; el frasquito
  flat, el piso
  fleet, la flota; la armada
to flick back again, volver
    (ue) a ocultarse
to fling, echar; arrojar
  floor, el piso; el suelo
  flung about (scattered),
    desparramado
  flutter (of wings), el batir
    (de alas)
to fly, volar (ue); to — a flag,
    ondear
to follow, seguir (i)
  food, los comestibles
  foot, el pie

  footstep, el paso
  foreign, extranjero
  foreigner, el extranjero
to forget, olvidar (20 k)
the former . . . the latter, el
    primero . . . el segundo
    (último)
  fort, el fuerte
  fortunately, por fortuna;
    afortunadamente
  fortune, la fortuna
to found, fundar
  fragment of the Cross, la
    reliquia de la Cruz
  frame, el marco
  frankly, francamente
  freely, libremente
to fret (active), irritar; (intran-
    sitive), estar irritado
  friendly, simpático
  fringe (surroundings), los
    alrededores
  front, el frente; to make —,
    hacer frente a
  fruit, la fruta; (profit), el
    fruto
  fugitive, el fugitivo
  funny, divertido; (strange),
    curioso; extraño
  furlong, medida de longitud
    de 200 metros
to furnish, proporcionar; pro-
    curar
  future, futuro; (noun), el (lo)
    futuro; el porvenir

to gain, ganar; (reach), llegar a
  gallery, la galería
  gardener, el jardinero
  garments, las prendas; la
    vestimenta
  gate, la puerta; la verja; el
    portillo
to gather around, rodear; —
    up, recoger
to gaze, examinar (con la
    vista); — at, contemplar
  gentle, dulce; apacible

to get (21c) (on the train), subir (al tren); — rid of, deshacerse de; — used (to), acostumbrarse (a)

ghost, el fantasma

giant, gigante

gift, el regalo

giggle, la risita

girl mother, la madre soltera

to be glad, alegrarse

to glance at, observar (a alguien)

at first glance, a primera vista

to glare, iluminar

glory, la gloria

to go (21d), ir; — away, irse; — for a walk, dar un paseo; — on, proceder; — on board, ir a bordo; — past, pasar por; — through, sufrir; — up to, acercarse a

goat, la cabra

goblin, el duende

goddess, la diosa

gold, el oro

to be good at, entenderse, (ie) bien; saber hacer bien

gooseberry, la grosella

gorge, el barranco

gospel, el evangelio

government, el gobierno

governor, el gobernador

gown (academical), la toga

grace, la bendición

grass, la hierba

grave, serio

to graze, pastar

to grease the palms of, sobornar

great-grandfather, el bisabuelo

to greet, saludar

greeting, el saludo

grey-haired, de pelo gris, canoso

grief, la pena, el dolor

grill, la verja

grimace, el gesto

grimly, ceñudo

to grin, sonreírse (i)

the grinding, el molido

ground, el terreno

group, el grupo

to grow old, envejecer; — up, criarse

growth, el avance

gruffly, malhumorado

grunt, el gruñido

guard, el guardia; el guarda

to guard, guardar

guarded (in expression), con cautela

guard's van, el furgón de los guardas

guess, la conjetura

to guess, sospechar

guide, el (la) guía

guilty, culpable

gulf, el abismo

gun, el cañón; shot —, la escopeta

hair, el pelo; el cabello

hairpin bend, la curva cerrada

half, medio; parcial; the — year, el semestre

hallucination, la alucinación

ham, el jamón

handkerchief, el pañuelo

to handle, desenvolverse (ue)

handsome, hermoso

to hang; colgar (ue); — around, andar por allí

hangover, el efecto de la embriaguez

to happen, suceder

Happy Christmas, Felices Navidades

hard, duro

hardly, apenas

harm, el daño

harmless, inofensivo

to hate, odiar

to haunt, rondar

to have to do with (st), conformarse con (algo)

hazardous, aventurado

headlight, el faro (del coche)

headlong, ciegamente

to hear, oír

heart, el corazón; **(courage),** el coraje

heartily, con gran apetito

heavy, pesado

hegemony, la hegemonía

help, la ayuda; **— ful,** servicial; **— less,** desamparado; **to —,** ayudar

to herd, cuidar

heritage, el patrimonio

hero, el héroe

heroine, la heroína

hidden, oculto

to hide ocultar (se)

highlights, los momentos culminantes

highly, sumamente

Her Highness, Su Alteza

hill, la colina; **— side,** la ladera de la colina

to hire, alquilar

to hit (a target), hacer blanco en

hitherto, hasta entonces

to hold, caber (20a); **— with s.o.** estar del lado de alguien

holidays, las vacaciones

home-coming, sentirse (ie) (i) en el hogar

Home Front, el Frente Nacional

home life, la vida familiar

honestly, de veras

honours degree, la matrícula de honor

to hoot, sonar (ue) la bocina

hope, la esperanza

horseman, el jinete

household (royal), la Casa Real

however, no obstante; sin embargo

huge, enorme

humanity, la humanidad

hump, la giba

hungry, hambriento

hurried, presuroso

to hurry, apresurarse

hurt, herido

husband, el esposo; el marido

iced, con hielo

idler, el desocupado

idly, distraídamente

to ignore, no hacer caso a (de)

ill, enfermo

illness, la enfermedad

to illumine, iluminar

to immerse oneself in; ensimismarse

imminent, inminente

to imply, significar; suponer

impoverishment, el empobrecimiento

to improve, mejorar

impulsive, impulsivo

incident, el incidente

inclination, el amor

incline, la pendiente

increased, ampliado

indeed, muy; ciertamente

indefatigable, incansable

Indian, el indio; **— corn,** el maíz; **Red —** el piel roja

to indicate, señalar

to induce, inducir

to be in industry, ser hombre de negocios

inexperienced, sin experiencia

inhabitant, el habitante

initiative, la iniciativa

inquirer, el preguntante

instead of, en vez de

instinctively, instintivamente

to intend, proponerse; tener intención

intent, absorto

to intercept, cortar el paso

interest, el interés

intermediate, intermedio
introduction, la presentación
inured, avezado
invader, el invasor
invaluable, sin precio
inverted, invertido
to invoke, invocar
to involve, envolver (ue); suponer
island, la isla

jealously, celosamente
jealousy, los celos
to jeer, mofarse
to jerk off, arrancar
jewel-case, el joyero
jewellery, las joyas
to join (up with), participar
to jostle, zarandear
journey, el viaje; to make a —, emprender un viaje
joy, el placer
to judge, juzgar
judgement, el juicio
just like, igual que
justice, la justicia

to keep, preservar; conservar; key, la llave; (small), el llavín; (clue), la clave
to kick, patear
to kill, matar
kind(ly), amable; bien; — hearted, de buen corazón
kindness, la benevolencia
king, el rey
kingdom, el reino
kinsman, el compatriota
to kiss, besar
knee, la rodilla
to kneel, arrodillarse
to knock (on a door), llamar (a la puerta); repiquetear
to know (21 e), saber; conocer
knowledge, el conocimiento
known, conocido

lace, el encaje
lack (of), la falta (de); to —, carecer de
lad, el chico
lake, el lago
lamp, la lámpara
land, el terreno; la tierra; el país
to land, desembarcar; aterrizar
landing, el rellano
large, grande; fuerte
to last, durar
late, tarde; (adj.) tardío
latter, este último; — years, los últimos años
to laugh, reír (i) (se)
laughter, la risa
to lavish, prodigar
law, la ley
to lay the foundations, echar los cimientos
to lead, conducir
leaden, plomizo
leading, principal
to lean forward, inclinarse; — on, apostarse (ue)
to leap, saltar
to learn, aprender; enterarse de
at least, al menos
to leave, marcharse; dejar; abandonar
leaving, yendo (se)
to lend, prestar
to let, dejar
on the level (in order), en orden
liberty, la libertad
lie, la mentira
liege lord, el señor feudal
light, la luz; (adj.), leve, ligero
to light, encender (ie)
lighter, el encendedor
like, como; — wise, también
to listen, escuchar
in litters, en litera
lively (adj.), vivo; animado
loaded, cargado
loafer, el gandul

to lock, cerrar (ie) con llave; — **up (in prison),** encarcelar

to lodge, alojarse; — **a complaint,** formular una protesta

loneliness, la soledad

lonely, a solas; solitario

long, largo

to long for, desear; — **to,** añorar

to look (at), mirar, contemplar; — **at life,** entender (ie) la vida; — **after,** cuidar; — **back (turn round),** volverse (ue); — **forward to,** desear

looking-glass, el espejo.

to loom, destacarse

loon, necio

loquacious, locuaz; — **stream,** una cascada de locuacidad

Your Lordship, su señoría

lorry, el camión

to lose, perder (ie)

loss, la pérdida

loud (noise), fuerte

love, el amor; **in —,** enamorado

low, bajo; — **ceilinged-roof,** de techo bajo

to lower, bajar

loyal, fiel; leal

luck, la suerte

lunch, el almuerzo

lying, acostado; — **back,** reclinado

machine, la máquina

magic, la magia

maid, la doncella

maiden-aunt, la tía soltera

main, principal

majesty, la majestad

major, el comandante

make, la marca

to make (*20j*) **(a difference),** cambiar; — **out,** distinguir; — **pay,** sacar partido

management, la dirección; **stage —,** la dirección escénica; — **skill,** la astucia

manager, el director; el gerente

map, el mapa

to march to(wards), avanzar

market, el mercado

marooned, detenido

to mask, ocultar

master, el amo; el dueño; el director

mate, el amigo; el compañero; el piloto

matron, la matrona

matter, el asunto

mayor, el alcalde

meal, la comida; **evening —,** la cena

to mean, significar

means, los medios; **by — of,** mediante; **by no —,** en absoluto no

in the meantime (meanwhile), mientras tanto

meekly, dócilmente

to meet, encontrar (ue); conocer; ver a

melancholy, melancólico

memory, el recuerdo

menace, la amenaza

merry, alegre

method, el método

methodical, metódico

middle, el medio

midnight, la medianoche

mile, la milla

milk, la leche

mind, la mentalidad; la mente; el pensamiento

miniature, el retrato en miniatura

minister, el ministro

ministration, el oficio

mischievous, travieso

misery, la desgracia

to miss, perderse (ie) algo; faltar (*20g*); echar de menos

mistake, el error

to misunderstand, entender (ie) mal

mixed up, revuelto

momentary, momentáneo; pasajero

monarchy, la monarquía

money, el dinero

monk, el fraile

monstrous, monstruoso

moon, la luna

Moor, el moro

Moorish, moro, árabe

moral, moral

moreover, además, por añadidura

mosque, la mezquita

most, la mayoría

to move about, andar por

moved (emotionally), emocionado

motionless, inmóvil

to mount guard, hacer guardia

mountain, el monte

mountaineer, el montañés; el montañero

mountainside, la ladera del monte

mule, la mula

to murmur, murmurar; — **softly,** susurrar

museum, el museo

music hall, la sala de variedades

musket, el mosquete

to mutter, murmurar

mystery, el misterio

as naked as a bone, desnudo como Dios le había hecho

name, el nombre, el apellido

narrow, estrecho

native, el nativo

nature, el carácter

to navigate, navegar

navigator, el navegante

near (*adv.*), cerca; — **er,** más de cerca

nearly, casi

neck, el cuello

necklace, el collar

need, la necesidad; **to —** necesitar

needless to say, excusado es decir

neighbour, el vecino

in the neighbourhood of, en las cercanías de

neighbouring, vecino

nephew, el sobrino

net, la red; la malla

news, las noticias

newspaper, el periódico, el diario

next, el siguiente; junto a

night before, la noche anterior

to nod, asentir (ie)(i) (de cabeza)

noisy, ruidoso

none, ningún

noon, el mediodía

no one, nadie

normally, corrientemente

northern, septentrional

not at all, ni siquiera

note, el billete (de banco); **to —,** advertir (ie) (i)

noted, notable

to notice, advertir (ie) (i)

novel, la novela

novelty, la novedad

nurse, la enfermera

to obey, obedecer

object, el objeto; **(aim),** el objetivo

obviously, evidentemente

occasion, la ocasión; —

occasionally, de vez en cuando

to occupy, ocupar

ocean, el océano; — **passage,** ruta transoceánica

offender, el delincuente

to offer, ofrecer

offering, la colación

office, la oficina; **(job),** el cargo

official, el funcionario
officious, oficioso
often, con frecuencia; muchas veces
old-fashioned, antiguo
olive (tree), el olivo
once, una vez
only, único
to **ooze,** manar
open, abierto
to **oppose,** oponer
opposite, opuesto
oppressive, opresivo
to **order,** encargar; pedir (i); dar órdenes
origin, el origen; (*pl.*) los orígenes
originally, al principio
ostensibly, en apariencia
other, otro
an **ounce of brain,** dos dedos de frente
outbreak, el estallido
outline, el contorno
outlying parts, las proximidades
outpost, la avanzada
outside, fuera
oval, ovalado
overnight, de la noche al día
to **owe to,** deber a
to **own,** poseer
of one's **own,** (suyo) propio; personal
to **pack,** empaquetar
package, el bulto
pad, el ruido de pasos
paint, la pintura; **— box,** la caja de pintura
to **paint,** pintar
painter, el pintor
pair, el par
pale-faced, pálido
palm tree, la palmera
paradox, la paradoja; **in —,** paradójicamente
parcel, el paquete
to **park,** aparcar
in **parley,** hablando con

parsimonious, parsimonioso
part, el papel; **to — with,** separarse de
party, el grupo; el cortejo; la fiesta
pass, el puerto; **to —,** pasar; **to — away the time,** matar el tiempo
patron of arts, el mecenas de las artes
patron saint, el santo patrón
to **pause,** hacer una pausa
to **pay attention,** prestar atención
peace, la paz; **— ful,** tranquilo; pacífico
peacock, el pavo real
peal, la campanada
pearl, la perla
peasant, el campesino
people, la gente; **— s,** los pueblos
penetration, la perspicacia
to be **penned in,** quedarse encerrado
perfume, el perfume
perpetuity, la perpetuidad
photograph, la fotografía
phrase, la frase
physical, físico
to **pick up,** apercibir
picturesque, pintoresco
Pied Piper, el Flautista de Hamelín
pig, el cerdo
pipe, la pipa
pirate, el pirata
pity, la lástima; la piedad
place, el sitio; **(post),** el puesto; **to take the — of,** sustituir
placid, plácido
plain, puro
to **plan,** planear
planter, el colono
plate, el plato
platform, el andén
play, la diversión; **— boy,** el señorito

plot (literary), el enredo; la trama; el juego

to pluck (nibble), mordisquear

to plunge, sacudir

pocket, el bosillo

to point out, indicar; — **at,** señalar con el dedo

police (force), la policía; — **station,** la comisaría

policeman, el policía; el guardia

politeness, la cortesía

port, el puerto

porter, el portero; el maletero

portrait, el retrato

to possess, poseer

postcard, la tarjeta postal

posterity, la posteridad; la descendencia

postman, el cartero

power, el poderío; — **s,** los poderes

practical, práctico

Praise be, Alabado sea

to pray, rezar

to preach, predicar

precocious, precoz

premonition, el presentimiento

presence, la presencia

present, el regalo; **to be —,** asistir

presently, después; pronto

to preserve, mantener

presumably, probablemente

to pretend, pretender; fingir

to prevent, evitar

price (reward), la recompensa

priceless, inapreciable

priestly, eclesiástico

to prime, dar instrucciones

prince, el príncipe

prison, la cárcel; la prisión

private, particular

to proceed, continuar el camino

to proclaim, proclamar

to procure, lograr

to produce, producir; sacar

profit, la ganancia; **to — from,** aprovecharse de

to promise, prometer

property, la propiedad

to prop (up), conservar

prophet, el profeta

prospect, la perspectiva

to protect, proteger

proudly, con orgullo

to prove, confirmar

province, la provincia

psychic, (p)sicológico; (p)síquico

pupil, el discípulo

purpose, el designio; **for the — of,** en lo que atañe a; **on —,** adrede

pursuer, el perseguidor

to push, empujar; dar un empujón; — **back,** rechazar; apartar

to put (2rg), colocar; poner; — **in,** meter en; interponer

quality, la cualidad

to quarrel, reñir (i)

quarters, la residencia

quiet, tranquilo; silencioso; (*noun*) la tranquilidad

quick (ears), el oído fino

race, la raza; el pueblo

radicalism, el radicalismo

railway, el ferrocarril; — **porter,** el maletero

rain, la lluvia; **to —,** llover (ue)

raised against, levantado en contra

rank, el rango; la fila

ravine, la barranca, el barranco

to reach, alcanzar

to read, leer

ready, preparado; dispuesto

to realize, darse cuenta

really, en realidad; de veras
reason, la razón
to **reassure,** tranquilizar
reckoner, el calculador
to **recognize,** reconocer
reconquest, la reconquista
record, el record
records, los archivos
to **refer to,** hacer referencia a
to **reflect,** reflexionar
refreshment, la colación
refuge, el refugio
refugee, el refugiado
to **refuse,** rehusar; — **to,** negarse a
to **regulate,** arreglar
to be **related to,** tener vínculos familiares con
to **relax,** descansar
reign, el reinado
reinforcement, el refuerzo
religion, la religión; la religiosidad; la fe
to **rely on,** contar (ue) con
to **remain,** seguir (i) siendo; mantenerse; quedarse
remarkable, formidable
to **remember,** recordar (ue); acordarse (ue) de
to **remind,** recordar (ue)
reminiscent, que recuerda
to **repel,** repeler; rechazar
to **require,** tener necesidad de
to **resemble,** parecerse a
reserves, las reservas
to **resist,** resistir
resolutely, resueltamente
respect, el respeto
responsibility, la responsabilidad
rest, el resto; lo demás; to —, descansar
to **retain,** retener
to **retreat,** emprender la retirada; retirarse
to **return,** volver (ue); regresar
in **reverse,** marcha atrás
reward, la recompensa
ribbon, la cinta

to **ride (a horse),** cabalgar; montar a caballo
rifle, el rifle; la escopeta; la carabina
right (legal), el derecho
ring, el anillo; **to — the bell,** tocar el timbre; **to — bells,** tañer campanas; **to — out (resound),** retumbar
to **rise,** levantarse; **(increase),** aumentar
risk, el riesgo
risky, aventurado
road, la carretera; el camino
to **roar,** rugir; bramar
roaring, retumbante
rock, la roca; la piedra
roof-top, el tejado
room, la habitación; el cuarto; **(space),** el sitio
root, la raíz
rough, burdo
round, la ronda; **to — the corner,** doblar la esquina
row, el jaleo; la riña
royal, real
rule, la dominación; el mando
rum, el ron
rumour, el rumor
to **run,** correr; — **headlong,** correr ciegamente
to **rush,** apresurarse

sacred, sagrado
sacraments, los sacramentos
saddle-bag, la alforja
safe, salvo
to **sail,** navegar
sailor, el marino; el marinero
for her **sake,** por cuenta de ella; para ella
same, mismo
sandalwood, el sándalo
sardine-boat, la lancha sardinera

to saunter, deambular; pasear; vagar

savage, feroz

to save, salvar; — **up,** ahorrar

savings, los ahorros

to say, decir; — **a word for somebody,** intervenir por alguien

scattered, desparramado

scene, el escenario

science, la ciencia

to scream, chillar

sea, el mar

search, la busca; **in — of,** en busca de; **to —,** buscar

seat, el asiento

in secret, a escondidas

to secure, afianzar(se); — **passage,** obtener pasaje

to seem, parecer

to send, mandar; enviar

separation, la escisión

seriously, gravemente

servant, el criado

to serve, servir (ie) (i) (20p)

service, el servicio

to set out, proponerse; — **fire to,** incendiar; pegar fuego a

to settle down, instalarse

settlement, la colonia

settler, el colono

severe, severo; — **looking,** de aspecto severo

shadow, la sombra

to shake, sacudir; — **off,** deshacerse de; — **hands,** estrechar la mano

shaped, en forma de

to share, compartir

sharp (steep), abrupto

to shed (blood), derramar (sangre)

shelf, una zanja

shell, la granada

shield, el escudo

ship, el barco; **merchant —,** el barco mercante

shock, la conmoción; el trastorno

shoe, el zapato

shop, la tienda

shore, la orilla; **(beach),** la playa

short, corto; **in —,** en resumen; **in a — time,** en poco tiempo

shot, el disparo

shoulder, el hombro

shout, el grito

to show, demostrar(ue); — **interest,** mostrar(ue) interés; **to make a —,** hacer alarde

shrewdly, agudamente

shrill, agudo

to shrug one's shoulders, encogerse de hombros

side, el lado; **ship's side,** el costado del barco

to sigh, suspirar

sight, la vista; la estampa; **in —,** a la vista; **to —,** avistar

sign, el signo; la señal; (*plural*) los indicios; **to —,** indicar

to be silent, callarse; estar sin hablar

silly, tonto

silver, la plata; (*adj.*) plateado; de plata

similarity, la semejanza; el parecido

single, solo

sinking (illness), perdiendo fuerzas

to sip, sorber

to sit, estar sentado; — **for s.o.,** posar para alguien

sitting-room, el cuarto de estar

skate, el patín; **roller —s,** los patines de ruedas; **to — patinar**

sketch, el esbozo; **to —,** esbozar

skill, el arte

slacks, los pantalones

slave, el esclavo

sleep-walk, la marcha de sonámbulo

sleeve, la manga

slim, delgado

to sling (stones), apedrear

slinger, el hondero

slope, la pendiente; **to — down,** descender

slowly, lentamente; despacio

small, pequeño

smile, la sonrisa; **to —,** sonreír

to smoke, fumar; humear

snatches (extracts), los trozos

snow, la nieve

soda, el sifón; la soda

so far, hasta ahora

soil, la tierra

soldier, el soldado

somehow, de algún modo

somewhere, en la cercanía de

son-in-law, el yerno

soon, pronto; **as — as,** en cuanto

sophisticated, adelantado

sorely, profundamente

sound, el ruido; el rumor; **— advice,** buen consejo

soup, la sopa

sour, amargo

south, el sur

southern, meridional; al sur

southward, hacia el sur

Spanish American, hispanoamericano

to speak; hablar; **— one's mind,** cantar las verdades

spectator, el espectador

speculator, el especulador

speech, el discurso

speed, la velocidad; **at great —,** a gran velocidad

spell, el hechizo

to spend (time), pasar; **(money),** gastar

sphere, la esfera

spinster, la solterona

spirit, el espíritu

to spoil, echar a perder; mimar

spoils, el botín

spoon, la cuchara

sports car, el automóvil de carreras

spot, el sitio

to spread on, cubrir

spring, la primavera

spy, el espía

spying, el espionaje

square, la plaza

stab, la puñalada

stage, la escena

to stain (with), manchar (de)

staircase, la escalera

to stand aside, hacerse a un lado

standing, de pie

star, la estrella

start, la antelación; el comienzo; **to —,** salir

state, el estado

statesmanship, la aptitud de estadista

station, la estación; **— master,** el jefe de estación

statistics, las estadísticas

statue, la estatua

to steady one's nerves, calmar los nervios

to steal, robar

steel, el acero

to stem, detener

stern, severo

stiff, rígido

still, todavía

stone, la piedra

stony, empedrado

to stop, parar; **— short,** parar(se) en seco

stork, la cigüeña

story, la historia; el cuento

stout, grueso; gordo; sólido

straight to, directamente a

strait (*geog.*), el estrecho

to be stranded, parar

stranger, el extraño; el forastero

straw, la paja
streak, la veta
street, la calle; **— lamp,** el farol
strength, la fortaleza
string, la cuerda; el cordel
strong, fuerte
stronghold, la plaza fuerte
to **struggle,** luchar
student, el estudiante
to **study,** estudiar; **(scrutinize),** escudriñar
style, el estilo
submission, la sumisión
subsequently, después; más tarde
to **succeed** (21 h), lograr; conseguir (i)
success, el éxito
successor, el sucesor
suddenly, de pronto
to **suffer,** sufrir
to **suggest,** proponer; sugerir (ie) (i)
to **suit,** ir (caer, venir) bien
suit-case, la maleta
sulkily, con desgana
sum, la suma; **to — up,** resumir
summary, el resumen
supply, la cantidad
to **support strongly,** confirmar ampliamente
supporter, el partidario
to **suppose,** imaginar(se); figurarse; suponer
supremacy, la supremacía
sure, seguro; protector
to **surprise,** sorprender; (*noun*) la sorpresa
surprisingly, inesperadamente
to **surround,** rodear
sweat, el sudor; **to —,** sudar
to **sweep on the floor,** tirar al suelo
to **swerve,** torcer (ue)
to **swim,** nadar; bañarse

to **swirl,** arremolinarse
sword thrust, la estocada
sympathetic, simpático; afín
sympathy, la simpatía; la comprensión

to **take** (21 i), tomar; coger; **— refuge,** hallar refugio; **— down a peg,** rebajar un grado
to be **taken with,** estar encantado de
talent, el talento
talisman, el talismán
talkative, hablador
tall, alto
task, la tarea
taste, el sabor
tax, el impuesto
tea, el té
to **teach,** enseñar
in **tears,** lloroso
to **tear,** rasgar; **— up,** arrancar
telephone, el teléfono; **to —,** telefonear
to **tell,** decir; contar (ue); referir (ie) (i)
tell-tale, revelador
tempter, el tentador
tense, nervioso
tent, la tienda de campaña
term, el trimestre (escolar)
to **terrify,** horrorizar
territory, el territorio
thank heaven, gracias a Dios
that is, es decir
theatre, el teatro
then, entonces; **(next)** después, luego
thence, de allí que
there, allí
therefore, por eso
thicket, la espesura
thief, el ladrón
thing, la cosa, el objeto

to **think**, (*21j*) pensar (ie); —
  much of, tener un alto
  concepto de
thoroughly, bien; por completo
though, aunque
thought, el pensamiento
thousand, mil
threat, la amenaza
to **threaten**, amenazar
threshold, el umbral
to go **through**, pasar por
throughout, por todo
to **throw**, echar; tirar; — **off**,
  desembarazarse
thus, así; así pues
ticket, el billete; — **collector**, el cobrador
tied, atado
time, el tiempo; la vez;
  from — to —, de vez en
  vez (cuando)
tinkle, el tintineo
tiny, muy pequeño
together, (todos) juntos
toiling, laboriosamente
tongue, la lengua
tonight, esta noche
top, la parte alta
to **touch**, impresionar
towards, hacia
towel, la toalla
tower, la torre
track, el camino
trade, el comercio
tragedy, la tragedia
tragic, trágico
trail, la vereda
tram, el tranvía
to **travel**, viajar
traveller, el viajero
tray, la bandeja
treachery, la traición
treasure, el tesoro
trench, la trinchera
tribesman, el hombre de la
  tribu
tribute, el tributo
trim, bien arreglado
trinket, la joya

triumph, el triunfo
trouble, la calamidad
trousers, el pantalón; los
  pantalones
true, cierto; auténtico; ver-
  dadero
to **trust**, confiar
trusted, fiel
to **try**, tratar (de); intentar
to **turn**, torcer (ue); volver (ue);
  not — a hair, no inmu-
  tarse; — **oneself away**,
  volverse (ue) de espaldas;
  — **(hand) over to**,
  entregar a; — **grey (hair)**
  encanecer
tutoring, el dar lecciones
twice, dos veces
type, el tipo
typical, típico

ugly, feo
umbrella, el paraguas
to be **unavailing**, no servir (ie) (i)
  de nada
unbearable, insoportable
uncharted, incontable
under, debajo de (*9i*)
to **undergo**, experimentar
to **understand**, comprender
to **undertake**, acometer una
  empresa; encargarse
undertaking, la empresa
undetected, sin ser descu-
  bierto
unfounded, sin (despro-
  visto de) fundamento
unhappiness, la desgracia
unhappy, infortunado
Union Jack, la bandera
  inglesa (británica)
unknown, desconocido
unlet, desalquilado
unmitigated, sin atenuantes
unmoved, impasible
unnoticed, desapercibido
unorganized, desorgani-
  zado

unreality, la irrealidad
unthinkable, inconcebible
until, hasta
unto, a
unusual, excepcional
to **upset,** hacer tambalear
upturned, panza arriba
to **use,** servirse (ie) (i) de; emplear; hacer uso; usar
useless, incapaz; inservible; inútil
usual, de costumbre
utterly, totalmente; por completo

vagabond, el vagabundo
value, el valor; **scale of — s,** la escala de valores
to **value,** dar aprecio
various, diversos; variados
vegetables, las legumbres
venture, la aventura
vestige, el vestigio
veteran, veterano
viceroy, el virrey
view, la vista; **to have in —,** tener a la vista
vile, repelente
village, el pueblo
vital, esencial
volley, la salva
votive, votivo

wage, el salario
to **wait,** esperar
waiter, el camarero
to **wake up,** despertar(se) (ie)
wakeful, despierto
walk, el paso; **to —,** andar
wall (indoors), la pared; **(outside),** la tapia; **(defensive),** el muro; la muralla
war, la guerra
warlike, belicoso
warm, cordial
warned, advertido
to **wash,** lavar
waster, el perdido

to **watch,** mirar; vigilar
waterfall, la cascada
waterproof, (el) impermeable
to **wave good-bye,** despedir (i) (con la mano)
way, la manera; **to have one's —,** salirse con la suya; **the — s of the world,** los medios mundanos
wealth, las riquezas
to **wear,** llevar puesto
weary, cansado; cansino
wedding-gift, el regalo de boda
as **well,** también; **— as,** así como
west, el oeste; el occidente
western, occidental; del oeste
wheel, la rueda
when, cuando; **— yet,** siendo todavía
while, mientras (que); **a —,** un rato
whisper, el cuchicheo; **to —,** cuchichear
whole, todo
wicked, malo; malvado
wide, ancho
widow, la viuda
window, la ventana; **— frame,** el marco de la ventana
will, la voluntad
wisely, juiciosamente
to **wish,** desear
wistfully, tristemente
to **withdraw,** apartarse
within, dentro de
wonder, la sorpresa; **no —,** no es de extrañar
to **wonder,** extrañarse
wonderful, estupendo
wondering, con curiosidad
to do **wonders,** realizar maravillas
wooden, de madera
wood(s), el bosque

word, la palabra; **to bring —,** llevar nuevas
work, la obra
working man, el obrero
world, el mundo
worried, preocupado
to **worry,** preocuparse
the **worst,** lo peor
to be **worth the trouble,** valer la pena (*20s*)
wrappings, las envolturas
wretched(ly), desgraciado
to **writhe,** revolverse (ue)
wrong, mal; equivocado; **to be —,** equivocarse

wound, la herida; **to —,** herir (ie) (i)

yard, el patio; la yarda
yet (still), todavía; **(however),** sin embargo; **not —,** todavía no
yonder, más allá
youth, el joven; la juventud

zest, el entusiasmo
to **zigzag,** serpentear